Active Aging: The Contribution of Psychology

About the author

Rocío Fernández-Ballesteros is Professor at the Autonomous University of Madrid, Spain. She researches and teaches in psychology of aging as well as psychological assessment and evaluation. She is the author of more than 250 publication, among them *Encyclopedia of Psychological Assessment* (2003) and *GeroPsychology: European perspectives for an aging world* (2007). She is the former President of the European Association of Psychological Assessment (EAPA), Founder and former Editor-in-Chief of the *European Journal of Psychological Assessment*, Past-President of the Division on Applied Gerontology of the International Association of Applied Psychology (IAAP), and a Fellow of the Gerontological Society of America (GSA). In 2005, she received the Aristotle Prize from the European Federation of Psychologists Associations (EFPA), and in 2006 the Award for Distinguished Contribution from the IAAP.

Acknowledgments

The manuscript for this book was prepared during a sabbatical awarded by the Autonoma University of Madrid and supported by the University State Secretary Program (PR2005-0031), in the Inter-University Center for Research on Motivation at the University La Sapienza, Rome. I would like to express my gratitude to the organizations that awarded and supported the sabbatical, as well as to Prof. Gian Vittorio Caprara and other colleagues at the research center and faculty in Rome.

Active Aging: The Contribution of Psychology

Rocío Fernández-Ballesteros
Autonoma University of Madrid, Spain

Library of Congress Cataloging in Publication

is available via the Library of Congress Marc Database under the
LC Control Number 2008927620.

Library and Archives Canada Cataloguing in Publication

Fernández Ballesteros, Rocío

Active aging : the contribution of psychology / Rocío Fernández-Ballesteros.

Includes bibliographical references.
ISBN 978-0-88937-360-0

1. Older people—Psychology. 2. Aging—Psychological aspects.
I. Title.
BF724.8.F47   2008   155.67   C2008-903560-7

© 2008 by Hogrefe & Huber Publishers

PUBLISHING OFFICES

USA:	Hogrefe & Huber Publishers, 875 Massachusetts Avenue, 7th Floor, Cambridge, MA 02139
	Phone (866) 823-4726, Fax (617) 354-6875; E-mail info@hogrefe.com
EUROPE:	Hogrefe & Huber Publishers, Rohnsweg 25, 37085 Göttingen, Germany
	Phone +49 551 49609-0, Fax +49 551 49609-88, E-mail hh@hogrefe.com

SALES & DISTRIBUTION

USA:	Hogrefe & Huber Publishers, Customer Services Department, 30 Amberwood Parkway, Ashland, OH 44805
	Phone (800) 228-3749, Fax (419) 281-6883, E-mail custserv@hogrefe.com
EUROPE:	Hogrefe & Huber Publishers, Rohnsweg 25, 37085 Göttingen, Germany
	Phone +49 551 49609-0, Fax +49 551 49609-88, E-mail hh@hogrefe.com

OTHER OFFICES

CANADA:	Hogrefe & Huber Publishers, 1543 Bayview Avenue, Toronto, Ontario M4G 3B5
SWITZERLAND:	Hogrefe & Huber Publishers, Länggass-Strasse 76, CH-3000 Bern 9

Hogrefe & Huber Publishers. Incorporated and registered in the State of Washington, USA, and in Göttingen, Lower Saxony, Germany.

No part of this book may be reproduced, stored in a retrieval system or transmitted, in any form or by any means, electronic, mechanical, photocopying, microfilming, recording or otherwise, without written permission from the publisher.

Printed and bound in the USA
ISBN 978-0-88937-360-0

Foreword

We all age. Active Aging, aging with well-being and a high quality of life, is one of the most important issues facing science and society in our time of increasing longevity and demographic change. Never before have so many people been able to live to such an advanced age. There has been an enormous extension of the life span during the last decades in all European countries, but also across the world. We live longer and remain more active into later life than our parents and grandparents. This is due to the progress of modern medicine, the improvement of socio-economic living conditions, and it is also very much influenced by lifestyles and human behavior. It is important to not just add years to life, but also to add life to years!

This very interesting and stimulating book, based on a critical analysis of the gerontological and especially psychological research literature on aging, emphasizes a new paradigm in scientific gerontology that has a more positive view of aging processes. What is "active aging," "healthy aging," "quality of life," "successful aging," "life satisfaction," "well-being," "positive aging"? Amongst many other things, this book also addresses these questions of definition. An analysis of the literature of the last decades shows an interesting development: In the 1960s, there were many articles on the subject of "life satisfaction," followed some years later by the topic of "successful aging." In the 1970s, the subject of "quality of life" came to prominence, originally introduced by medical doctors; and then in the 1980s and beyond, the topic of "subjective well-being" became dominant. Life satisfaction (in the sense of satisfaction with the development of one's life as well as with the current situation) is recognized as an indicator of successful aging. Life satisfaction (often measured with a so-called "life satisfaction scale") in this context is valued as an aspect of adjusting successfully to the aging process. As is shown in the following, the definition of all these concepts is very difficult. In the literature, they sometimes overlap and it is not possible to differentiate between them, and there is some confusion regarding theoretical and methodological concepts.

In this book, Rocío Fernández-Ballesteros makes a convincing case for a multidimensional, multilevel model of active aging, including several theoretical constructs, and states: "In conclusion, positive aging can be defined as the life-course adaptation process for arriving at an optimal physical (including health), psychological (optimal cognition and emotion-motivation regulation), and social functioning of the individual. Therefore, the promotion of active aging will imply the optimization of those conditions through biomedical, physical, psychological, and socio-environmental interventions. It should also be emphasized that promoting active aging is preventing illness and disability, and increasing well-being in old age."(p. 58)

Aging is not only a biological process; it is a process determined by a number of biological, social, psychological, and ecological factors. Healthy aging is active aging! The focus of this book is on active, healthy aging and the behavioral and psychosocial factors that contribute to it. Healthy aging is the result of a lifelong process. It is therefore necessary to optimize the development of the individual from early childhood on. We know that a variety of influences in early childhood, in adolescence, during early and middle adulthood, but also in the current living circumstances of the aged determine the processes of aging and well-being in old age.

Achieving healthy aging is a challenge for society but also for every individual. Measures of health promotion and primary prevention are necessary to maintain and increase competencies in later life. What can be done to secure a high quality of life in old age?

There are many studies that demonstrate that physical activity is a prerequisite for successful aging. Age-determined physical changes – such as functional impairments of the organs, changes in the motor and muscular system as well as changes in the respiratory organs (which, of course, depending on the individual, can appear at any age) – are similar to the effects brought about by a lack of exercise. A young but physically inactive individual seems old, just as an old but active individual appears young. Physical activity also has positive effects on psychological well-being by promoting mental abilities, subjective well-being, social skills, and self-concept.

Cognitive activity is another prerequisite for successful aging. Many studies have found that mentally active individuals who have a wide range of interests, a time perspective reaching farther into the future, and a larger number of social contacts reach old age with greater feelings of psycho-physical well-being than those who lack such activity and perspective. It has been established that cognitive activity is essential for healthy aging. It is therefore, important that older people have mental tasks – they must be challenged to mental activity, as a reduction in such activity can speed up the process of aging.

Emotional and motivational functioning influences healthy and active aging. Aging is associated with life-change units and such changes require adaptation and adjustment; elderly people sometimes have to cope with multiple critical life events. Last but not least, social functioning and social participation also have an influence on healthy and active aging.

"Promoting active aging" is the main goal of this very important book, which aims to strengthen a theory- and research-based practical approach, a program for healthy active aging. Overall, we need a more positive view of aging; we have to do everything we can to change the negative image of the aged into a more realistic one. Old age is every young person's future, so we have to strengthen every individual's physical, cognitive, emotional-motivational, and social development from very early on in life. In this, health promotion is the most important prerequisite for active aging. This is a challenge for psychologists, who can contribute to effecting behavioral changes towards healthier behavior. To promote aging well, to achieve long life as free of disability as possible, and to reduce morbidity at the end of life should be the aim of the necessary multidomain-based, multidimensional intervention programs. "The process of aging well, at the individual, community, and population level, depends on complex psychological self-regulation functioning because the individual is always an active agent who requires the exercise of control." (p. 154)

Old age and longevity should not be seen as a problem but as a chance and a challenge – a challenge for everyone: for the aging individual, for their family, and for our society. We should not only talk about the losses, problems, and deficits of aging and old age. We have to talk about – and we have to open our eyes to – the potentials of the elderly, and also the competencies and potentials of the very old. We have to see the aged of the 21st century as human capital. This book will help to such a new view of the older population.

Ursula Lehr
June 2008

Table of Contents

Foreword v
Table of Contents ix

PART I: CONCEPTUAL ISSUES 1

1   A New Paradigm in the Study of Aging 3
    Traditions in the Study of Aging, Age, and the Aged 3
    Evolution in Research on Active Aging 6
    Empirical Bases of Active Aging 9
    Concluding Remarks 14

2   Population Aging: Facts and Projections 16
    Life Expectancy Enlargement 16
    Population Aging 17
    Years to Life and Life to Years 18
    Morbidity Hypotheses 21
    Determinants of Morbidity 26
    Concluding Remarks 28

3   Working, Empirical, and Lay Definitions, and Theoretical Models . . . 29
    Introduction 29
    Controversial Issues 30
    Working Definitions 32
    Empirical Definitions 36
    Lay Concepts 44
    Theoretical Models 49
    Toward a Multidimensional-Multilevel Proposal of Active Aging 55
    Psychological Domains Contributing to Active Aging 57
    Concluding Remarks 58

PART II: BEHAVIORAL AND PSYCHOLOGICAL DOMAINS
OF ACTIVE AGING 61

4   Behavioral Health and Physical Fitness 63
    Introduction 63
    Physical Exercise 64
    Diet and Nutrition 69
    Smoking and Drinking 72
    Concluding Remarks 72

5	Cognitive Functioning	74
	Introduction	74
	Education and Socioeconomic Status	77
	Physical Exercise	80
	Activity	84
	Cognitive Training and Interventions	88
	Concluding Remarks	97
6	Emotional and Motivational Functioning: Affect, Control, and Coping	98
	Introduction	98
	Positive Emotions and Positive Aging	102
	Personal Control	107
	Coping with Stress	112
	Concluding Remarks	119
7	Social Functioning and Social Participation	120
	Introduction	120
	Social Functioning and Positive Emotions Across the Life Span	121
	Social Functioning and Health	123
	Social Functioning and Cognitive Impairment	126
	Concluding Remarks	128

PART III: PROMOTING ACTIVE AGING 129

8	Active Aging Promotion Programs	131
	Introduction	131
	Lifelong Health Promotion	133
	Promoting Healthy Aging During Adulthood	135
	Cognitive Impairment	137
	Active-Aging Promotion Projects	145
	Population-Based Projects	150
	Concluding Remarks	153

Conclusions 155

References 159

Selected Websites on Active Aging 192

PART I
CONCEPTUAL ISSUES

1
A New Paradigm in the Study of Aging

Traditions in the Study of Aging, Age, and the Aged

Assumptions about aging have two main scopes, based in two main philosophical traditions of thinking. From Plato (427–347 BC) a tradition emerges of a positive and individualistic view of aging in which the human being ages as he/she lives, and that he/she must prepare for aging throughout the lifespan. Following this tradition, Cicero (106–43 BC) wrote "De Senectute" describing how human virtue grows through age. By contrast, from an Aristotelian (384–322 BC) point of view, it is stated that old age, as the last stage of human life, could be considered as a natural illness. In the same line Seneca (4 BC–65 AD) proposes physical and mental impairment in the individual as consequences of aging.

From these two traditions, across the history of the study of aging, theories and authors can be found who emphasized a positive view of aging (e.g., the activity theory, Havighurst, 1963; or the continuity theory, Atchley, 1989, 1999) and those who underline the negative aspects that explain the decline in social participation and engagement during old age (e.g., disengagement theory, Cummings & Henry, 1961; see also Fernández-Ballesteros, 2000; Lupien & Wand, 2004; Juengst, 2005).

Aging is a biological phenomenon and throughout aging there is a decline in the efficiency and efficacy of all biological systems, therefore, during this process there is an increase in vulnerability to chronic and acute disease. Nevertheless, it can also be stated that within the biological aging process of decline there are wide individual differences and, therefore, there are also broad differences in vulnerability.

However, a human being is not only a biological organism but he/she is also a bio-psycho-cultural entity; moreover, an active agent who is constructing him/herself throughout the lifespan, in interaction with an active world, and in an ongoing and dynamic process (Bandura, 1986; Gould, 1977, 1981). Intraindividual and interindividual differences attributed to age are not exclusively the result of age but of the ongoing and dynamic process through which the individual as a biological organism and his/her behavioral and psychological conditions interact with the external factors – sociocultural, economic, environmental, etc. During the process of aging, what the human being does, thinks, and feels and how he/she interacts with the environmental and its historical circumstances are decisive for aging outcomes.

As Birren (1996) pointed out, the science of gerontology is mainly devoted to the multidisciplinary study of aging, age, and the aged, therefore, even the scientific subject of gerontology embraces primary aging (caused by age), secondary aging (caused by disease), and their individual differences as well as the process of aging itself and aged people. This diversity in the subject of study has influenced a certain bias in the selected topics: authors studying the "aging" process emphasize small intraindividual changes; authors studying differences between "age" groups are going to find high interindividual differences attributed to age, and finally, those authors studying "the aged" are devoted to illnesses, impairments, and needs of care, therefore, they are going to focus on impairment and suffering during the process of aging.

Moreover, the intrinsic characteristic of gerontology is to have a complex subject of study but also to be multidisciplinary; that is, aging, age, and the aged should be studied from a bio-psycho-social perspective. Nevertheless Juengst (2005) emphasized that "from a biomedical model of pathology, human senescence carries all the hallmarks of a disease process: Specific underlying molecular changes create abnormalities in cells that inhibit the functional efficiency and structural resiliency of tissues and organs, causing disabilities, deformities, and distress" (p. 3). Also, Blazer (2006), in his Introduction to a Special Issue of the *American Journal of Geriatric Psychiatry* devoted to successful aging, stated that "success in late life has, therefore, been tied to the success of physicians and other health care providers in treating the maladies of late life" (p. 3). However, although as people age biophysical systems become less efficient and illness and age are covariants, since the human being is a bio-psycho-social entity not all human functioning fits into this biomedical model. Therefore, it can be concluded that this biomedical reductionism cannot be generalized to the entire field of study.

Thus, a biomedical model of aging cannot be transferred to all aging conditions; as Gould (1981) emphasized, psychosocial functioning cannot be understood under the same principles that those guiding organisms as biological entities since human functioning is also determined by sociocultural context. In fact, as Bandura (1986) posited from his sociocognitive theory, psychological functioning is determined by the reciprocal interactions between the biological organism, his/her basic learned behavioral repertoire and the sociocultural context.

Finally, the mere concept of "age," the process of aging, or the individual differences in how a given person, in a given society, ages are, to some extent, sociocultural phenomena. The importance of sociocultural factors on aging does not ignore – as seems to be claimed by some constructivistic authors such as Gergen and Gergen (2001) – the existence of illness, decline, or impairment linked to biological aging. Nevertheless, the ways in which the human organism ages are modulated by psychosocial and cultural factors. The process of aging cannot be reduced to biomedical conditions but neither can it be reduced to sociocultural ones.

As Lupien and Wan (2004) pointed out, gerontologists' speech is promoting the spread of negative views of age and aging and reinforcing the existing stereotypes in society as a whole. These authors recall Butler's statements accusing health professionals of promoting these stereotypes when he coined the concept of "ageism" as the process of discrimination against the elderly as a consequence of systematic stereotyping (Butler, 1969). Moreover, as is demonstrated by empirical evidence (e.g., World Health Organization [WHO], 1990b), negative views of aging have a perverse repercussion in society in a double sense: They reinforce negative beliefs and negatives views at the macro and micro levels, they threaten individuals and groups, and act as self-fulfilling prophecies during aging (Levy and Langer, 1994). A common schema or script is: Illness (as a main biological condition) is unavoidable in old age, cognitive impairment is normative, old individuals cannot learn, social withdraw is a standard situation at the end of life; social responses to these images go from nihilism to paternalism. Finally, the individual is threatened by this profile into acting as predicted and society is also threatened by an increase in the aging population under the assumption that they spend more than they contribute to society. In fact, all these assumptions come from one of the more extensive sociological theories in gerontology: the disengagement theory mentioned above.

Unfortunately, these negative images seem to be very common; for example, in one of our studies more than 60% of the individuals surveyed – from a representative sample (by age and sex) of people older than eighteen – agreed that people older than 65 are cognitively impaired, have serious memory problems, cannot learn, are rigid and inflexible, are worse than younger people in problem-solving, have bad humor, and are "as children" (Fernández-Ballesteros, 1992, 2006). Most important, after covariant analysis, no differences were found between age groups, gender, social position, and education. Although this negative view has improved in the last decade, it can be considered as a social threat and, therefore, any policy on aging should be preceded by changes in this negative view of aging (e.g., UN, 2002; UNECE, 2003; WHO, 1990b). Finally, and most important, this negative view is against scientific evidence and, therefore, comes from false beliefs.

In conclusion, from an Aristotelian tradition, gerontology (the scientific study of aging, age, and the aged), has been more devoted to those biomedical and psychosocial negative covariants that decline through age than to those that show positive development or are stable across aging. It can be assumed that this bias has been disseminated in society through negative images. However, it must be emphasized that an opposite perspective (taking into consideration only the positive conditions) would also be biased. In our view, positive aging is not a superficial, simplistic, and reductionistic conceptualization about aging, age, and the aged. On the contrary, it is an empirically based concept of aging that includes not only decline and losses but growth, stability, and positive events as part of the aging process. Moreover, without denying the probability of negative conditions, they can be prevented and/or modified since human beings have, throughout the lifecycle, high levels of plasticity (Baltes & Baltes, 1990b; Fernández-Ballesteros, 1986, 2003; Fries, 1989; Lehr, 1980, 1982; Whitebourn, 2005).

As a result of human and social development – including biomedical and technological progress in education, health care, hygiene, nutrition, etc. – during the twentieth century, all over the world, human lifespan increased and, in those developed countries, life expectancy at birth has doubled. Also, since the second half of the twentieth century, the fertility rate has been going down all over the world, approaching the level of replacement in most of the developed countries. These two demographic changes have produced an increase of older people, both in absolute and relative numbers, all over the world. The aging population can be considered as one of the most important demographic revolution throughout human history.

Since science is *accumulative* and *historical,* new findings about a scientific subject under study can change its conceptualization. From an individual point of view, a 70-year-old man or woman born at the beginning of the twentieth century, who had about 40 years of life expectancy at birth, today has not only a high probability of living longer than his/her parents but, also, of living in better bio-psycho-social conditions. Both multicohort and family studies have shown results in this direction (Schaie, 2005a, 2005b).

In sum, these changes from both demographic and individual points of view support the existence of a new perspective in the study of aging, age, and the aged.

Evolution in Research on Active Aging

From an evidence-based point of view, it has been during the last decades of twentieth century that the so-called "new paradigm" or "revolution" in the field of aging research and, in a broader sense, in the science of gerontology started: a positive view. Pioneers in this new paradigm are from several gerontological disciplines, including the fields of biomedicine and social sciences such as Fries and Crapo (1981); Fries (1989); Rowe and Khan (1987), or Baltes and Baltes (1990b).

This positive view of aging adopted several verbal rubrics: "healthy" (WHO, 1990b), "successful" (Thomae, 1975; Rowe & Khan, 1987; Baltes & Baltes, 1990a), "optimal" (Palmore, 1979), "vital" (Erikson et al., 1986), "productive" (Butler & Gleason, 1985), "active" (WHO, 2002), "positive" (Gergen & Gergen, 2001), or simply "aging well" (Fries, 1989) or "good life" (Bearon, 1996). It is important to emphasize that all these terms are taken almost interchangeably by experts when they review the field and in this text all of them are considered under the term "active aging" (e.g., Depp & Jeste, 2006; Lupien & Wan, 2004; Peel, McClure, & Bartlett, 2005).

Taking into consideration all these verbal key words, two searches were conducted: on the Internet and within scientific literature. On the Internet (Google, May, 2007), the most often cited term was "active aging" (4,250,000) followed by "healthy aging" (2,650,000), "successful aging" (2,150,000), "optimal aging" (2,010,000), and "productive aging" (1,800,000).

The search of scientific literature was conducted in three scientific data bases: PubMed, PsycINFO, and Sociological Abstract. This search were performed from 1970 to 2007 by decades using aging/aging and successful, healthy, active, optimal, and productive[1] in all fields (the last period covers from 2000 through 2007).

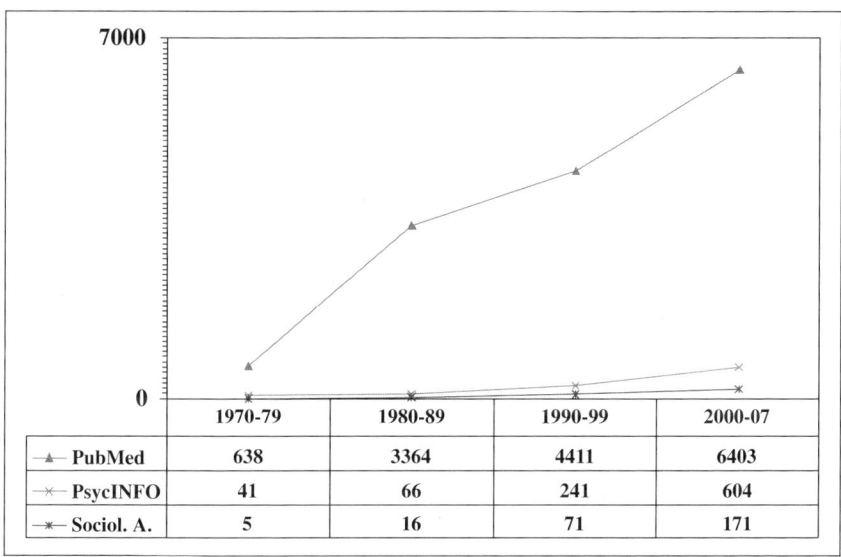

Figure 1. Active aging and related concepts in three scientific databases (1970–2007).

Figure 1 shows comparisons between the three databases. PubMed yielded the highest number of references going from 638 (70–79) to 6,403 (00–07) which ist ten times more. In the same line, the PsycINFO database started from about 40 publications in the first decade and had the greatest increase, to about 600 publications, during the last period (2000–2007). Finally, Sociological Abstract yielded the lowest numbers, running from 5 to 171 publications in the whole period.

Making a comparison between the terms used, we examined these publication databases separately. Figure 2 shows references published in PubMed. As can be observed, "healthy" aging is the term most used, followed by "successful," "active," "optimal," and "productive" aging. It is interesting to note that in the last period there is an inverse trend in the use of "successful" and "active"; while the use of "successful" aging is decreasing, "active" aging is increasing.

1 "Aging well" and "positive aging" were not used because they are both very general terms.

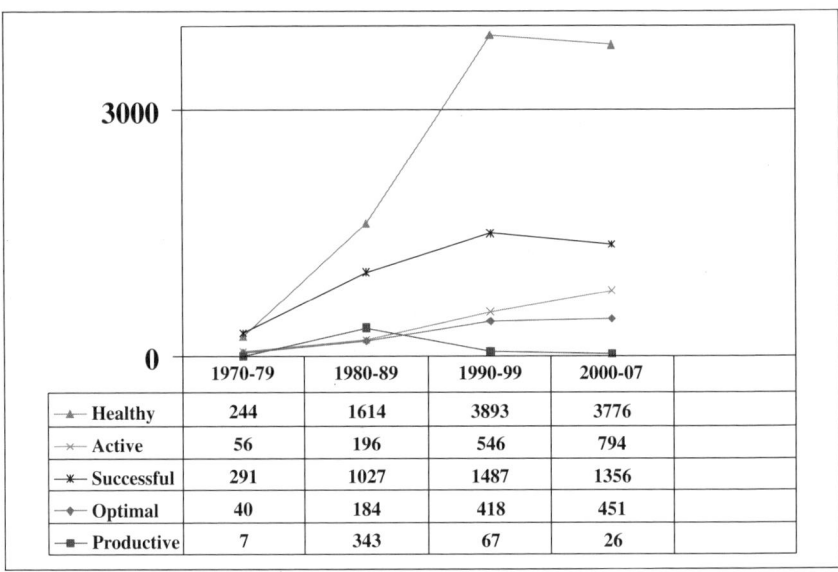

Figure 2. Active aging and related concepts research in PubMed scientific databases (1970–2007).

As we can see in Figure 3, there is an exponential growth in references to the field in PsycINFO. "Successful" aging is the most often used term, followed by "healthy" aging; there are minor references to "active," "optimal," and "productive" aging.

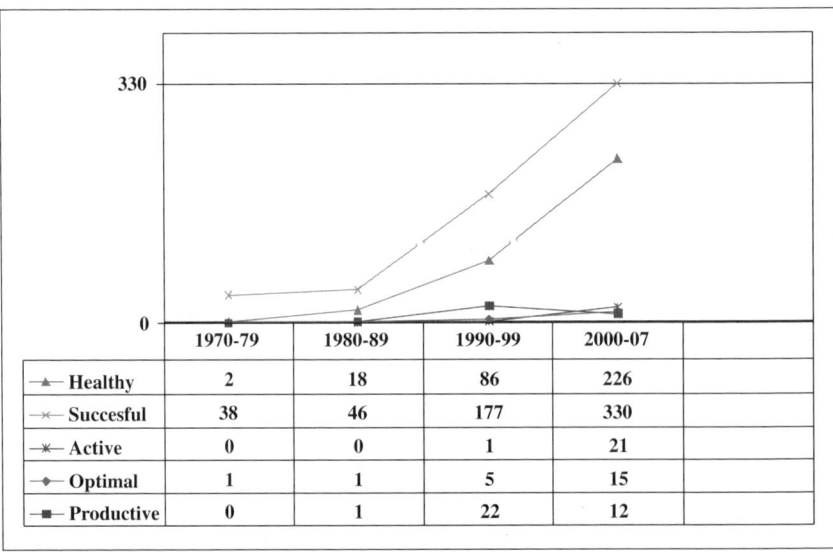

Figure 3. Active aging and related concepts research in PsycINFO scientific databases (1970–2007).

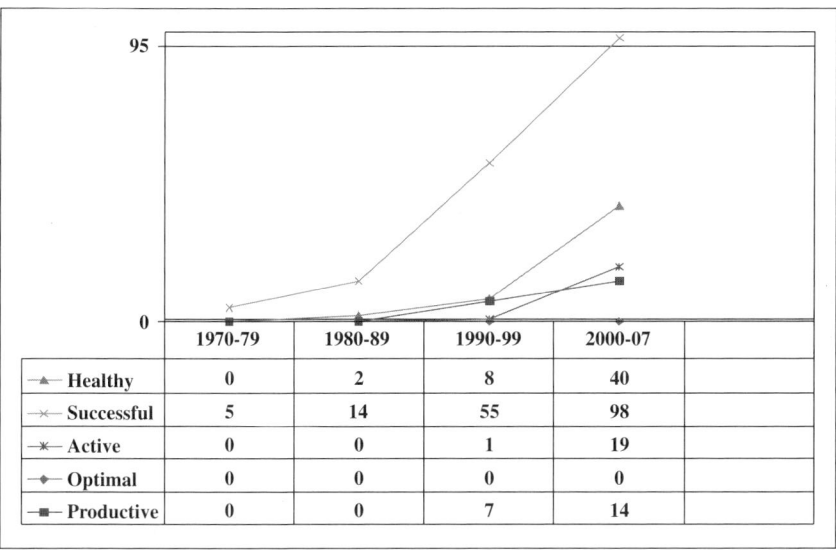

Figure 4. Active aging and related concepts research in Sociological Abstract scientific databases (1970–2007).

Finally, Sociological Abstract yielded the least results. The most often used term was "successful" aging followed by "healthy" and "active" aging (see Figure 4).

This review shows that research in the field of positive aging has increased from the 1970s to the present in all bibliographical databases. Also, it can be stated that the terms are linked to a concrete scientific field: "healthy" aging is a consolidated term within a biomedical context but use has declined in the last decade. "Successful" aging is the most extensively used term in psychological and social literature, and "active" aging appears more often in most of the databases in the last decade; this is congruent with the fact that "active aging" is linked to the *II International Plan of Action on Aging* (UN, 2002) and with the document *Active Aging* published by the WHO (2002) at the occasion of the *UN II General Assembly on Aging,* where the II International Plan of Action was approved. Also, these figures are in agreement with the search preformed on the Internet where the highest figures reference "active aging."

Empirical Bases of Active Aging

Baltes and Baltes (1990b) in the seminal Introductory chapter to their book *Successful Aging* suggested a framework of seven propositions from a psychological point of view:

1. The first proposition emphasizes the major differences between normal, optimal, and sick (pathological) aging.
2. The second proposition emerges from the first and refers to a broad interindividual variability in level, rate and direction of change. In sum, there is much heterogeneity (variability) in aging.
3. The third proposition assumes the concept of plasticity and latent reserve across the lifespan and, therefore, in old age.
4. The fourth proposition emerges from the empirical research establishing limits for behavioral plasticity and adaptive capacity.
5. With the fifth proposition authors try to reconcile propositions 3 and 4, that is, knowledge-based pragmatics and technology can compensate for decline.
6. The sixth proposition argues that with aging the balance between gains and losses becomes less positive. This decline or negative balance is in accord with individuals' subjective evaluation as well as with social stereotypes.
7. Finally, the last proposition is based on empirical evidence that there are minor age differences between life satisfaction and other positive psychological characteristics, therefore, it is assumed that the self remains resilient in old age.

Some of these propositions have also been supported from a biomedical perspective. Fries (Fries & Crapo, 1981; Fries, 1989) emphasized the variability of the ways of aging (1 and 2), plasticity of aging under the assumption that major manifestations of senescence are shown to be modifiable (3 and 4), diseases of aging may be postponed by personal decision (for example, changing lifestyles), and, therefore, he supports the other assumptions (5 and 6). Moreover, Fries introduced a new source of information about population aging: the rectangularization of the survival curves, which means that the shapes of survival curves are expressing not only longevity but the compression of morbidity and, therefore, that *sociohistorical development coincides not only with more years to life but, also, more life to years.*

Trying to make a synthesis, this positive view on the field of aging emerges from three main observed facts supported by empirical research (demographic, epidemiological, cross-sectional, longitudinal, and experimental studies): the *compression of morbidity*; the extreme *variability* of any bio-psycho-social condition in old age, and the *plasticity* of human beings expressed through *modifiability* of most of those declined or impaired conditions.

1. The first assumption states that, at the population level, across history, human beings are living longer and in better conditions. Fries and Crapo (1981) argue against the medical model for the study of aging. Using new knowledge about aging (morbidity, mortality, and survival) they arrive at a syllogism:
1. The human lifespan is fixed,
2. The age at first infirmity will increase,
3. Therefore, the duration of infirmity will decrease and, as a conclusion,
4. The period of vitality may be prolonged.

This syllogism can be tested through the improvement of life expectancy in good health, which is supported by the *postponement* of chronic disease and morbidity and, therefore, the "rectangularization" shape of the survival curve across time, which means that survival rate in humans is increasing not only throughout history but across ages as well (see Figure 10, in Chapter 2). The decline in mortality (not only infant mortality but mortality at all ages) has raised life expectancy almost all over the planet (Kannisto, 1996; Jeune & Vaupel, 1995). But, living longer does not mean living well; and increase in life expectancy could be and increase in morbidity and disability and, therefore, in suffering at the individual, family, and population levels. Presently, the increase in life expectancy is not only a general phenomenon but, most important, there are data supporting that morbidity has been concentrated in the later years of life; disability-free life expectancy and healthy life expectancy are slowly increasing in several of the countries with high life expectancy and, at least, for severe disability (see Chapter 2, Fries & Crapo, 1981; Fries, 2002; Robine, 2003; Meslé & Vallin, 2003; Robine & Michel, 2004).

As is well known, this demographic revolution should be attributed to social development, improvements in living conditions (hygiene, health services, education, etc.) but also should be taken as a consequence of the plasticity and modifiability of human being throughout the lifecycle, at all ages.

2. Therefore, our second assumption emerged from the well-tested variability of the aging phenomenon itself, which can be classified as: usual, pathological, and optimal aging (e.g., Baltes & Baltes, 1990b; Fries, 1989; Lerner, 1984; Plomin & Thompson, 1986; Rowe & Khan, 1997). Any pattern of decline across ages has high variability and variability increases throughout the lifespan (Smith & Baltes, 1999). As Vaupel et al. (1998) said from a bio-demographic point of view, "even genetically identical populations display phenotypic differences ... Some individuals are frailer than others, innately or because of acquired frailty" (p. 857). Therefore, there is high heterogeneity in the way of aging, as expressed at the level of individuals: from successful aging to disability.

As an example, Figure 5 shows the variability (*SD*) in three physical (speed assessed by tapping test), health (number of health problems reported), and social (social interaction frequency) conditions from the EXCELSA study performed in 7 European countries ($N = 672$), ages ranging from 30 to 85 years. Standard deviation increases by age in these three measures (Fernandez-Ballesteros, Zamarrón, Rudinger, Schroots et al., 2004).

Although this heterogeneity could be considered a continuum[2], under the assumption that any individual would have a true score on this continuum (based on the mean and standard deviation of a standard distribution), we are

---

2 For example, Smith and Baltes (1999) required 9 subgroups to describe a set of psychological dimensions in persons older than 70.

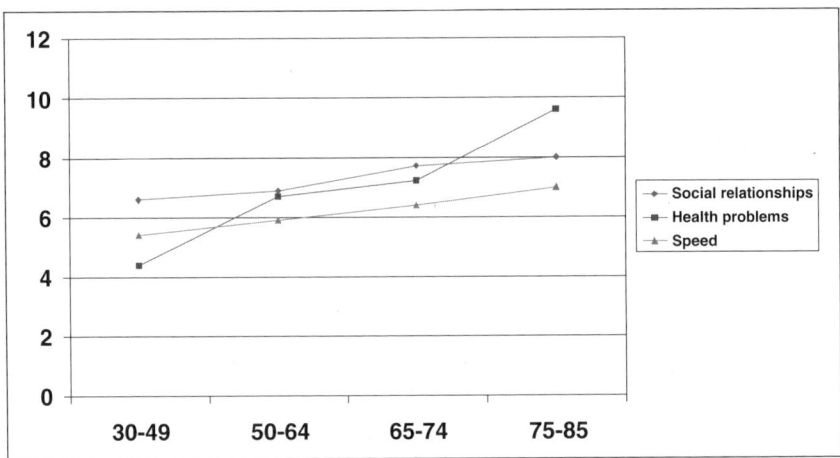

Figure 5. Variability *(SD)* in three bio-psycho-social conditions from the EXCELSA-P Project (30–85 years; N = 672) (Fernández-Ballesteros, Zamarrón, Rudinger et al., 2004).

able to classify the aging process as under, over, or on the average in a standard distribution, as has been claimed by Kubik (2006). Perhaps, a cut-off in a standard distribution would be preferable than calling these three trajectories "usual," "pathological," and "optimal" (or active, successful, etc.) as has been commonly accepted in the field (Rowe & Khan, 1987; Whitbourne, 1985). These three broad categories seem to maintain their descriptive power even in very old persons (see for example, Baltes & Smith 2003[3], for persons older than 70; Motta, Bennati Ferlito, Malafuarnera, & Motta 2005[4], for centenarians). Briefly, this classification has been disseminated for expressing this variability and heterogeneity as emerging from differences in plasticity, adaptability, and resilience of the organism.

In sum, there are large individual differences in adaptive mechanisms across the lifespan, which express the diversity of aging trajectories (e.g., Baltes & Baltes, 1990a; Carstensen, 1993; Greve & Staudinger, 2006).

3. Finally, the third assumption implies a condition emerging from empirical research from psychological and neurobiological perspectives: There exists a broad plasticity and reserve capacity of human functioning. In other terms, research in gerontology supports the existence of a basic multilevel principle of plasticity at the

---

[3] They considered that the oldest old are at the limits of their functioning, so the very old individuals of the BASE study could be classified following these three categories.

[4] In their study of centenarians (N = 602), they classified 20% as being in good health, independent, and maintaining good cognitive functioning, but they do not maintain any social or productive activity; 33.4% as having intermediate functioning, and 46.6% as being in bad health and functional status.

biological level, including the central nervous system (CNS), which is expressed, at a phenotypical level, through cognitive, emotional, and behavioral plasticity.

In fact, plasticity is also the basis for the results indicating that most of the conditions that decline over the lifecycle can be modified through environmental interventions. This broad plasticity of the human being, his/her modifiability of his/her biophysical functioning, reserve capacity or/and compensation preceding dysfunctions is the keystone of positive aging (e.g., Stern, 2003).

Learning potential and cognitive plasticity have been broadly tested through cross-sectional experimental designs using testing-the-limits, learning potential, or dynamic assessment procedures (e.g., Kliegl, Smith, & Baltes, 1989; Fernández-Ballesteros & Calero, 1995). Also, in the biomedical field, as Fries stated, across the aging process, any future capability of the individual "is not fixed, predestined, and inevitable, but may be modified" (Fries & Crapo, 1981, p. 111). These biomedical results on plasticity come from longitudinal, cohort, and intervention studies. From a broad, historical point of view, referring to physical standards, the modern Olympic Games show good examples of the improvement of the new cohorts in comparison with the oldest. Also, all longitudinal, time, and cohort sequential aging studies showed that the elderly in a younger cohort performed significantly better in most of the assessment variables. In addition, the elderly in younger cohorts have fewer disabilities (Crimmins, Saito, & Reynolds, 1997; Manton, 1997; Manton et al., 2007) and have higher cognitive performances (Shaie, 2005a, 2005b).

These three main assumptions could be reduced to the third one, since it is plasticity and modifiability of human being, taken as an adaptation mechanism of human life (both from population and individual perspectives), which determine both a human being's life expectancy and healthy life expectancy, as well as their individual differences. This fact has been pointed out by the pioneers of the paradigm.From a biomedical perspective, Fries and Crapo (1981), in their seminal paper *Vitality and Aging*, emphasized that the "rectangularization" of the survival curve is the expression of the modifiability and adaptation capacity of humanity. Likewise, Baltes and Schaie (1974, 1976), from a psychological perspective, emphasized that plasticity and modifiability is behind individual differences expressing multidimensionality and multidirectionality in human functioning. Baltes and Baltes (1990b) described the successful aging process through three strategies selective optimization with compensation (SOC) locating, behind them, the plasticity of human nature. Also from a sociological point of view, Kahana and Kahana's (2001, 2003) model of successful aging lies in the proactive principle of adaptation.

All these authors pointed out that across the lifespan there is evidence of wide individual differences in growth and decline in most bio-psycho-social characteristics. However,it is important that this does not occur at random but it is the agentic human being who is involved in and committed to his/her trajectory

(Bandura, 1986). Although this agentic condition of the human being is essential for active aging, it is highly important to emphasize the relevance of sociohistorical changes for increasing life expectancy and, also, the inequalities of sociocultural and environmental conditions for active aging. Paraphrasing Bandura (1986), active aging requires an active person in an active world.

Concluding Remarks

From different sources of data it can be stated that there is a new paradigm in scientific gerontology called active, successful, healthy, optimal, vital, or positive aging. In short, this new paradigm is based in new gerontological evidence supporting, at the individual level, the variability, plasticity, and modifiability of elderly functioning, as well as, at the populational level, the compression of morbidity at the end of life. This new paradigm is also involved in the study of positive components of aging and their determinants, as well as how health, well-being, and quality of life can be promoted throughout the lifecycle, including old age.

It is important to point out from the very beginning that we considered successful aging as an active and proactive way of aging and not as a simplistic and unrealistic, socioculturally constructed paradigm that avoids the reality of aging, as has been considered by some authors (Gergen & Gergen, 2001). In the scientific literature of this new paradigm, there are very few authors ignoring or neglecting biological age concomitant with system deterioration, with illness, with cognitive decline or impairment, and with other negative events (loss of position, family and friends, etc.), all of them covariant with age (Kane, 2003).

This renewed view considers that:
1. Organisms age at different rates as a function of the interaction between active individuals in active worlds where life circumstances can be changed;
2. Individuals have different forms of coping with these losses and declines but the way individuals cope can also be trained;
3. Not all covariants with aging are negative and throughout the lifespan several positive changes occur; and finally
4. Some of the negative consequences of aging are determined by illness (not only by age) and it is well known that illness (and other negative age covariants such as disability), can be prevented.

In summary, this renewed view or new paradigm stated that some of the concomitants of aging could be attributed – from an individual perspective – to illness (not to age) and/or to socioenvironmental conditions embracing aging, claiming that both type of covariants with age can be prevented and/or changed by means of the agentic individual will in interaction with social policies and, therefore, their negative consequences eliminated or postponed.[5]

---

5   It can, therefore, be stated that the two faces or views of aging continue nowadays within the positive aging paradigm. For example, Baltes and Smith (2003) propose less action through policies promoting successful aging in the younger elderly (the so-called third age), emphasizing the lack of plasticity and modifiability of the so-called fourth age, and alerting one to the "negative consequences of pushing biological aging or sheer longevity to its limits" (p. 133). Any political policy restriction ought to come from clear data – that is already well known – about the prevalence of certain illnesses (such as dementia and Alzheimer's disease) and high disability rates in very old age. Could it be said: "Do not push too much health and well-being into old age because, at the end of life, people will have a 50% chance of suffering from Alzheimer's and this will create a very big burden on society." What about the 50% who do not have AD and severe chronic disease and continue to live satisfactorily?

2
Population Aging: Facts and Projections

Life Expectancy Enlargement

During the twentieth century, as a consequence of the mortality decline at all ages, life expectancy increased dramatically. However, life expectancy has a ceiling: The human lifespan is about 115 years and it is fixed in all species (at least for the last 100,000 years). Therefore, although human longevity has a maximum life potential (Fries & Crapo, 1981; Olshansky, Carnes, & Desesquelles, 2001) life expectancy projections indicate it will continue to grow during the next decades: The average lifespan is expected to extend another 10 years by 2050 (Report on MIPPA; UN, 2002).

Figure 6 shows examples of life expectancy (LE) at birth for the year 2005 and projections for the year 2025 in a set of selected countries. It must be emphasized

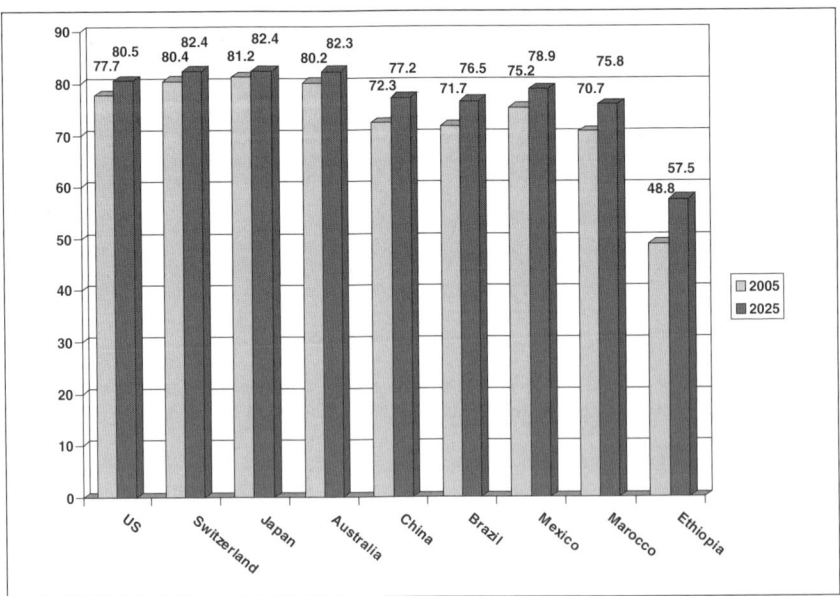

Figure 6. Life expectancy at birth in 2005 and projection to the year 2025 (data from US Bureau of the Census international database, 2006).

that there are important differences in life expectancy according to socioeconomic development. Some "developed" countries have a LE around 80 years (Japan, North America, Western European countries, and Australia), some other countries have around 75 years of LE and, finally, some countries have less than 50 years of LE (for example, Ethiopia). Without doubt, these differences express socioeconomic inequalities among different regions of the world.

Population Aging

This trait of life expectancy, together with a decline in fertility, will produce, during the first 50 years of the twenty-first century, a new "silent revolution": the population older than 60 is going to rise from about 600 million in 2000 to almost 2 billion in 2050; at that point the world will contain more people over 60 years old than under 15. The fastest growing group of the older population is the oldest old, that is those who are 80 or more years old. In 2000, this group was 70 million but they will increase five times by the 2050. Moreover, as Vaupel and Jeune (1995) showed, centenarians were an exception about the middle of the twentieth century but they have been doubling every 10 years since the 1950s.

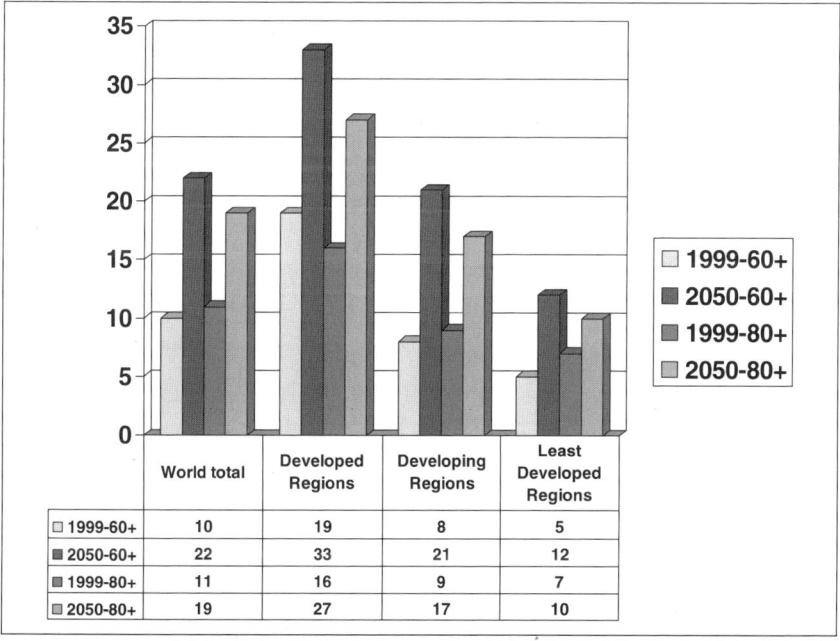

Figure 7. Percentage of the total population older than 60 and 80 in 1999 and projections for 2050, worldwide and in individual regions (data from UN, 2002).

As Perry (1995) stated, this longevity revolution is still in its "infancy." This new and exciting phenomenon has being called the "aging of aging" and is provoking many questions arising from this new population revolution; as Robine and Michel (2004) emphasized, much more research on the oldest old through longitudinal and cohort studies will be required in the forthcoming decades.

Figure 7 shows comparisons between 1999 and 2050; percentages of elderly who are older than 60 and 80 years are increasing in all regions of the world, both for developed and for developing countries.

Without doubt, the enlargement of life expectancy is the success of humanity, but age is also associated with disease and disability; therefore, an important question emerges: To what extent are population aging and life expectancy influencing the increasing prevalence of morbidity and disability at the end of life? In other (more poetic) words, to what extent does increasing "years to life" not mean enlarging "life to years." This question can be examined through demo-epidemiological indicators, that is, calculating the life expectancy without disability and/or through life expectancy in good health.

Years to Life and Life to Years

Population aging can be considered as a consequence of the success of human life and human society. However, as Fries and Crapo (1981) stated, adult life can be divided into two (not well-defined) periods: independence and vigor, and disease, diminished capacity, and dependence. Therefore, as mentioned in Chapter 1, a key issue is to what extent this infirmity period is going to be postponed and/or reduced (as predicted by Fries & Crapo, 1981), or enlarged or any other intermediate possibility.

Since the 1980s, WHO has been working on a set of demo-epidemiological indicators, extending the concept of life expectancy to morbidity and disability and, therefore, calculating "disability-free life expectancy" (absence of disability) and "healthy active life expectancy" (optimal health perception). Therefore, nowadays, the most extensively used demo-epidemiological population indicators are disability-free life expectancy (DFLE) or healthy active life expectancy (HALE), exploring whether the years lived at the end of life are years with or without disability or in poor or good health. Comparisons between life expectancy, DFLE, and HALE allow us to predict the number of years with disability or unhealthy years in a given population. Following-up these indicators also allows us to test hypotheses about the period of infirmity at the end of life.

Making comparisons of these demo-epidemiological indicators between countries, Figure 8 shows life expectancy at birth and DFLE (European Communities Council, 2007) in both Western (EU-15) and Eastern European countries

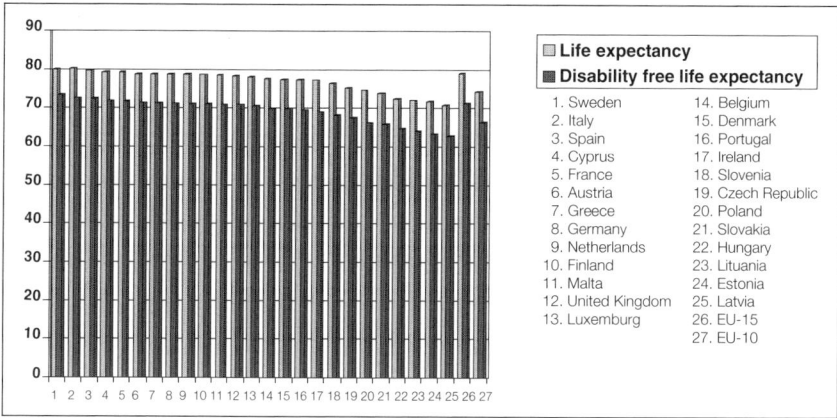

Figure 8. Life expectancy at birth and disability-free life expectancy in Western and Eastern European countries, EU-15 and EU-10 (data from ECC, 2007).

(EU-10). There are large differences between countries in both indicators; for example, Sweden has, on average (men and women), about 80 years life expectancy at birth and 73 years of DFLE (that is, about 7 years with disability) meanwhile Latvia has about 71 years of life expectancy and 63 years of DFLE (that is, around 8 years with disability). This means that a Swedish person born in 2004 has almost 10 years more of life expectancy and 1 year less to suffer disability than a person born in Latvia. In summary, regions on the same continent have broad differences in both demographic and health indicators, while Western European in comparison with Eastern countries have on average 8 years more of life expectancy and 1 year more DFLE.

Healthy Active Life Expectancy (HALE) is a another demo-epidemiological indicator developed by WHO (2003). As well as life expectancy at birth, HALE comparisons show tremendous differences between continents and countries. Figure 9 shows HALE and life expectancy at birth for a set of selected countries on the five continents. Life expectancy ranges from 84 years (Japan) to 33 (Sierra Leona); more than two and a half times more, and HALE ranges from 25.8 years in Sierra Leona (a country at that time at war in Africa) to 73.5 in Japan. In other terms, while in some countries an individual born in 2000 can expect to have 10 years in poor health in other countries this expectancy is reduced to less than 7 years. Without doubt, these differences are the result of contextual differences among countries (socioeconomic, educational, health and social conditions, etc.).

Nevertheless, the examples are given to emphasize the value of HALE and DFLE as important indicators for assessing health and well-being in population aging as well as economic and social development influences on quality of life for older populations. HALE and DFLE are also considered as indicators for evaluating policies and programs developed from the Madrid International Plan of

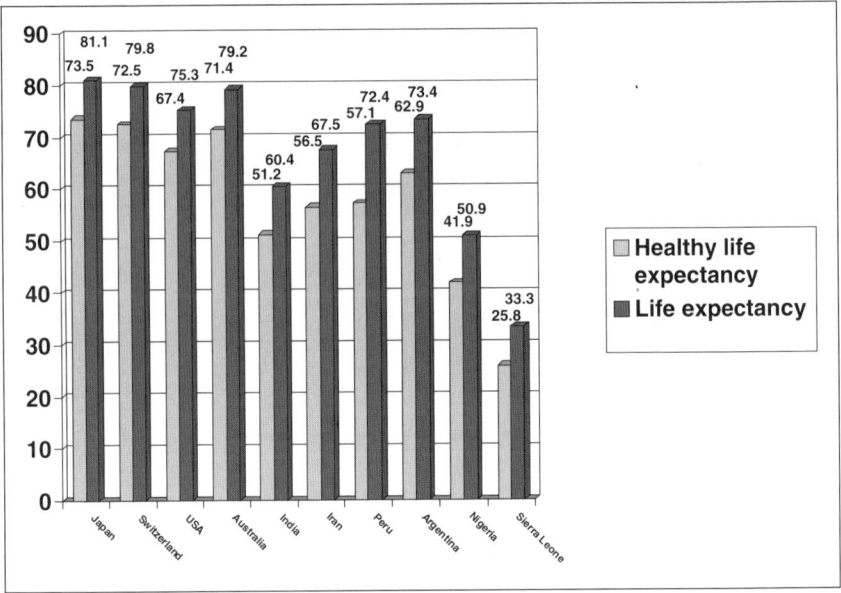

Figure 9. Healthy life expectancy and life expectancy at birth in countries of 5 continents (data from WHO, 2002).

Action on Aging (UN, 2002) in these areas (European Center-Monitoring RIS: http://www.monitoringris.org/; Marin & Zaidi, 2007).

As has been noted previously, projections in life expectancy predict an enlargement of human life and there is an important debate regarding the degree to which this enlargement (adding years to life) – that is, longevity – would have negative repercussions in DFLE and/or HALE. In other words, whether adding years to life is going to determine more years of illness and disability at the end of life.

Consequences of population aging in health and illness, disability, and well-being are taken as a threat for old individuals, families, and the entire society and not only because one of its consequences is individual and group suffering. From a socioeconomic point of view, an increase in longevity has repercussions in health care costs (Miller, 2001). Scientists, policy makers, and civil organizations (national and internationally) have emphasized that the impact of the aging population in formal (health and social services) and informal care will be extraordinary. We will briefly introduce these economic consequences and some particular conditions that could make the threat less dramatic.

Lubitz (2004), pointed out that in the USA the highest expenditure in medical care was for the last year of life. Moreover, this cost in the last year was lower for the elderly, for the simple reason that less aggressive and costly interventions are provided to the elderly than to younger clients[1]. Moreover, healthy elderly (more than 70 years old) lived longer than unhealthy elderly and, therefore, they spent more because unhealthy elderly lived one-third less than healthier elderly did and their cost per year was higher (see also Lubitz, Cai, Kramarow & Lentzer, 2003).

Therefore, the problematic situation emerges not from the fact that unhealthy people are more costly than healthier people but that healthier people lived more years than unhealthy. In sum, is not being healthy or unhealthy but the number of years the individual is going to be alive[2].

Although there are discussions about healthcare projections, it seems to be commonly accepted that, parallel to this "salient revolution" runs a public health problem (UN, 2002; WHO, 2002; Center for Disease Control and Prevention, 2003; Manton, Lamband, & Gu, 2007). Therefore, it is extremely important both to attend to those elderly with disability with the best long-term care system but, at the same time, to promote active aging as well as to prevent illness throughout the lifecycle. Improvements in healthy habits are low cost and, thus, authors (e.g., Daviglus et al. 2003) consider that favorable health-risk profiles in middle age may result in both longer life and, at the same time, that medical costs in the last year of life would be lower for persons with favorable risk profiles in middle age.

This demographic transition is explained by progress in biomedical and technical knowledge as well as by the extension of education, healthy habits, and welfare. Without doubt, as has been repeated, changes in demographic patterns can be considered the product of human and social development, but this demographic revolution might have a negative repercussion: Life expectancy increases and population aging *might* determine a higher prevalence of disability and long-term care costs.

Morbidity Hypotheses

It is extremely important to determine whether increasing life expectancy in the population is going to increase, be reduced, or remain stable morbidity and disability at the end of life (with its correspondent increase in health expenditure and social cost). Manton (1982) established three hypotheses: *enlargement* (years added to life are going to be years with disability), a *dynamic equilibrium* (between prevalence and severity), and a *compression of morbidity* (disability rates will be reduced). Obviously, morbidity enlargement is the most important threat for population aging, while compression of morbidity will be the most beneficial.

---

1   This is not the right place to discuss this fact, which perhaps is an "ageist" medical practice.
2   It is difficult to estimate the situation of future cohorts of elderly because modern younger generations display more risk behaviors (mainly those related with diet – overweight – and drugs) than current cohorts.

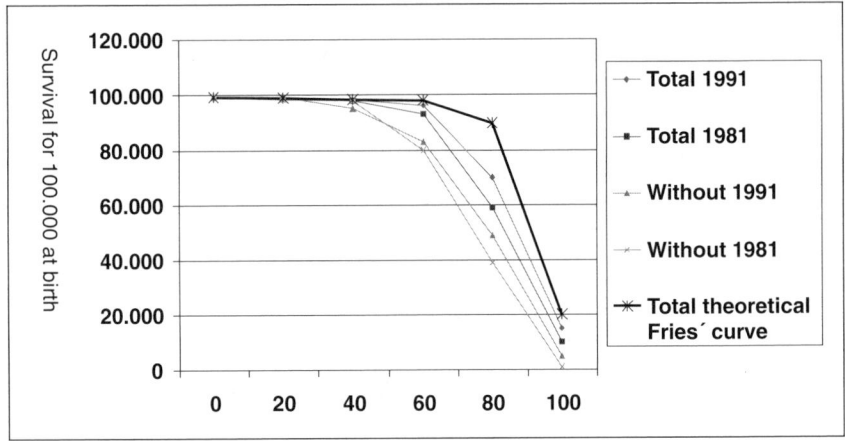

Figure 10. "Rectangularization" of survival curve: Total survival and survival without disability in 1981 and 1991 (France, females, data from Robine & Michel, 2004) and theoretical Fries curve.

Behind these three hypotheses there are sociopolitical and behavioral assumptions based on predictions about outcomes of health promotion and illness-prevention programs. In behavioral terms, whether lifestyles or promotion of healthy habits and/or other salutogenic practices are going to be implemented and whether they will decrease or compress morbidity in old age is one of the most intriguing topics in the field (Manton, 1982; Robine & Michel, 2004). These three hypothesis about morbidity have been examined through several methodologies (e.g., Cheung, 2005; Land, 2001; Zeng, 2004; Robine & Michel, 2004).

As has been stated by Fries and Crapo (1981), *compression of morbidity* was based on changes in the shape of the survival curve during the twentieth century. That is, from 1900 through the present time, the percentage of survival has increased at all ages, and the survival curve for the twentieth century has adopted a quasi-rectangular shape. These data suggest, at an individual level, the possibility of a long life with a relatively short period of terminal decline.

Figure 10 shows data of total survival and survival without disability for two periods (1981 and 1991), for French women in comparison with the ideal curve proposed by Fries and Crapo (1981, p. 7). Although total survival is higher than total survival with disability, both types of survival are increasing and approaching to the expected curve shape predicted by Fries and Crapo (1981).

As has been emphasized by Fries (2003), although the concept of compression of morbidity has sometimes been portrayed as naively optimistic and, even, a threat to the preparation required to care for ever-larger elderly populations, it is still working. Let us now discuss the results supporting morbidity compression stemming from several countries and several data sources.

As suggested by Manton (1982, 1997) disability is a source for testing morbidity compression. Taking the evolution of disability during the twentieth century from a historical point of view and from a population perspective, Fogel (2005) stated: "Prevalence rates of chronic diseases were . . . lower at the end of the 20th Century than they were at the beginning or during the last half of the 19th century and there has been a significant delay in the onset of chronic diseases over the course of 20th Century." From the early twentieth century to the early 1990s, Costa (2002) estimated the functional limitation decline in men, in the US, at an annual rate of 0.6%. All these findings and others have led investigators to posit a synergism between technological and physiological improvements, which will continue through the twenty-first century.

Even so, some inconsistencies found in the morbidity compression hypothesis in the US have been solved by a technical working group. After a revision of all existing studies, the panel reported "consistent declines on the order of 1–2.5% per year for two commonly used measures in the disability literature (disability with daily activities and help with daily activities). The panel also found agreement across surveys" (Freedman et al., 2004, p. 417; Robine, Mormiche, & Sermet, 1998).

Other sources for testing morbidity hypotheses comes from observations of cohorts (Hubert, Bloch, Oehlert, & Fries, 2002), changes in health differences during different periods of time (Cambois, Robine, & Hayward, 2001), studies in individual differences on socio-economic status (SES: education, income, profession), professional status across time (Geronimus, 2001), and education (Peres, Jagger, Lievre, & Barberger-Gateau, 2005), broad studies in long-term care and health surveys, longitudinal studies (HALE Report, see Bogers et al., 2006), as well as intervention studies analyzing the impact of health promotion programs in mortality and morbidity (RAND, 2002). All of them support the compression of morbidity at least in so-called first world or in developed countries (EU-15, Switzerland, USA, Canada, France, Japan, and Australia).

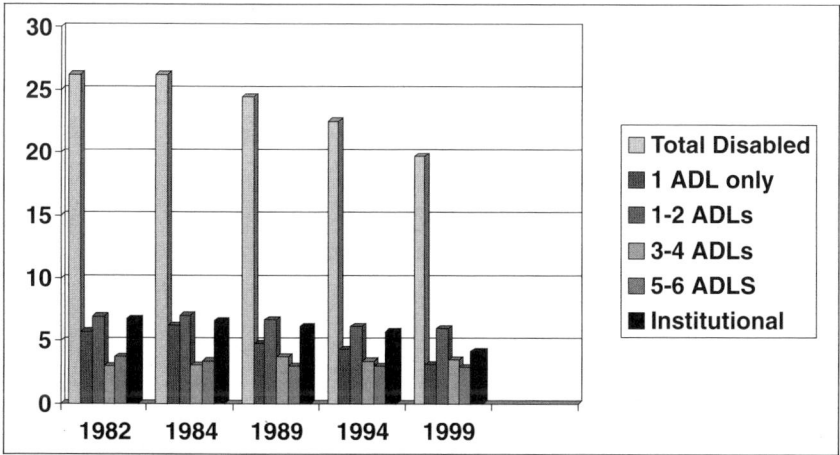

Figure 11. US population distribution of disability (age standardized to 1999 over-65) (adapted from Manton & Gu, 2001).

As an example, Figure 11 shows the reduction of disability in several cohorts from results from the National Long-Term Care Survey on Disability (USA, Manton & Gu, 2001). Total disabled as well as several levels of Activity of Daily Living (ADL) impaired have been reduced from 1982 through 1999 in the USA.

An important issue is which factors contribute to the decline in disability prevalence. Manton, Gu, and Ukraintseva (2005) consider that the decline in chronic disability prevalence that occurred from 1982 to 1999 in the US elderly population parallel to declines in severe cognitive impairment yielded 310.000 fewer severely cognitively impaired elderly in 1999 than in 1982. The average decline in prevalence was from 5.7 to 2.9 for this period. This was associated with a significant decline in mixed but not Alzheimer's dementias. Several explanations of such data are:
1. Increase in the proportion of better educated people,
2. Decline in stroke rates,
3. Decline in vascular and mixed dementias resulting from preventive behaviors of vascular diseases, and
4. Expanding use of neuro-protective medications working prophylactically for selected dementia.

Also, trying to identify those factors that must be controlled in order to reduce morbidity and disability, the Medical Research Council Cognitive Function and Ageing Study Investigators (Jagger, Matthews, Matthews, Robinson, & Robine, 2007) examined the relative impact of different diseases in disability. To this end, 13,004 individuals aged 65 years and older were interviewed in five UK centers starting in 1991. Disability was assessed through basic ADL and instrumental ADL assessment devices at baseline and at 2, 6, and 10 years of follow-up. At baseline, participants also reported their disease conditions and their current treatment and diagnoses, in addition diagnostic scales were used for angina, peripheral disease-and for cognitive impairment. First of all prevalence (weighted by sampling design) of chronic conditions at baseline were examined for nine diseases: coronary heart disease, stroke, cognitive impairment, diabetes, peripheral vascular disease, chronic airway obstruction, arthritis, visual and hearing impairment. To assess the relative impact of different diseases on disability, DFLE and extra years free of any disability without disease were calculated for each of the nine diseases. For example, while the expected number of years free of any disability for those without cognitive impairment was 12.0, those with cognitive impairment had only 7.8 years. In other words, the extra years free of any disability in participants without cognitive impairment was 4.2 years. The most relevant conclusion from this paper is that eliminating or reducing stroke, cognitive impairment, arthritis, and/or visual impairment results in a reduction of disability.

Although these studies give supportive arguments to the compression of morbidity resulting from specific health problems, it would be difficult to establish the amount of variance from all different causes for this total decline in disability.

As has been recognized by several authors, this phenomenon might be multifactorial, with no single identifiable cause. For example, Costa (2002) gives very this general calculation: 24% of this decline is attributable to reductions in debilitating effects of chronic disease, and 37% to reduced rates of chronic disease.

After a review of research studies about disability and morbidity at the end of life, Fries (2003) concluded that the decline in disability is about 2% per year, contrasted with a decline in mortality rates of about 1% per year in the last three decades, thereby documenting a 1% rate of compression of morbidity in the United States at the population level. All of this supports the compression of morbidity and increasing active aging. However, it should also be emphasized that for Fries (2003), compression of morbidity requires a research agenda including:

1. Monitoring disability trends through national survey programs, with addition of more quantitative disability measures to the instruments and inclusion of quality-of-life measures;
2. Attempting to more precisely define the causes behind the trends, possibly using econometric techniques; and
3. Performing systematic studies of specific primary prevention interventions, with the goal of identifying population-based approaches to compression of morbidity that are most effective and most cost-efficient. To these three items a fourth item must be added:
4. Evaluating active aging programs, looking for their impact on disability at population and at individual levels, and searching for their efficiency through cost-benefit analysis.

Until here, the supporting evidence of compression of morbidity hypothesis, nevertheless, there are other results introducing supportive evidence not only for compression but also for equilibrium and enlargement hypotheses.

From the *International Network on Health Expectancy (REVES)*, Robine and Michel (2004) showed that a universal and regular increase in life expectancy can be found in the low mortality countries, but this positive view cannot be generalized to DFLE because only "severe" disability follows a shape parallel to life expectancy in Australia, Canada, France, Japan, the UK, and the US. They found that the three hypotheses could be supported by the differential profiles in different countries. For example, comparing chronological series coming from some European countries: Life expectancy at 65 increased from 1980 and 1990 in Austria (from 15.2 years in 1978 to 17.5 in 1998) and in Great Britain (from 8.5 years in 1981 to 9.5 years in 1999); DFLE and HALE changed in opposing ways in that Great Britain increased in DFLE (8.5 years in 1981 to 9.5 years in 1998), Austria (from 3.5 years at 65 in 1978 to 8.3 in 1998) and Great Britain increased in HALE.

These data from population aging supports both the equilibrium and compression hypotheses with two conclusions:

1. A control of the progression of chronic diseases, which would explain a subtle equilibrium between the fall of mortality and the increase in disability; and
2. An improvement in health status and health behaviors of the new cohorts of old people, which would support the compression of morbidity.

Nevertheless, some data coming from some other countries support the expansion of morbidity and disability resulting from the increase in the survival rates of sick persons and/or to the emergence of very old and frail elderly. Unfortunately, as authors have stated, all these elements coexist today, but future salutogenic scenarios promoting active aging could incline the balance to the compression hypothesis.

In conclusion, much more effort must be made to reduce morbidity at the end of life. This is a challenge for science and society, in humanitarian, biological, psychological, social, and economic terms. Population aging at the beginning of the twenty-first century will require public policies in reducing morbidity to extend health and well-being over the lifecycle and in old age.

Determinants of Morbidity

A last question refers to information about factors influencing morbidity. In brief:
1. *Education* attainment and lifelong learning have an enormous influence on the way people age. Low levels of education are associated with poor biological and health conditions, and low psychological functioning (e.g., Kubzansky, Berkman, Glass, & Seeman, 1998).
2. *Socioeconomic development* is highly related to life expectancy at the population and at the individual levels. There is a gradient with similar shape between health and SES and there is a strong relationship between national or regional socioeconomic development and DFLE and HALE (Adler & Snibbe, 2003). Gregg (1992) even suggested the introduction of the concept *well span* in order to demonstrate its relevance to the financial dimensions of successful aging and the responsibility of public policies through pension systems.
3. *Biomedical advances and medical measures* (from environmental safety to cancer screening, better treatment of hypertension, diabetes, coronary artery disease, and rheumatoid arthritis influenza and pneumococcal vaccines, and cardiac-dose aspirin) are biomedical and environmental sources of morbidity compression.
4. *Social policies* on environmental and economic safety, health, and education across the lifespan as well as in active aging promotion necessarily reduce mortality as well as morbidity. As and example, the *Madrid II International Plan of*

Action on Aging (UN, 2002; UNECE, 2003) has been planned and approved for integrating aging and development, for enhancing health and well-being in old age, and for enabling friendly environments for the elderly.

5. *Behavioral lifestyles* are recognized as determinants of morbidity for most chronic diseases (see Chapter 4). Postponement of chronic disease is associated with risk factors such as cigarette smoking, excessive alcohol consumption and other unhealthy dietary habits, and low physical exercise. Risk factors can be removed by changes to healthy lifestyles. As Fries (2003) pointed out, those people who do not smoke and who drink moderately, follow a diet, and exercise regularly show four times less disability than those who smoke, drink too much, do not exercise, and are obese.
6. The last kind of factors refer to those *behavioral and psychosocial* conditions that are associated with mortality, survival, and morbidity. As we can see in Chapter 3, WHO (2002) considers behavioral lifestyles among the determinants of active aging. Moreover, among personal factors (together with genetic and biological), WHO posited, as determinants of active aging, psychological factors such as coping styles, perception about self-control, self-efficacy, and other personality characteristics such as optimism. It can be assumed that the promotion of these factors can contribute in some extent to the reduction of mortality and morbidity.

In sum, reducing risk factors (for stroke, CVD, diabetes, etc.), changes in behavioral lifestyles (increase in physical and intellectual activity, diet improvement, etc.) give better expectations for longevity and for healthier aging. Also, education, lifelong learning, cognitive activity, perceived control and self-efficacy, adaptive coping styles, and social participation are personal factors influencing health and well-being in old age. Synergies among all these empirically based factors could be an accumulative source of variance of the morbidity compression and, therefore, on an increase in positive and healthy aging.

Throughout this section we have focused on the following two empirically based issues:
1. The way people age is not random but depends on a set of risk and protective factors (some of them well-known factors) and
2. Not only mortality can be postponed but disability and dependency as well. In conclusion, implementation of public policies for increasing health and well-being in old age and decreasing chronic disease and dependency is an important goal at the population and individual levels. These policies should incorporate the promotion of personal, protective behavioral and psychological factors (such as a sense of control, health management, positive coping styles, etc.) throughout the lifecycle.

Concluding Remarks

Population aging is a universal phenomenon. In the coming years, life expectancy at birth will increase all over the world. Indicators such as Disability Free Life Expectancy (DFLE) and Healthy Life Expectancy (HALE) show that there are large differences between countries, regions, and continents. These differences are mainly because of contextual differences among these countries, regions, and continents: environmental, socioeconomic, sociocultural, educational, health and social policies, etc. These differences also determine wide differences in the way people age; therefore, a more egalitarian world should be pursued.

A review of the facts and projections of demographic and epidemiological indicators has been introduced and discussed examining morbidity hypotheses. As researchers in positive aging we could be positive regarding the future. As Lubitz (2004) concludes: "if morbidity is indeed becoming compressed, medical costs should be affected – possibly reducing them . . . the morbidity hypothesis posits that the amount of time in poor health will be less among the future elderly than among today's elderly (p. 7)."

It can be concluded that the hypothesis of morbidity compression seems to be the most plausible hypothesis with the existing data for most of the developed countries, but new research is needed in order both to evaluate policies and programs for preventing illness and disability and for promoting successful aging.

This positive panorama requires the promotion of active aging as well as the prevention of disability, which is the only avenue not only for reducing and postponing disability but for increasing well-being and quality of life across aging.

Policies for aging well should be developed and implemented all over the world for ensuring adequate environmental conditions, income, lifelong education, health and social care services, and support and opportunities for independent living and participation.

The socioepidemiological indicators reviewed are broadly recommended by experts and by international organizations as outcome measures for evaluating human development and the fulfillment of the II International Plan of Actions on Aging (UN, 2002; UNECE, 2003; Marin & Zaidi, 2007; Nusselder & Peeters, 2006). These measures of population aging (DFLE and HALE) reflect both survival and human functioning throughout life, as well as across time, and allow us to test the evolution of one of the most important factors of progress for human life: active aging.

3
Working, Empirical, and Lay Definitions, and Theoretical Models

Introduction

As usually happens when a new concept in science emerges, successful aging not only has a variety of synonymies (healthy, successful, optimal, productive, active aging) but still does not have a definition or a commonly accepted theoretical model.

Based on our previous bibliographical analyses, three periods can be distinguished in the constitution and development of the conceptualization of successful aging:

1. A first period, until the end of the 1970s, when research on aging focused on biomedical, psychological, and social changes among age groups with very few references to the ways of aging. In this period the two main theoretical approaches "disengagement" and "activity" theories can be considered as opposed conceptions in the study of aging (for a review see Freund & Riediger, 2003).
2. During the 1980s, a second period based on the activity theory can be identified; the concept of successful aging emerged and some definitions, predictors, and theoretical models about this new concept were developed.
3. Finally, from the 1990s until now, large studies on healthy and successful aging are still publishing conclusions and more reliable empirical definitions, tested predictors, and theoretical models of successful aging have been posited.

During all these periods, scientific conceptualizations about aging have been disseminated; politicians, newspapers, and lay audiences have adopted some of these conceptualizations and those concepts have been embedded in peoples' vocabulary and in their minds. Lay concepts about aging well are important because they can be considered as an expression of social images about aging and are necessarily related to self-perceptions about aging. Therefore, one avenue of inquiry is to examine lay conceptualizations across different population groups.

In this section the most extensive definitions of positive aging and related terms will be reviewed. First of all, two controversial issues are going to be discussed; secondly, working definitions are given by authors within the scientific community will be described. Thirdly, empirical definitions emerging from cross-sectional and longitudinal research on successful aging will be reviewed. Also, "lay" concepts of positive aging will be examined, under the assumption that they are explicit conceptualizations of this scientific concept shared by group of individuals. Finally, elaborated theoretical models will be presented and, on the basis of those conceptualizations, from a lifespan perspective, a multidimensional-multilevel model of aging well will be proposed.

Controversial Issues

At the beginning of this chapter, two main controversial topics should be discussed as preconditions for our understanding of successful aging:
1. Confounding successful (optimal, active, productive) aging with other constructs such as well-being, life satisfaction, or quality of life and
2. Reductionism vs. multidimensional components of successful aging.

Confounding Successful (Optimal, Active, Productive) Aging with Other Constructs such as Well-Being, Life Satisfaction, or Quality of Life

Historically, the successful aging concept has been developed at the same time and in connection with other positive constructs such as quality of life, or has been reduced to one of its components such as life satisfaction or well-being. Therefore, it has been conceptualized as sharing certain components with those, also new, constructs.

In his seminal article regarding determinants of well-being in old age, Lawton (1983) defined "good life" through psychological dimensions such as behavioral competence (health, motor, and cognitive), psychological well being (optimism, happiness, accordance between desire and obtained goals) perceived quality of life (family, friends, work, activity, income, and home conditions), but adding objective environmental conditions (housing, neighborhood, income, etc.). Therefore, this concept of "good life" developed by Lawton cannot be distinguished from the concept of quality of life nor can those criteria be distinguished from its determinants (see also Abeles et al., 1994).

In a similar line, Ryff (1989a), attempting to search for the integration of a definition of successful aging, established six criteria: self-acceptance, positive relationships with others, autonomy, environmental mastery, purpose in life, and personal growth.

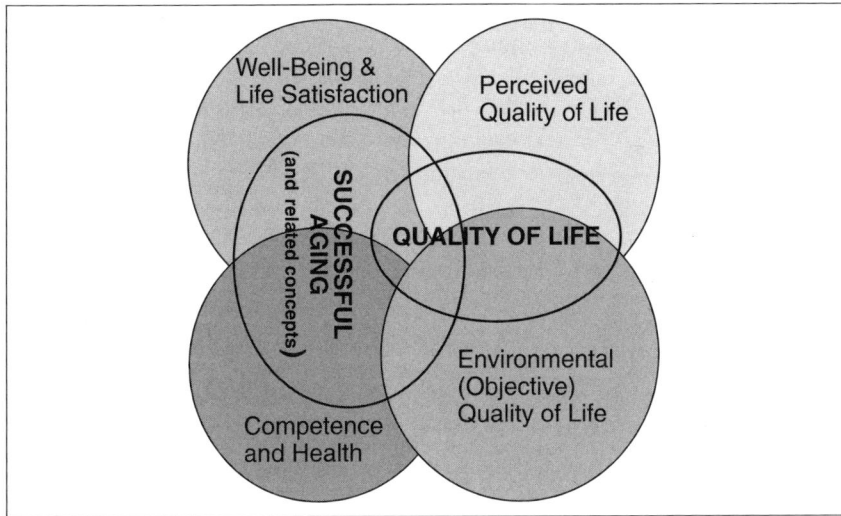

Figure 12. Theoretical relationships between quality of life, well-being and life satisfaction and successful aging (adapted from Lawton, 1983, and modified from Fernández-Ballesteros, Kruse, Zamarrón, & Caprara, 2007).

Figure 12 is a theoretical proposal by Fernández-Ballesteros et al. (2007) summarizing the theoretical relations between quality of life (QoL) and successful aging (and related concepts) on the basis of Lawton's four-sector model. First of all, well-being and life satisfaction, and competence and health are personal conditions both for successful aging (and related concepts) and for QoL. But while QoL also embraces environmental conditions (both perceived and objective), successful aging can be considered as an individual's multidimensional and multilevel concept.

As pointed out by Walker (2005), QoL is an umbrella or meta-level concept embedding a broad set of conditions, from the individual and from the environment. Successful aging is (also) a multidomain, multilevel concept, but it refers mainly to the individual as a bio-psychosocial agency, and it cannot be reduced to any of its components (such as health, physical competence, or well-being). Finally, environmental circumstances can be considered an antecedent, determining successful aging, but successful aging can also enhance quality of life in old age.

Biomedical Reductionism vs. Multidimensional Components of Successful Aging

As is recognized by several authors in the field (e.g., Baltes & Baltes, 1990b), successful aging must be addressed by interdisciplinary collaboration. Nevertheless, some working definitions have been developed for a specific field (biomedical, psychological, or sociological) reducing aging well to only one domain. For example, from a biomedical point of view, Guralnik and Kaplan (1989) considered two main criteria for aging well: low level of disease and disability and high physical functioning. Williams and Wirths (1965) offered a psychosocial definition when they stated that successful aging means life satisfaction, life and social engagement, feeling well about oneself, and behavior according with one's own values and beliefs. Lehr et al. (2000) also suggest life satisfaction as the central constituent of successful aging. From a social perspective, Butler and Gleason (1985) propose three main criteria for defining productive aging: productivity, participation, and engagement with life. In sum, although there are working definitions of active or successful aging from specific disciplines, multidimensionality is considered as an essential characteristic of successful aging.

Aging could be considered as a long bio-psycho-social process through which reciprocal transactions between the biological organism, the person, and the environment occur (Bandura, 1986). Therefore, the attributes "successful," "active," "productive," "healthy," etc. should be examined from a variety of outcomes, components, expressions, or ingredients for describing successful aging (good health, independence, coping with stress, etc.).

The person who is becoming old successfully must be considered as a complex active agent (constituted by multiple biological and psychological dimensional systems) interacting with a multilevel environment (family, community, society). Therefore, those multidimensional or multidomain outcomes defining successful aging and its multilevel determinants operating multidirectional transactions must be distinguished.

Working Definitions

A working definition refers to a list of intuitive *outcomes* or *criteria* or *proposed processes* for achieving successful aging suggested by authors. As Ryff (1989a) stated, most of these definitions do not arise from a guiding theory and, therefore, are only attempts to describe an existing, but not yet tested, concept.

In this section we examine those working definitions of successful aging (and related concepts) that refer both to intuitive *criteria* or *outcomes* and to the *process* for aging successfully.

The Outcomes

Authors from this field accept that it was Havighurst (1963) who proposed the first conceptualization of successful aging: "adding life to the years" and "getting satisfaction from life." Both ingredients are highly abstract and mainly subjective.

Based on the Bonn Longitudinal Study of Aging, Thomae (1975) defined patterns of successful aging in terms of biological, social, and perceptual-motivational processes. However, it was Palmore (1979) who first listed a set of biomedical and psychological conditions for successful aging: longevity, health, and life satisfaction. He also posited a multidimensional theoretical framework in which these criteria are a function of social, economic, physical, and mental health systems.

Fries (1989, 1990) was one of the first authors to distinguish not only the concept of vital aging and aging well but also its potential determinants through prevention and healthy lifestyle promotion (Fries & Crapo, 1981; Fries, 1989). Fries (1989) pointed out six basic criteria for vital aging:
1. Maintain independence,
2. Moderate habits,
3. Keep active,
4. Be enthusiastic,
5. Have a good image of one's self, and
6. Be individual.

Baltes and Baltes (1990b) listed a more extensive set of criteria for successful aging: length of life, biological health, mental health, cognitive efficacy, social competence and productivity, personal control, and life satisfaction. But most important, they introduced one of the most extensive and tested theories for successful aging when they includes the Selective Optimization with Compensation (SOC) model, which we will describe later.

One of the most well-known definitions of successful aging was proposed by Rowe and Khan (1987, 1997, 1998). They gave a formal and multidimensional set of criteria: low probability of disease and disability, high physical and mental functioning, and active engagement with life. This model has been tested through longitudinal research (as, for example McArthur Studies USA, see Brim, Ryff, and Kessler, 2004; Albert et al., 1995; in Australia: Andrews, Clark, & Luszcz, 2002) but has also received broad criticism mainly for not considering external conditions of the individual or the historical process for becoming successful (e.g., Scheidt, Humphreys, & Yorgason, 1999).

M.M. Baltes and Carstensen (1996) also have a criterion-based definition of successful aging with the following multidimensional conditions: psychosocial factors, such as life satisfaction and subjective well-being, perceived social support, and involvement in life; physical health, functional abilities and lifestyle; biophysical conditions, such as strength or vital capacity; and social conditions, such as social network or education.

Vaillant and Vaillant (1990), defined vital aging through three bio-psychological outcome variables: physical health, mental health, and life satisfaction. Subsequently, they proposed a set of empirically detected predictors: to have long-lived ancestors, the maintenance of family relationships, absence of alcohol and depression, and mature defence mechanisms (Vaillant, 2002).

Schulz and Heckhausen (1996) considered the following multidimensional outcome variables for successful aging: cardiovascular and pulmonary functioning, absence of disability, cognitive and intellectual performance, primary control, and achievements in physical and artistic domains.

Yoon (1996) proposed the following list of key elements for successful aging: physical health, personal income and financial stability, family dynamics and cohesiveness, social support networks, meaning of life, optimal cognitive functioning, personal control, prevention of depression, coping strategies, mastering bereavement, and self-justification mechanism for negative life outcomes. Yoon considered a working definition in which determinants or strategies for successful aging are also posited; however, as noted previously, there is a confusion between successful aging and quality of life.

The last outcome consideration of successful aging has been formulated, very recently, by Kahana and Kahana (2003). Moreover, they posited the preventive and corrective proactivity (PCP) complex model of successful aging, but they proposed a set of outcome variables: affective states, meaning in life, and maintenance of valued activities and relationships. Also, they posited a set of proactive options from which these outcomes derive.

The Process

Based on a developmental life-cycle perspective, there are authors who point out intuitive approaches to the process of aging well. For example, Williams and Wirths (1965) considered successful aging as the adaptive process of developing capacities for solving difficulties and minimizing the effects of deficits. Also, successful aging was defined by Palmore (1979) as the process of maximizing longevity, health, and life satisfaction.

A broader process definition is given by Ryff (1989a) who considered successful aging as the positive and ideal functioning of the individual across the lifespan and, in the same line, Fisher (2002) defined successful aging in terms of coping strategies throughout the lifecycle.

The broadest process definition of active aging has been proposed by WHO (2002) "...... the process of optimizing opportunities for health, participation, and security in order to enhance well-being and quality of life as people age..." (p. 12). This process is dependent on a set of macro environmental, economic, social, health and social services, personal (genetic and psychological), and behavioral determinant factors.

Finally, there are other process definitions that can be considered as much broad theoretical conceptualizations of successful aging as processual definitions, such as Baltes and Baltes' (1990b) SOC theoretical framework or Kahana and

Table 1. Summary of active aging (and related terms) outcomes and procedural conditions proposed by authors

SOURCE	OUTCOME CONDITIONS	PROCESS
BIO-MEDICAL	– Longevity – Biological health – Cardiovascular and pulmonary functioning – Mental health – Functional abilities – Physical strength – Vital capacity – Absence of disability – Autonomy	– Long life ancestors – Maximizing health across lifespan
PSYCHOLOGICAL	– Subjective health – Activity – Competence (motor and cognitive) – Mental and physical positive functioning – Life and social engagement – Behave according with own values and beliefs – Coping – Purpose in life – Personal growth – Psychological well-being – Life satisfaction – Perceived quality of Life – Adaptation capabilities – Mature defense mechanism – Family relationships – Affective states – Meaning in life – Maintenance of valued activities and relationships	– Selective optimization with compensation – Development and maintenance of primary control – Socioemotional selectivity – Adaptive process developing capacities for solving difficulties and minimizing the effects of deficits – Coping strategies across life cycle – Behavioral lifestyles
SOCIAL	– Social productivity – Social networks – Education – Material security – Environmental mastery	– Optimizing opportunities for health, participation and security

Kahana's (2001, 2003) theory of PCP. These theories are going to be described in the next section.

Table 1 shows a summary of the most consistent criteria and process proposals for describing and understanding successful aging. They are classified by scientific contexts (biomedical, psychological, and social). Thus, there are four general characteristics common to the majority of these definitions:

1. Positive aging is preferably considered a multidimensional concept and must not be reduced to any of its components (life satisfaction, health, etc.);
2. Several authors confound positive aging with life satisfaction or quality of life and this fact should be considered as a conceptual flaw (see also, Fisher, 2002);
3. Some definitions include, without clear distinction, what is defined and what are its determinants, and
4. Several of the characteristics of successful aging outcomes and process mechanisms imply psychological conditions.

Empirical Definitions

At the same time as positive aging was being developed as a new concept, several research projects for investigating this way of aging were also conducted; most of them started with a working definition of positive aging (or related concepts) in order to examine individual differences in successful, healthy, optimal, active, or productive aging. Also, project leaders distinguished between criteria and predictors variables, risk factors, or determinants of successful aging through both cross-sectional, longitudinal, or even sequential designs (see Baltes, Reese, & Nesselroad, 1977).

As has been pointed out by Lupien and Wan (2004) in a thorough review of successful aging, individual differences is a central issue when successful aging research is examined. There are several sources of bias when different studies are compared and, also, when older people are classified according to a set of domains or components of successful aging. Therefore, any comparison between research studies should take into consideration these potential source of bias.

First of all, age is the first demographic condition accounting for variability: Young older adults likely will receive higher scores in successful aging than the elderly. Secondly, education, income, or other components of SES (Socioeconomic Status; e.g., see Adler & Snibbe, 2003) are mediating any aging domain. It is well known that throughout the lifecycle there are individual differences in health, physical, cognitive, and social functioning highly associated with SES, especially with education and with income. Also, the empirical definition of successful aging, as well as any other considered multidimensional variable, must be operationalized through a set of assessment instruments or measures but, very rarely, different constructs are assessed through different measures and, therefore, multitrait-multimethod analysis is rarely performed (e.g., Fernández-Ballesteros, Van de Vijver, & Hambleton, 1999).

Finally, it is possible to hypothesize that those individuals with high education and high income are successful people throughout life and, therefore, they are going to aging successfully. Nevertheless, as has been pointed out by Lupien and Wan (2004), there are individual differences in cognitive reserve or in learning potential and "one could become a successful ager later in life" (p. 418). Therefore, successful aging could have different trajectories; for example, in order to assess changes in functional status Shaw et al. (2003) assessed a broad sample of Japanese older adults, from 60 to 102 years old, examined through five waves, between 1987 and 1999 ($N = 2,000$). They found three major trajectories of functional change: (1) early onset of functional impairment (or, in other words, 20% pathological aging), (2) no decline or minimum functional decrement before 75 (60%), and (3) late onset of functional impairment after 75 (13%). In other words, when different individuals belonging to different cohorts are classified as aging successfully this condition should refer to age.

Recently, Peel et al. (2005) and Depp and Jeste (2006) reviewed most of the posited cross-sectional and longitudinal studies on successful aging. These reviews are going to be followed in order to reach both empirical definitions and predictors, or determinants, of successful aging.

Peel et al. (2005) searched for "healthy" and "successful" aging as well as "aged" or "elderly" (older than 60 years); "longitudinal" or "follow-up" or "prospective"; "risk" or "predictors" or "determinants"; and "behavioral" or "lifestyles" in peer-review scientific journals, writing in English, in PUBMED, MEDLINE, EMBASE (bio-medical), CINAHL (nursing and health), PSYCINFO (psychological abstracts), SOCIOFILE (sociological abstracts), and AGELINE (gerontological abstracts) from 1985 to 2003. The study outcome was healthy or successful aging defined and measured as a multidimensional construct. Dependent variables were defined as measures across several domains of health to identify the subset of individuals who were functioning well in most or all measured domains. Risk/protective factors or determinants measured included behavioral factors, defined as those that can be manipulated and changed and measured as independent variables. In order to overcome reverse causation, studies were reduced to longitudinal design. Following this method, a total of 341 articles were identified. When selection criteria were defined requiring associations between baseline behavioral risk factors and subsequent healthy aging in a cohort of people aged 60 years or more at outcome assessment, only eight studies fulfilled these criteria. The selected studies were primarily from the United States and only one study was developed in Europe (SENECA, Haveman-Nies et al., 2003). Table 2 shows authors, outcome definition of health or successful aging, length of the follow-up, percentage of subjects classified as healthy or successful and determinants.

As Peel et al. emphasized, "although a detailed critique of the quality of the

Table 2. Studies identified by Peel, McClure, and Bartlett (2005): Authors, outcomes, and determinants identified

Author, publication year	Outcomes	Baseline-follow-up interval and subjects classification	Risk factors/ determinants
Guralnik & Kaplan, 1989	Healthy aging: Survival, high level of functioning	19 years Healthy: 12.7%	Smoking, Alcohol consumption, Weight, Eating breakfast, Snacking, Hours of sleep
Strawbridge, Cohen, & Shema, 1996	Successful aging: Survival with high level of functioning	6 years Successful: 35%	Smoking, Alcohol use, Exercise
Reed et al., 1998	Healthy aging: Surviving, free of major life-threatening illness and maintaining physical and mental capacities	28 years Healthy: 19%	Smoking, Physical activity, Alcohol intake, BMI, Diet
Leiveille, Guralnik, & Ferucci, 1999	Aging successfully: Living to an advanced old age and having little or no disability prior to death	2 to 8 years Successful: 49%	Smoking, Alcohol, Activity level, BMI
Ford, Haug, & Stange, 2000	Successful aging: Sustained independent living in the community	2 years Sustained independence: 20.1%	Smoking, Alcohol, Exercise
Vaillant & Mukamal, 2001	Successful aging: Survival with high level of physical, mental, and social well-being	60 years Happy well: 26/29%	Smoking, Alcohol, Exercise, BMI
Newman, Arnold, & Naydeck, 2003	Successful aging: Remaining free of major life-threatening disease and having normal physical and cognitive functioning	8 years Successful: 48%	Smoking, Physical activity
Haveman-Nies, De Groot, & Van Staveren, 2003	Healthy aging: Maintenance of health at old age (being alive, remaining independent)	10 years Remaining independent: 381	Physical activity, Diet, Smoking

evidence presented in these selected studies is beyond the scope of this paper" (p. 303), among the eight studies examined there are strong differences in the design, the follow-up period, the population sampled, and moreover, the cohort followed. Therefore, it is understandable that there would be differences in the rates of healthy elderly (from 12.7% to 49%).

Summarizing, most of definitions focus on bio-medical dimensions, "successful" and "healthy" aging were operationalized through survival and independent living, three studies considered mental capacities and only one study (Vaillant & Mukamal, 2001) took into consideration a subjective or emotional condition such as "well-being" (physical, mental, and social). Moreover, most of the posited determinants are rather consistent lifestyles: not smoking, moderate alcohol consumption, being physically active, maintaining weight within normal ranges. That is, all of these are behavioral lifestyles very well-known as risky factors from a biomedical framework; no other conditions usually present in the working definition described above – such as education, social participation, cognitive functioning, control, coping styles, etc. – were examined (see Vaillant, 2002).

Depp and Jeste (2006) have recently published a report with very similar objectives: to review larger, quantitative studies on successful aging and to examine the proportions of subjects meeting criteria and individual components of definitions as well as correlates of these definitions. A search on PubMed and www.scholar.google.com was conducted (1978–2005) using the following terms: successful aging, healthy aging, productive aging, optimal aging, and aging well. Criteria for inclusion were: published in English in peer-review journals, reporting quantitative data from adults over 60; use of operationalized definition as continuous or categorical dependent variable; studies that expressed an intent to study positive outcomes in aging; both cross-sectional and longitudinal predictors of successful aging were accepted.

Some 407 articles were identified for "successful aging," 490 for "healthy aging," 12 for "productive aging," and 1 for "aging well" or "robust aging." From this list, 28 articles (7 of them were coincident with those reviewed by Peel et al.) were selected, giving 27 categorical definitions and 2 dimensional measures (Almeida, Norman, Hankey, Jamrozik, & Flikcker, 2006; Andrews et al., 2002; Avlund, Holstein, & Mortensen, 1999; Berkman, Seeman, & Albert, 1993; Baltes & Smith, 1999; Burke, Seeman, & Albert, 2001; Day & Day, 1993; Ford et al., 2000; Garfein & Herzog, 1995; Grundy & Bowling, 1999; Guralnik & Kaplan, 1989; Hogan, Fung & Ebly, 1999; Jorm, Christiansen, & Henderson, 1998; Lamb & Miers, 1999; Leveille et al., 1999; Liang, Shaw, & Krause, 2003; Menec, 2003; Montross et al., 2006; Newman et al., 2003; Palmore, 1979; Ross & Havens, 1991; Strawbridge, 1996; Tate et al., 2003; Uotinen, Suutama, & Ruoppila, 2003; Von Faber et al., 2001; Valliant & Mukamal, 2001).

The components of the definitions were classified in 10 different domains, each measured in various manners from self-report to performance-based and other objective indicators. These domains were present in a limited number of studies: disability/physical functioning (studies 26), cognitive functioning (15), life satisfaction/well-being (9), social/productive engagement (8), presence of illness (6), longevity (4), self-rated health (3), personality (2), environment/finances (2), and self-rated successful aging (2). It is interesting to notice that physical, cognitive, emotional, and social functioning are the multidimensional domains with more presence in the studies reviewed.

Taking into consideration those 22 studies that had disability/physical function enclosed as a domain and reported a proportion of successful agers, it can be concluded that the mean proportion was 27.2% (range: 0.4–63; median: 20.8; SD: 27.1). The proportion of successful agers among those studies that included both cognitive and disability/physical functioning ranged from 3 to 95% (mean: 20.4; median: 19, SD: 14.8). The broad range of successful agers is explained by variability in sampling (rate of young elderly in comparison with old elderly) and by differences in measurements.

A set of independent variables were examined for their relationship to dependent or outcome variables. The significance of predictor variables was tested separately in relation to the different descriptions of successful aging. Effect sizes depended on the comparison group, the definition of successful aging, and the independent variables posited in the equation. Predictors or correlates of successful aging definitions were: younger age (10 of 10 longitudinal; 3 of 5 cross-sectional), higher income (2 of 5 longitudinal, 2 of 4 cross-sectional), education (3 of 7 longitudinal, 1 of 2 cross-sectional), gender/female (4 of 8 longitudinal, 0 of 2 cross-sectional), gender/male (1 of 1 longitudinal, 1 of 1 cross-sectional), creactive protein (2 of 2 longitudinal), ankle-arm index (2 of 2 longitudinal), presence of medical conditions (2 of 3 longitudinal, 2 of 4 cross-sectional), diabetes (4 of 6 longitudinal, 1 of 1 cross-sectional), cardiovascular disease (0 of 2 longitudinal, 0 of 1 longitudinal), cancer (1 of 3 longitudinal), hypertension (1 of 3 longitudinal, 1 of 1 cross-sectional), stroke (1 of 3 longitudinal, 0 of 1 cross-sectional), arthritis (2 of 3 longitudinal, 1 of 1 cross-sectional), hearing problems (4 of 4 longitudinal), and depression (2 of 3 longitudinal, 3 of 4 cross-sectional).

It should be noted that presence of illness is one of the domains of dependent variables but is sometimes included as an independent variable; income is considered in the domain of environmental conditions as a dependent variable but, also, income is considered one of the independent variables. This methodological confusion makes any distinction between successful aging outcomes and predictors or determinants circular. Obviously, it is possible to use disability as an outcome variable and presence of illness (arthritis, absence of hearing problems, etc.) as a determinant, but it is unsound to use the same variable in different roles.

Not all studies on successful aging, and related terms, were considered in the reviews by Peel et al. (2005) or Depp and Jeste (2006). There are also many other studies, mainly European (both at national or European levels), dealing with topics related to successful aging (life satisfaction, well-being, quality of life); most of them are cross-sectional or longitudinal studies, supported by the "Ageing

Well" project (developed under the auspices of the European Commission-FP5, which estimates the direct causal contribution of five key components for aging well: physical health and functioning, mental efficacy, life activity, material security, and social support). All of these studies had the main objective to identify those factors and how they contribute to competence, life satisfaction, or well-being in old age. Therefore, most of these European projects, although primarily dealing with QoL, subjective well-being, or life satisfaction, also consider successful aging as a key word, or as a subproject or outcome of QoL (for a review, see Fernández-Ballesteros, Kruse et al., 2007). However, two of these studies have as their primary goal the study of healthy aging (HALE; Bogers, Tijhuis, van Gelder, & Kromhout, 2005) or the study of competence, health, and aging (Fernández-Ballesteros, Zamarrón, Rudinger et al., 2004). We will next examine some results from these two studies developed from a European scope following the review already made by Fernández-Ballesteros, Kruse et al. (2007).

The HALE study (Bogers et al., 2005) had the main objective to study changes in and determinants of usual and healthy aging in 13 European countries. It is, mostly, a secondary analysis because it combines data from three longitudinal studies collected in the period 1995–2000 (from the Seven Countries Study, the FINE study (Van Gelder et al., 2004), and the SENECA study (Haveman-Nies et al., 2003)) in a total of 13 European countries; data on 7,047 men aged 40–90 collected in Finland, Greece, Italy, the Netherlands and Serbia and data on 3,805 men and women aged 70–99 collected in Belgium, Denmark, Finland, France, Greece, Hungary, Italy, the Netherlands, Poland, Portugal, Spain, and Switzerland.

Although HALE had a very broad scope (healthy aging), base studies were mainly designed for assessing diet and nutrition in Europe, taking into consideration Northern and Southern European regions with different cultural and behavioral habits. The main findings from HALE are the following:
1. In general, low systolic blood pressure and serum cholesterol levels were related to a low cardiovascular-disease mortality risk.
2. A Mediterranean type of diet, moderate consumption of alcohol, not smoking, and regular physical activity were related to lower mortality risk.
3. Health and functional status decreased with age, although in the younger cohorts the proportion of healthy agers increased.
4. Regular physical activity, moderate coffee consumption, being married, and living with others were associated with smaller cognitive decline in the older men.

In sum, the HALE study was developed from a biomedical perspective and findings were in accord with those studies reviewed by Peel et al. (2005)

EXCELSA (Fernández-Ballesteros, Zamarrón et al., 2004), under the auspices of the European Union PF-5, was planned as the first stage of a cross-European longitudinal study on aging. The central research objective was arriving at an empirical definition of competence and its potential determinants (distal factors such as sociodemographics and education, and proximal factors such as psychosocial and biophysical variables), but a previous purpose was to translate and adapt the European Survey on Aging Protocol (ESAP) to seven participant countries (Austria, Finland, Germany, Italy, Portugal, Polonia, and Spain). A total of 672 individuals, aged 30–85 years, was selected by quota sampling (by age, gender, education, and living conditions) in each country (96 participants per country). In order to assess reliability of each scale and instrument, retest to a third of the sample was performed. A basic research protocol (the ESAP) for assessing competence and its potencial determinants from a multidisciplinary point of view was developed and administered. The main domains assessed were: biophysical (anthropometric and biobehavioral objective measures); health, hearing, and vision; perceived capacity; lifestyles; and psychosocial variables (social relationships, cognitive abilities, personality, the self, well-being, and control).

After reliability and validity evaluations, exploratory and confirmatory analysis were performed. Competence was described as physical and cognitive competence and, as in the majority of models on successful aging, as outcome variables (Rowe & Khan, 1997,1998), and the following conditions were posited as determinants of cognitive and physical competence:
1. Education, income, and age were understood as historical distal determinants in accordance with the literature (Seeman, Charpentier, Bekman, & Tinetti, 1994).
2. Social relationships, internal control, lifestyles, and illness were considered as proximal factors following a majority of optimal aging assumptions (Rowe & Khan, 1997; Schulz & Heckhausen,1996).
3. Finally, although subjective appraisal of competence is not loading the same factor as objective competence, it seems to play a role of *buffer* for social relationships, internal control, and illness but is posited as proximal and not as distal factor.

From our examination of working definitions and the complementary reviews from the studies collected by Depp and Jeste (2006) and Peel et al. (2005), and other studies, the following conclusions are emphasized:
1. In some of the working definitions, a tacit confusion emerges between positive aging and other (also positive) concepts such as well-being, life satisfaction, or quality of life. As has been emphasized by several authors (Fernández-Ballesteros, Kruse et al., 2007; van Kraayenoord, 2006), this confusion is linked to several conceptual overlaps within the field: (a) well-being and life satisfaction are two subjective and evaluative properties attributed to a given individual, these two psychological conditions are shared both by successful aging and by quality of life (as happen with other characteristics such as competence or health, see Figure 12); (b) successful aging refers to the individual's process of aging, which is determined by transactions across the life cycle between the person and his/her socio-environmental context (see Figure 16), and (c) quality of life in old age refers to

the total quality of the individual's life, which includes not only her/his characteristics (such as health, well-being, functional abilities, etc., see Figure 12) but also her/his external and environmental circumstances (such as income, environmental quality, health and social services, etc., see Figure 15); quality of life could be considered both as antecedent of successful aging and, during old age, as consequence of aging well (WHO, 2002). Maintaining differences among these constructs is extremely important because using different concepts within similar conceptualizations is not scientifically sound.

2. As was stated in the review of working definitions, it is the common consensus that successful aging is multidimensional construct, both in its constituents and in its determinants. Also, research on successful aging has been planned as multidimensional, both in the operational definition of the concept used and in the predictors or risk factors considered. However, in one third of positive aging research, outcome or dependent variables are operationalized through biomedical indicators (survival and disability measures) as well as emergent predictors such as behavioral lifestyles (smoking, drinking, and diet). It should be taken into consideration that some of these studies were planned from an epidemiological scope or that their main goal was to search for the influence – per se – of lifestyles (e.g., Haveman-Nies et al. 2003, Jeste, 2005) in health. All these studies have been reconsidered and reanalyzed in order to reach conclusions in this new field of successful aging. As Depp and Jeste (2006) emphasized, a definition of positive aging "should be acceptable to clinicians, researchers, and older adults" (p. 15); it must be added that the definition should be also be acceptable to gerontologists as well as to experts coming from different branches of science (physicians, psychologists, sociologists, etc.) working in this interdisciplinary field.

Also, hypothetical determinants (risk factors, predictors, etc,) included in a given research study must be also multidimensional. Inui (2003), in his contribution to the "Determinants of Successful Aging: Developing an Integrated Research Agenda for the 21st Century" (*Annals of Internal Medicine, 2003*), emphasized that:

"successful aging must be defined not by longevity alone but also by sufficient well-being in multiple domains to sustain a capacity for functioning adequately in changing circumstances... the determinants of such well-being and functional status are manifold and include the genetic endowment, physical environment, social environment, population and individual response to challenges, the occurrence of disease, availability and effectiveness of health care, and personal prosperity (p. 391)."

3. Finally, from this revision two conceptual and methodological flaws can be noted:

    a. In the common literature on successful aging a conceptual confusion can be found between positive aging and other constructs (such as quality of life or well-being) and also between definitions of successful aging and its determinants, making any potential cause/effect links circular. The next section will be devoted to a more carefully discussion of this issue in order to clarify this misleading conceptualization.

b. If successful aging is a complex multidimensional construct, not only are several (bio-psycho-social) domains required but they should be assessed through different methods. This would prevent confusion between the construct assessed and the method used. Particularly, this introduces an important bias when the method is reduced to self-reports without triangulation with other objective procedures. This triangulation is recommended even when self-rated health is a good predictor of mortality (Schoenfeld, Malmrose, Blazer, & Gold, 1994). Moreover, this procedure would allow multi-trait-multimethod analysis and, therefore, assure the construct validity of the whole system (Cook, 1985; Fernández-Ballesteros, 2004; Fernández-Ballesteros & Botella, 2007).

Lay Concepts

As Bowling (2007) pointed out, literature on successful aging reveals a wide range of definitions, most of them reflect a theoretical, academic, or scientific bias. Thus, biomedical researchers mainly emphasize health and physical functioning as key areas for successful aging; psychologists usually limit their interest to subjective dimensions of successful aging such as life satisfaction or well-being, and, finally, social scientists consider socioeconomic conditions such as social participation, as key criteria of active aging. But aging well is also an abstraction in the minds of elderly and, therefore, it is expressed in common verbal reports. When a 75-year-old person completes a marathon, or wins on a "math" TV show, he/she and others say: "he/she is aging very well!" (even, he/she thinks: "I am really aging well!"). In fact, the concept "aging well" (and most related concepts) is a lay concept.

Sternberg (1990) proposes that scientific concepts are also mental constructions within people's cognitive system and, therefore, aging well could be assessed through elderly (or other groups) opinions or views. Based on Molden and Dweck's (2006) work on the effects of social perception on lay theories, it can be stated that the view of "aging well" – as a lay concept – can be highly helpful from three different perspectives:
1. As an expression of how lay people learn a disseminated scientific concept,
2. As an expression of social views about aging, and
3. As a procedure for self-classification as a "successful ager."

It is important to emphasize the difficulty in conducting research on lay concepts because even open questions necessarily imply a verbal formulation linked to a more or less elaborated concept. Moreover, when open questions are used, content analysis should be performed classifying open answers by preestablished scientific concepts. However, usually researchers use questionnaires in where they introduce a list of attributes or scientific criteria of successful aging. All these aspects contaminate research on lay concepts. For example, Knight and Ricciardelli (2003) investigated older adults' perceptions ($N = 60$; Age range = 70–101 years) on successful aging and the relationship of these perceptions to common definitions from scientific literature. When subjects were asked for a definition with an open question, most of them used only one or two components of successful aging but when authors used a list of potential conditions, individuals rated as very important almost all those components emerging from the literature (adjusting to situations, compensating for losses, and selecting activities according to capabilities). The authors concluded that lay theories of successful aging given by elderly are similar to those given in the scientific literature but this occurs only when a specific methodology is used. One must be aware of these difficulties when reaching conclusions in this area.

Several studies have been conducted in order to test how older adults and other social groups define or describe successful aging or what are the "ingredients" for aging well or aging positively. Also, in some of these studies, questions of self-evaluation allow a double portrait: what is successful aging, and to what extent participants are aging well. Finally, several studies have made comparisons among countries or cultures or about lay people and experts.

Ryff (1989b) was one of the first authors to research how older adults define well-being and positive functioning. She interviewed 171 middle-aged (Mean age = 52.5 years) and older (Mean = 73.5 years) men and women. Questions referred to general evaluation of life, past experiences, conceptions of well-being, and views of the aging process. Responses indicated that both age groups and sexes emphasized social dimensions (e.g., having good relationships). The middle-aged group considered "self" dimensions (self-confidence, self-acceptance, self-knowledge) and older participants stressed the acceptance of change. Ryff concludes that positive relationships, sense of humor, enjoying life, and accepting change are criteria for well-being and successful aging.

Tate, Lah, and Cuddy (2003), surveyed an elderly male population ($N = 1.771$ Mean age = 78 years, in 1996), taken from the Manitoba follow-up study. Survivors were surveyed and asked about their definition of successful aging and their opinion about how they had aged. Successful aging conditions most frequently cited by participants were the following: health and disease, physical, mental, and social activity were more likely to be found, but also interest, having goals, family, or diet. Other issues described referred to subjective functioning such as attitudes toward life and aging. Regarding self-evaluation of aging, the authors found a strong association between definition of successful aging and rated life satisfaction, subjective health, and activities of daily living. In sum, lay definitions of successful aging seems to be *multidimensional* and in accordance with scientific literature.

Bowling (2006) compared lay perceptions with theoretical models in a British community-dwelling population sample ($N = 854$) of men and women older than 50 years. They were assessed by administering an open-ended questionnaire. Two thirds of respondents defined successful aging in term of health and functioning; half distinguished psychological aspects (in terms of life satisfaction, active life, etc.); others considered it in terms of social relationships and/or finances. From the study it is concluded that a biomedical perspective of successful aging emerged, but it needs balancing with a psychosocial perspective, and vice versa (p. 57).

Phelan, Anderson, Lacroix, and Larsen (2004) performed a cross-sectional survey mailed to 1,985 Japanese-Americans older than 65 (from 1992–1994) and to 2,581 White Americans (from 1994–1996). Participants were asked three types of questions:
1. Whether they had ever thought about aging or aging successfully, and whether these thoughts had changed over the previous 20 years;
2. How important twenty attributes, taken from the published literature, were in characterizing successful aging, and
3. Finally, authors asked for a ranking of the five most important conditions of successful aging.

Briefly, results were: 90% had previously thought about aging and successful aging and 60% said their thoughts had changed over 20 years. Both groups rated almost the same attributes for defining successful aging but White Americans added "learning new things." Also, more than 75% of both samples supported two thirds of the 20 attributes found in the published literature as important for successful aging. The authors concluded that the definition of successful aging is multidimensional and comprises physical, functional, psychological, and social components as well as that this view is almost shared by two cultural and ethnic groups of subjects.

In order to test whether this view of successful aging is also shared by Asian Japanese, Matsubayashi, Ishine, Wada, and Okumiya (2006) conducted the same survey as Phelan et al. (2004) in 5,207 community-dwelling, independent subjects 65 or older living in four towns in Japan. Results indicated that Asian Japanese shared 7 attributes of the 20 listed (while Japanese and White Americans rated as important 13 or 14, respectively, of the 20 items listed – exception "having the kind of genes (heredity) that help me age well"). Less than 75% of Asian Japanese did not consider important the following items most cited for American Japanese and White: "staying involved," "making choices," "able to meet needs and wants," "feeling good," "able to cope with challenges," and "able to act according to own inner standard." In summary, from this study, culture (and perhaps not race) seems to be a source of variance for lay theories.

Trying to find the extent to which acculturation affects the concept of successful aging, Bull (2005) examined how Chinese-Americans – as a minority in the

United States – experience and describe successful aging. Conclusions were that Chinese-American elderly showed similar patterns of aging to the dominant culture with minor idiosyncratic components.

Hsu (2006) explored the concept of aging well among Taiwanese elderly. The sample was proportional to the population aged 65 or more. Two type of questions were asked:
1. An open-ended question: "What do you think are the essential components of an ideal and satisfactory life in old age?"
2. 23 successful-aging criteria were listed, asking for these to be ranked by order of importance.

Open-ended questions were grouped in six categories: physical health and independence, economic security, family and social support, engagement with life, spiritual well-being, and environment and social welfare policies. The most highly rated successful-aging criteria were the following: physical health, independence, living without chronic disease, living with family, and receiving emotional care. After performing a factorial analysis, five factors accounted for 58.7% of the variance: family and social support, mastery over life, health, enjoyment of life, and autonomy. The author concludes that successful aging in Taiwan means being healthy and independent, with economic security and family support and, therefore, seems to be in accordance with theoretical and empirical characteristics of successful aging.

Cultural differences found in these studies inspired Fernández-Ballesteros et al. (2008) to make comparisons between European and Latin-American, and US and Japanese older people. A total of 1,189 people older (495 men and 694 women) than 55 (Mean age = 68.18) participated in this study from seven Latin American (Brasil, Chile, Colombia, Cuba, Ecuador, México, and Uruguay) and three European (Greece, Portugal and Spain) countries. In order to make comparisons with US and Japanese samples, Phelan et al.'s (2004) questions were included. Results yielded minor differences in the views of aging well between European and Latin American and US samples countries. Also, significant differences were not found between US, Latin-American, and European samples in the ranking order of the five more important outcomes of aging well: good health, satisfaction with life, being independent, and good relationships with family and friends.

On the basis of this consensus among different countries and cultures Litwin (2005) explored to what extent the concept of successful aging is universal. He compared three population groups in Israel (Jewish and Arab Israelis and a new immigrant group) examining background and health status, social environment factors, and activity variables. The analysis performed yielded a similar portrait of successful aging in the three groups, especially based on the importance of health status in all groups. However, an idiosyncratic characteristic within the immigrant group was also found: the importance for this group of searching for social ties beyond family members.

Folk theories of a given concept can be assessed through the opinions of other group of individuals. Snow and Pan (2004) administered a questionnaire with open-ended questions and rating scales regarding successful aging to 31 physicians of internal medicine and geriatrics. First of all, most participants thought that successful aging cannot be achieved by all older adults. All participants agree that the most important factor defining successful aging is staying engaged with life and having strong social networks. Other factors cited were being spiritual, sexually intimate with a partner, and having a healthy diet. When participants were asked to give an example of a successfully aging person, typical examples were given but, interestingly, some respondents included sick or even demented patients. In conclusion, in this study physicians have a negative view about aging and they are less coincident with older adults and the scientific literature in their view of successful aging.

Von Faber et al. (2001) compared the meaning of successful aging from two perspectives: expert criteria and opinions of the elderly. Data come from the first cross-sectional baseline of the longitudinal Leiden Study (599 participants aged 85 years old). First of all, participants were classified as successful, or not, based on expert criteria: physical, social, cognitive functioning, and well-being. Interesting, although 45% of them had optimal scores in well-being only 10% met the four criteria used. On the other hand, qualitative interviews showed that older persons defined "success" as the process of adaptation with outcomes in physical, cognitive, emotional, and social domains. Taking into consideration their definition, a higher percentage of successful agers were found. These results suggest the need to include both objective and subjective criteria when individuals are classified regarding successful aging conceptualization (Pushkar, Arbuckle, Rousseau, & Bourque, 2003).

Finally, although successful aging is considered as a multidimensional concept, some authors have equated it to one of its components: life satisfaction. Fisher (2002) tried to research how older people define and can distinguish life satisfaction from successful aging. Nineteen older people at a senior center were interviewed. Although there is an overlap of criteria used for describing both concepts, taking into consideration qualitative data, respondents described life satisfaction in term of past expectation and present circumstances while successful aging was more oriented to strategies for coping in later life as well as in maintaining a positive view about life and aging. In fact, results are in accordance with scientific literature regarding similarities and differences between life satisfaction and successful aging.

In sum, after reviewing research on lay perceptions of successful aging, the following conclusions can be reached:
1. A multidimensional conceptualization of successful aging clearly emerged;
2. Health, physical, emotional, cognitive, and social domains are present in most studies, therefore, lay definitions cannot be reduced either to biomedical indicators such as health, survival, or physical disability or to subjective conditions such as life satisfaction or well-being;

3. This view is concordant with most working and empirical definitions of successful aging;
4. Although there are minor cultural differences among studies, lay persons on several continents and in several cultures seem to share most of the components of expert definitions of successful aging. In conclusion, contrary to the Ryff (1989a) assumption that conceptions of successful aging are open to cultural variation, it can be stated that central components (such as health, physical and cognitive functioning, life satisfaction, social relationships) of successful aging can be considered embedded in the minds of people as well as emerging in international empirical research (Butt & Beiser, 1987; Fernández-Ballesteros, Caprara, & García, 2004; Fernández-Ballesteros et al., 2008; Lehr, Seiler, & Thomae, 2000; Li, Zhang, He, & Zhang, 2001).

Theoretical Models

As has been pointed out in previous sections, some definitions of successful aging (and related terms), both working and empirical, do not distinguish clearly between the outcome and its determinant explanatory factors, etc.; that is, there is no distinction between dependent and independent variables (or mediator or intervening variables; see MacCorquodale & Meehl, 1948). In other words, from an epistemological point of view, it is not clear which is the *explanans* and the *explanandum* and, frequently, there is confusion between the type of aging and its determinants.

Also, the nature of these determinant factors are not taken into consideration; that is, whether a given factor belongs to different *context* levels (e.g., available health and social services, healthy environment, family SES, etc.) or to the *person* (e.g., subject's education, healthy habits, self-efficacy) in other words, most authors do not have a multilevel framework.

Finally, authors do not usually consider at what point in life a given predictor or determinant acts on the process of aging, if it is a distal or historical or proximal condition. In this section, we are trying to emphasize some of the theoretical assumptions distinguishing between these elements.

Diehl (1998) developed a complex model for everyday competence, making distinctions between *antecedents* (e.g., individual factors such as health and cognition), *components* or level of competence (e.g., intraindividual: physical and mental, contextual: social and physical), mechanisms (e.g., attributions, control beliefs), and *outcomes* (psychological well-being).

Also, Baltes and Baltes (1990b) distinguished between *antecedent* conditions (e.g., reduction in general reserve capacity), *processes* (the mechanism acting through the aging process: SOC), and the *outcomes* (effective life). Although Baltes and Baltes considered these three conditions for successful aging, as has been already described, the Baltes and Baltes' SOC theoretical framework has received more attention and empirical support. Let us describe this process model.

From a psychological perspective, Baltes and Baltes (1990b) conceptualize successful aging through a meta-model considering three mechanisms regulating the adaptive-aging process: selection, optimization, and compensation (SOC model; see also Riediger, Li, & Lindenberger, 2006). These three mechanisms are understood as universal conditions of developmental regulation, which can vary in their expression depending on the sociohistorical and personal circumstances of the individual, the domain implied, and the unit examined (see also Freund & Baltes, 2002; Freund, 2006).

Selection is a universal mechanism present all through the lifecycle; required in the face of a multi-stimuli world and limited resources, it could be considered as a precondition for specialization. Therefore, when individual resources are declining, selection has special importance as an adaptive mechanism. Baltes and Baltes distinguish two type of selection: elective and loss-based selection. With the former the individual assumes the required balance between his/her needs and wishes with available resources. Loss-based selection acts when the individual's competencies are declining or impaired and his/her demands and preferences should be adapted to a new situation. It is considered an essential part of the process of adaptation, coping, and mastery. Defining (or redefining) and adjusting personal (biological and behavioral) needs and resources to social and environmental pressures and demands is essential for successful aging.

Across the lifespan, most of the effort invested during individual growth and development as well as in adulthood refers to the *optimization* of individual knowledge, skills, and any other human characteristic and virtue. In old age, the optimization of one's own potentialities is one of the motives for investing time and energy in lifelong learning programs and, therefore, is a requirement for successful aging.

Finally, *compensation* is a mechanism for counteracting losses and declines and, in spite of these facts, continuing to function well. Since both compensation and optimization require the individual's efforts, a carefully selective process should be performed before deciding what should be optimized and what should be compensated. This complex process requires decision making and problem solving procedural knowledge and could be considered also as basic strategy for successful aging.

The SOC model has been considered a motivational system leading to a higher level of functioning in the individual. Also, selection, optimization, and compensation can be conceptualized as coping mechanisms or life-management strategies, with protective functions and, therefore, as determinants for active aging and well-being (Jopp & Smith, 2006). These three mechanisms can be posited as sources of individual differences in the ways of aging at different times of life.

During the last 15 years the SOC model has been tested not only by the Baltes' and their group (for a review, see Freund & Baltes, 2007) but also by other researchers working in several settings from long-term care to older worker contexts (Abraham & Hansson, 1995; Collins & Smyer, 2006, Rothermund & Brandstadter, 2003).

Very close to the Baltes' SOC theory, is the optimization in primary and secondary control (OPS) developed by Heckhausen and Schulz (1995; Schulz & Heckhausen, 1996). Two of the main features are the conceptualization of two modes of control (primary and secondary) and the special focus on "optimization" as a central regulatory process for active aging. They emphasize the basic need the human being has for control of environmental circumstances by specifying two forms: primary control is the attempt to the instrumental control of the environment for adjusting to one's own needs while secondary control is the attempt to protect one's own resources for primary control.

Schulz and Heckhausen define successful aging as the development and maintenance of control and describe two forms of primary and secondary control: *selective and compensatory*. Selective primary control implies actions or resources performed by the person for controlling external events whereas compensatory primary control implies that others are substituting the person for fulfilling needs and requirements. When the individual is losing capacities, selective secondary control is acting when efforts are made for enhancing or improving the person's resources for obtaining important needs. Nevertheless, in the same case, compensatory secondary control can also act when the individual is transforming needs and goals or is re-evaluating them in order to adapt him/herself to the new situation. This theory of optimization of primary and secondary control has received broad empirical support (for example: McConatha & Huba, 1999).

As a derivation of SOC theory, Carstensen's theory of socioemotional selectivity (Carstensen, 1991,1993) has as its central postulate that as people age (and their cognitive functioning and primary control decline) they are regulating their emotions, concentrating their social functioning to closer relationships, and, therefore, increasing secondary control mechanisms. This theoretical approach is going to be introduced in Chapter 7, which deals with the importance of social functioning for active aging.

From a sociological perspective, Kahana and Kahana (2001, 2003; Kahana et al., 2005) have developed a comprehensive model of successful aging called preventive and corrective proactivity, shown in Figure 13. The authors specify the following explanatory conditions:

1. Historical context (temporal: history, biography; and spatial: demography, community) influences other determinants through the causal chain;
2. Long-term and recent stressors and person-environmental relationships;
3. Internal resources such as hopefulness, altruism, self-esteem, life satisfaction, and coping (that is, personality);
4. External resources, such as financial and social support as well as availability of technology, and social and health services;

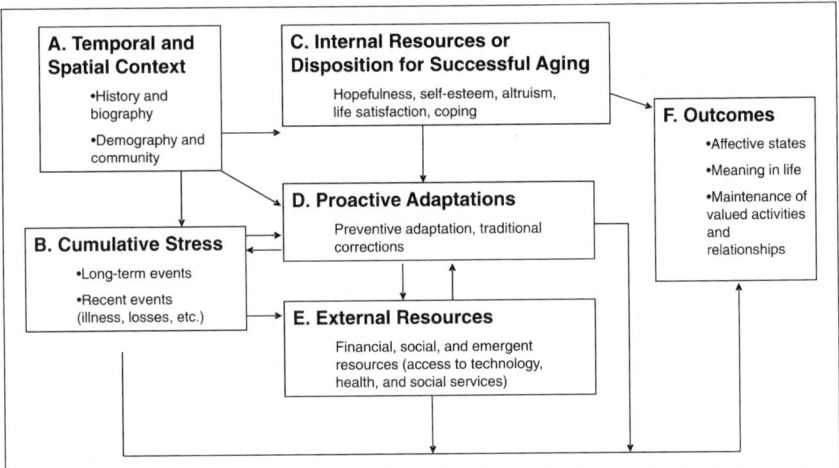

Figure 13. Model of preventive and corrective proactivity adapted from Kahana and Kahana (2001, 2003).

5. Proactive adaptation is a central explanatory site where preventive (health promotion, planning ahead, helping others, etc.) and corrective adaptation (role substitution, environmental modifications) take place; and finally
6. The outcomes (already described above) of these five explanatory sites are: affective states, meaning in life, maintenance of valued activities, and relationships.

This is not the right place to go more deeply in this theoretical model; it is an example of the complex relationships between multiple (both internal and external, and historical and concurrent) dimensions, acting in different directions, in multiple systems, and distinguishing among determinants (independent variables or *explanans*) and outcomes (dependent variables or *explanandum*).

As has been presented previously, the WHO postulated a process definition, a life-course approach for maintaining optimal functioning, a theoretical model about determinants of active aging, and the political response to the challenge of an aging world, all of these theoretical considerations developed in the document *Active Ageing. A Policy framework* (WHO, 2002). Since the definition of active aging has already been introduced, we will present here these other theoretical proposals.

First of all, WHO set out a life-course approach on aging, shown in Figure 14. This approach recognizes that "older people are not one homogeneous group and that individual diversity tends to increase with age" (p. 14). Throughout the lifespan, some individuals who have not reached high functional capacities can overcome the disability threshold. Nevertheless, those individuals who, during their lifespan, reach high levels of physical, cognitive, emotional, and social growth and development can remain above the disability threshold in old age,

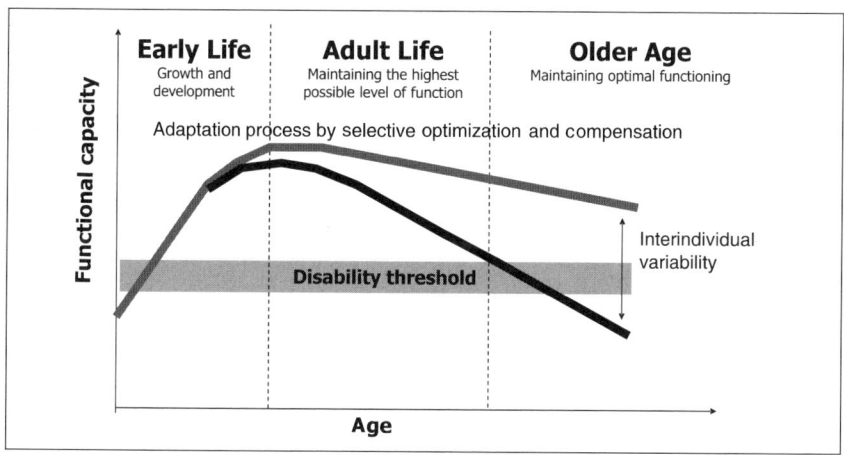

Figure 14. Life course approach to active aging (WHO, 2002) (adapting elements from Kalache & Kickbusch, 1997, and from the SOC model by Baltes & Baltes, 1990).

with a high level of functioning and well-being. Also, this model recognizes that individuals have a broad plasticity, and that "interventions that create supportive environments and foster healthy choices are important at all stages of life" (p. 14).

This theoretical approach is in accord with those other process definitions which support that aging is an adaptation process (e.g., Kahana & Kahana, 2001, 2003) and it is compatible with the three mechanisms proposed by Baltes and Baltes, therefore, on Figure 14 it could be assumed that selection, optimization, and compensation are adapting mechanisms acting throughout the lifecycle to reach the highest human functioning.

On the basis of this approach, Figure 15 shows the set of factors posited by WHO, in a circular manner but expressing multiple directions of multiple systems at both micro and macrolevels. Among external (macrolevel) factors are considered social, environmental, economic, health, and social services conditions. Among individual or internal factors are posited behavioral (or lifestyle) factors, and personal determinants including, at the microlevel, biogenetics and psychological factors (cognitive capacity, solving problem abilities, adaption to change, self-efficacy, and coping styles, including resilience, etc.). WHO also introduced two cross-cutting determinants – gender and culture – as sites acting both from the individual (gender) and from the context (culture).

In the document *Healthy Aging,* on the basis of the hypothetical determinants suggested, WHO proposed a set of policies for promoting active aging. Table 3 shows those aspects where psychology and psychologists are involved, related to four main domains: behavioral health and physical fitness, cognitive functioning, positive affect and coping, and social participation.

This proposal for active aging promotion is based on the WHO documents but

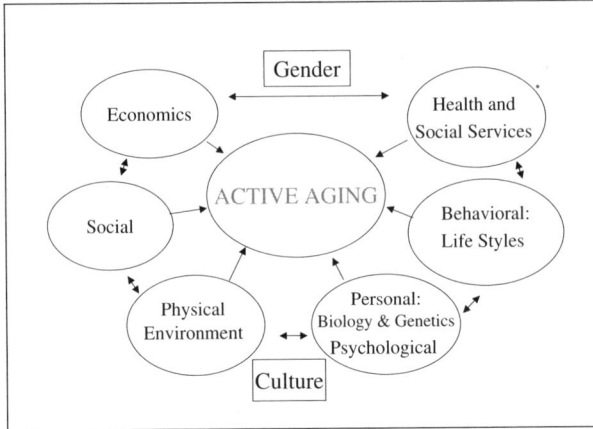

Figure 15. Determinants of active aging (adapted from WHO, 2002).

Table 3. Policy actions referring behavioral and psychological factors as potential determinants of active aging (adapted from WHO, 2001)

Reduce risk factors associated with major diseases and increase factors that promote *behavioral health and physical fitness*
- Ensure adequate nutrition through the life course
- Prevent the use of tobacco and determine the extent of healthy use of alcohol
- Policy for health monitoring and the use of medication and correct adherence to medical treatments
- Promote physical activity throughout the aging process

Promote *protective factors of cognitive functioning*
- Promote literacy programs throughout the life course, lifelong learning programs
- Promote the use of cognitive exercises in old age
- Promote engagement with cognitive demanding tasks
- Exercise communication and verbal skills

Promote *positive affect and coping*
- Promote pleasant events in old age as preventive factors of depression and loneliness
- Promote active and competent coping with stress, anxiety, and conflict
- Promote self-efficacy beliefs
- Promote positive thinking and sense of control

Promote *psychosocial functioning and participation*
- Encourage old-age empowerment and combat negative stereotypes
- Enable people to build collective efficacy beliefs
- Promote prosocial behaviors
- Promote social participation

also has empirical support and has been mentioned by lay people, experts, and empirical definitions. In other words, following Inui (2003), different stakeholders (elderly, researchers, gerontologists from different disciplines, and policies makers) agree that longevity, avoidance of disease and disability, as well as behavioral, psychological, and social factors are important conditions for successful aging.

Toward a Multidimensional-Multilevel Proposal of Active Aging

Trying to embrace several theoretical constructs proposed by various authors, a historical multidimensional-multilevel life-cycle model for successful aging will be posited with the following constructive elements.

1. First, this model takes into consideration historical or distal and proximal factors as elements of Gibson's (1979) ecology perception theory. Distal factors are those historical or longitudinal conditions that accompany the individual across his/her life course because they are relevant in his/her development. Proximal factors are those cross-sectional conditions, or short-term determinants, or predictive variables, for successful aging outcomes.
2. Following Bronfenbrenner (1977), both distal and proximal factors refer to macro (society), meso (context), and micro (person) systems or levels. Macrolevel distal conditions consider those sociohistorical circumstances in the individual's life course influencing his/her growth and development. At the mesolevel, community and family are distal factors that, in transaction with the person, determine his/her bio-psychological growth and development. Finally, microlevel alludes to the person as a biological, behavioral, and psychological active agent.
3. A fourth constituent element of this model comes from the social cognitive theory provided by Bandura (1986) and his principle of reciprocal determinism. This principle states that individual functioning depends on transactions between the environment (physical and social, etc.); personal functioning (cognitive, emotional, etc.), and the individual's behavior. These three conditions reciprocally determine one another. From this principle it can be deduced that a human being is an active agent in active world. In other words, across the lifespan human beings develop adaptive basic behavioral repertoires (cognitive-language, emotional-motivational, and sensory-motor, see also Staats, 1971, 1975, 1996), that influence the selection and creation of environments and situations through his/her behavior. Therefore, causality is never unidirectional but depends on the transactions between the person, his/her behaviors, and his/her multilevel contexts.

4. The final theoretical elements are those posited by Baltes and Baltes (1990b): the adaptive mechanisms of selection, optimization, and compensation. As already described, these process elements act throughout the life course as determinants of the selected ways of aging and act as sources for individuals' development or decline, as expressed in the diagram as an arrow that introduces individual freedom and differentiation.

Trying to organize hypothetical determinants of active aging, Figure 16 shows a diagram of this multidimensional, multilevel life-course model of active aging integrating potential transactive determinant factors where positive or active aging is an output or outcome. In all these sites, several examples are given to illustrate this complex model in its constituent elements. Also, it should be emphasized that all theoretically relevant sites proposed here have received empirical support. At the microlevel, there are personal (e.g., biogenetic, gender, cognitive-language, emotional-motivational, and sensory-motor basic behavioral repertoires, healthy habits during childhood) and contextual (family and group socialization rules, schooling, health care, family social position, social support, stressor events, family and community physical environment, health care, and environmental) factors. All these interactive person-context distal factors are supported by other macrolevel factors such as education, health, and social systems, cultural values, etc.

Moreover, proximal factors are organized also as personal (e.g., biogenetic, basic behavioral repertoires – such as cognitive abilities and reserve capacity, control and self-efficacy, positive emotions, coping skills, prosocial behavior, etc.) or

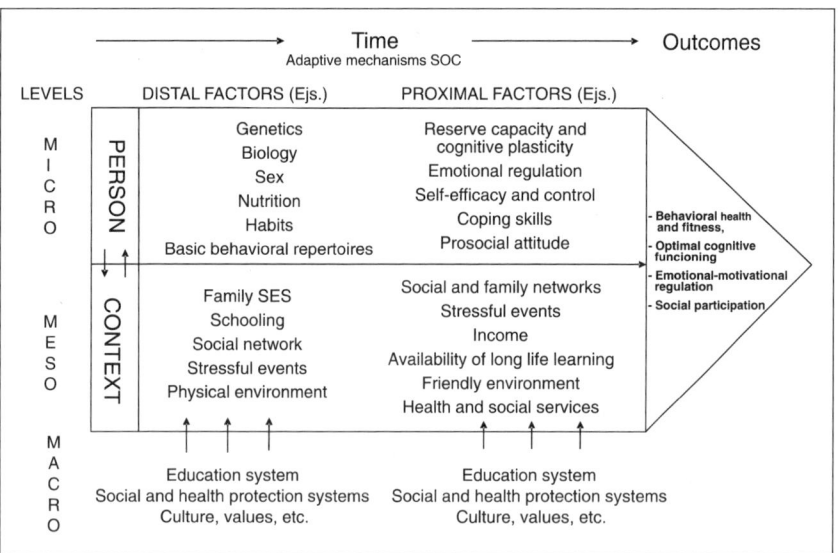

Figure 16. Multidimensional-multilevel life course model for active aging (adapted from Fernández-Ballesteros, 2002, p. 43).

contextual (e.g., social/ family support, stressful events, pension/income, lifelong learning availability, friendly environments, health, and social services). Also at the macrolevel, environmental, social, economic factors (such as public protection, health and social care systems, aging policy and programs, lifelong leaning system, cultural values, etc.) support the personal factors. Throughout the lifecycle, adaptive mechanisms (SOC) are functioning and, as Figure 16 shows, selective optimization with compensation are considered as the most important adaptive mechanisms for aging successfully.

Finally, after myriads of transactions among the person, his/her behavior, and his/her distal and proximal multilevel environments, he/she arrives at a certain age that could be described through four multidimensional domains: health and physical fitness, optimal cognitive functioning, emotional-motivational optimal regulation, and high social functioning and participation.

Psychological Domains Contributing to Active Aging

Across this chapter, working, empirical, and lay definitions, as well as theoretical models of active aging have been reviewed, and on the basis of this review a multidimensional-multilevel lifecycle model of successful/active aging has being introduced. Within this model, as an output of all posited determinants, a set of domains for successful aging are enclosed, most of them are psychological. These domains have been introduced by most of the reviewed works; they are supported by broad empirical evidence and national and international organizations of professionals (e.g., COP, 2002; Gething et al., 2003), and they are also addressed by the World Health Organization (WHO, 2002; see Table 3).

Therefore, taking into consideration the four domains introduced as active aging output (health and physical fitness, cognitive, emotional-motivational, and social functioning), psychology is one of the core disciplines not only because cognitive and emotional-motivational functioning are definitively psychological in nature but because health and physical fitness and social functioning also have important psychological and behavioral components.

Most of the health risk factors are behavioral habits, learned and maintained through learning principles as basic behavioral repertoires (e.g., WHO, 2002). Chapter 8 will deal with those conditions that should be promoted as healthy lifestyles (WHO, 2002; Figure 18) shows how most world deaths are attributable to selected behavioral risk factors. In this case, behavior is a determinant for health. Behavioral health and behavioral medicine are subdisciplines of psychology involving the integration of information regarding cognitive, affective, and behavioral functioning vis-à-vis health, illness, and disability (e.g., Andersen & Haley, 1997). In conclusion, behavioral health is necessarily committed in active or successful aging. In the same line, social functioning (social participation, so-

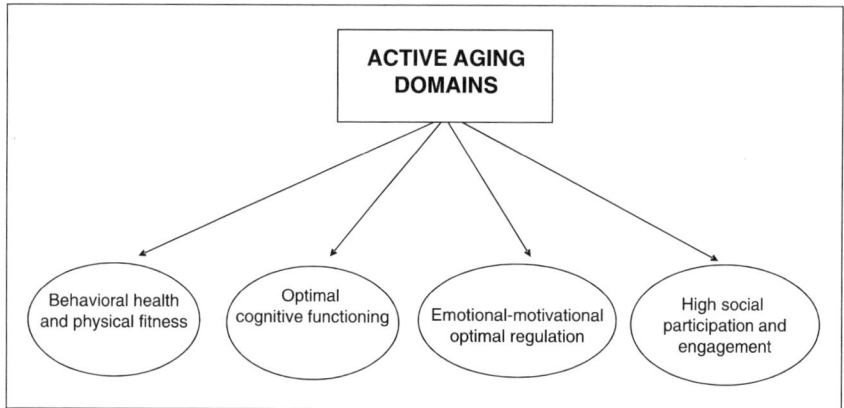

Figure 17. Active-aging psychological domains (adapted from Fernández-Ballesteros, 2003).

cial involvement, etc.) is also highly related and usually dependent on cognitive, emotional, and motivational processes, and behavioral skills.

From the proposed theoretical model, we will amplify the domains introduced as output of the whole process in Figure 16. Figure 17 shows the postulated four domains in which psychological and behavioral conditions are organized: behavioral health and physical fitness, optimal cognitive functioning, emotional and motivational (affect, control, and coping) optimal regulation, and high social functioning.

In conclusion, positive aging can be defined as *the life course adaptation process for arriving at an optimal physical (including health), psychological (optimal cognition and emotion-motivation regulation), and social functioning in old age.* Therefore, the promotion of active aging will imply the optimization of those environmental conditions through biomedical, physical, psychological, and socioenvironmental interventions. It should also be emphasized that promoting active aging is preventing illness and disability through biomedical interventions but, also, optimizing behavioral health, cognitive, emotional-motivational, and social conditions.

The next sections deal with empirical evidence about the importance of those psychological domains for active aging as well as for its promotion.

Concluding Remarks

Based on our previous bibliographical analyses, three periods in the conceptualization of active aging have been distinguished and, from them, several definitions and theoretical models have been discussed. Lay perception studies on aging-well reveal that it is a multidimensional concept integrating biomedical, psychological, and socioenvironmental elements, and this conceptualization seems to be present throughout the world.

When working and empirical definitions of active aging (and related terms) are reviewed some confusion between active aging and other concepts – such as life satisfaction or quality of life – can be found. Also, for several authors there is not a clear distinction between *explanans* and *explanandum* of positive aging that is, between its definition and determinants.

In conclusion, two conceptual and methodological flaws must be underlined:
1. The confusion between positive aging and other constructs should be discussed and clarified and the distinction between positive or active aging and its determinants should be considered.
2. Since there is a broad consensus about the multidimensionality of positive aging, its assessment requires not only the inclusion of bio-psycho-social domains but, also, the use of multimethods preventing confusion between the construct assessed and the method used.

After the review of theoretical models, a life course, multidimensional, and multilevel framework of active aging has been proposed in which, throughout the lifespan, proximal and distal multilevel and multidimensional factors are determinants of psychological and behavioral outcomes.

Finally, as the culmination of this chapter, we conclude that four psychological domains emerge as relevant for active aging: behavioral health and physical fitness, optimal cognitive functioning, emotional-motivational optimal regulation, and social participation and engagement. Part III will be devoted to these most important behavioral and psychological active aging domains and Part IV will deal with how to enhance them. Empirical evidence coming from observational, experimental, cross-sectional, and longitudinal studies will be reviewed to examine to what extent behavioral and psychological factors implied in active aging can be promoted through interventions.

PART II
BEHAVIORAL AND PSYCHOLOGICAL DOMAINS OF ACTIVE AGING

4
Behavioral Health and Physical Fitness

Introduction

All systematic reviews on active aging have emphasized the importance of lifestyles or behavioral habits (Aldwin, Spiro, & Park, 2006; Fries, 1989; Rowe & Khan, 1998; Brim, Ryff, & Kessler, 2004); the WHO (2002), in the same sense, considers them behavioral determinants of active aging. These determinants of active aging can be examined through the subdiscipline of scientific psychology: behavioral health.

One of the most relevant topics in behavioral health is health promotion and illness prevention. Therefore, healthy habits and other behavioral aspects influencing health and illness, and physical fitness, are a bridge from psychology to the promotion of active aging.

All longitudinal research on active aging includes healthy habits (regular physical activity, weight and diet control, moderate drinking, and not smoking) as determinant factors. Obviously, these four habits are considered important healthy lifestyles throughout the lifecycle and not only in old age (Bogers, Tijhuis, Van Gelder, & Kromhout, 2006; Ferrucci, Izmidian, Leveille, Phillips, Corti, Brock, and Guralnik, 1999; Nusselder, Looman, Marang et al., 2000; Hubert et al., 2002; Vaillant & Mukamal, 2001).

The promotion of healthy lifestyles over the lifecycle depend on complex psychological self-regulation processes that determine adherence to those healthy lifestyles (Bandura, 1997,2005). Therefore, as Maes and Karoly (2005) emphasize, psychological components of emotion and motivation are important factors for the development and maintenance of physical health and illness. These components will be developed further in Chapter 8.

In general terms, Fries (2003) pointed out that effects of good heath habits on subsequent disability are extremely large: The cumulative lifetime disability for those who do not smoke, drink moderately, follow a diet, and exercise shows four times less disability than those who smoke, drink too much, do not exercise, and are obese. Moreover, the onset of initial disability was postponed 7.75 years in the best one third compared with the worst one third of the sample. Independently, using an exercise club cohort, there was a postponement of mild disability by 12.8 years in comparison with more sedentary controls (Wang, Ramey, Schettler, Hubert, & Fries, 2002). From a psychological point of view, it can be stated: *"for aging well just do it yourself."*

Nevertheless, there is a false belief, or general negative image or stereotype that old age is too late for learning new habits as well as that even if new habits could be adopted, they would not have any influence on health. Both ideas are contradicted by empirical data supporting broad plasticity or modifiability even during old age (Baltes & Willis, 1982; Schaie, 1990b, 2005b) as well as the positive effects of behavioral health intervention programs in old age (Sherman, 1997). Next we will examine the research that supports the importance of behavioral habits or lifestyles for active aging.

Physical Exercise

Bortz (1982) collected a large body of evidence showing that decline in physical functioning attributed to the process of aging is very close to the effects of inactivity and concluded that physical activity could be considered as one of the key determinant and action for active aging. Moreover, longitudinal and experimental evidence supports that regular physical activity reduces mortality and increases longevity, producing benefits to physical and mental health, and cognitive, emotional, and social functioning (e.g., Bouchard, Shepard, & Stephens, 1994; Sunquist, Quist, Sundquist, & Johansson, 2002; WHO, 1997).

A general effect of regular physical exercise is longevity because it's high associated with mortality. Thus, Rowe & Khan (1998) state: "There is a simple, basic fact about exercise and health: fitness cuts the risk of dying. It does not get much more 'bottom line' than that . . . The substantial protective effect of physical activity was found to persist even to advance age" (p. 97). We will next introduce the type of effects of physical exercise on health and physical fitness.

A primary outcome of physical exercise is muscle strength, flexibility, and standing balance; still more regular physical exercise can optimize and compensate the decline in physical functioning (muscular strength and resistance, endurance, flexibility, cardiac response, and other physical parameters). For example, Pahor et al. (2006) conducted a randomized moderate-intensity physical activity intervention followed for an average of 1.2 years. Participants were 424 sedentary persons at risk of disability (age 70–89 years) and were assessed through a battery of physical performance tests. After treatment, experimental individuals significantly improved in most of the physical measures and, moreover, they had a lower incidence of major mobility disability.

These positive effects can also be found in "oldest" groups (aged 72 to 98) who follow 10 weeks of resistance training. As reported by Fiatarone et al. (1994), participants showed an increased in local muscle strength of 113%, gait velocity of 11.8%, and stair-climbing power of 28.4%. These benefits have been found after regular training, regular sport practice (running, bicycling, tennis playing, etc.) or even, some of them, in 48 weeks intense Tai Chi training (Wolf et al. 2006; Motivala, Sollers, Thayer, & Irwin, 2006).

Also, physical exercise not only increases physical fitness but reduces cardiovascular diseases and stroke (Berlin et al., 1990), diabetes (Seals et al., 1984), arthritis (Fisher et al., 1991), osteoporosis (Nelson et al., 1994), and, in general terms, disability (Fries et al, 2004). Physical exercise also has a positive effect on risk factors such as high blood pressure (Hagberg et al.,1989) and lack of balance (Tinetti et al., 1994). Exercising not only has a positive effect on illness and risk factors but also benefits the immune function (Bruunsgard & Pedersen, 2000) and is a protective factor of pulmonary function and increases vital capacity (VO2 max.). Some of these results of physical training have been found even in frail 85-year-old elderly (Puggaard, Larsen, Stovring, & Jeune, 2000).

These beneficial effects of physical exercise on physical health continue when individuals who present risk factors start physical exercise late in life. For example, Bijnen et al. (1999) investigated the association of physical activity and all-cause mortality during 5 years in 472 Dutch men. After adjusting the baseline for chronic diseases, functional status, and lifestyle factors, those people with a higher level of physical activity reduced their mortality risk to 0.44. Moreover, recent levels of physical activity were more important for mortality risk than activity 5 years previously (in the baseline).

Moreover, physical exercise benefits not only physical health but mental health, emotional functioning, well-being, and quality of life. Netz, Wu, Becker, and Tenenbaum (2003) performed a meta-analysis of those studies linking physical activity to mental health and well-being. Older adults showed effect sizes for physical-exercise treatment groups that were almost 3 times the mean for control groups. Aerobic training was most beneficial and moderate-intensity activity was the most beneficial activity level. Longer exercise duration was less beneficial for several types of well-being. Also, physical activity interventions have had positive influences on mental health problems (Atlantis et al., 2004) in people with depression (Brosse, Sheets et al., 2002), and old adults with anxiety and stress (Salmon, 2001).

Finally, regular physical exercise not only has effects on mental health and well-being but in social interactions and participation. For example, Bertera (2003) examined how physical activity level is associated with network relationships in an interview survey of 6,596 people older than 60 years. Social contacts were assessed through the number of phone calls, family relationships, and visits with neighbors. Physical activity was operationalized by frequency and intensity of the five most common activities in the past month. Results yielded that gardening, walking, and biking were positively associated with three measures of social contacts. The author concluded that physical activity positively influences social interactions. These and other results are supported by WHO (1999) in its recommendations of physical exercise as a protective factor across the aging process.

These benefits of physical health on physical and mental health, well-being, and social participation have been tested not only in Western societies but also in other Asian countries and have shown effects also for the very old (Fukukawa et al., 2004).

So, physical activity prevents and delays disability even at a very old age. Thus, evidence coming from cross-sectional and longitudinal studies (Fries et al., 2004; Kaplan et al., 1987; Sundquist, Jan, Sundquist, & Johansson; 2004), as well as from intervention studies (randomized experiment: Berlin et al., 1990; Leon et al., 1991; LIFE Study Investigators, 2006) support these statements. For example, Berk, Hubert and Fries (2006) performed a prospective study from 1984 to 2000. A total of 549 individuals participants in the study (end-of-study average age of 74 years) were assessed through disability measures. At baseline and at the end of the study, participants were classified following their exercise level as well as following the exercise changes. Authors concluded that inactive participants who increased exercise achieved excellent end-of-study values with decrements in disability similar to those participants who were more active throughout. These results suggest a beneficial effect of exercise, even when begun later in life, on postponement of disability.

For 12 years, Fries et al. (2004) followed-up on older persons (ages ranged from 50 to 72 years old) who engaged in vigorous running and other aerobic activities. Both cross-sectionally and longitudinally they had lower mortality and slower development of disability than members of the general population and control group. The authors suggested that this association is probably related to increased aerobic activity, strength, fitness, and increased organ reserve rather than to an effect of postponed osteoarthritis development. These results are in accord with those yielded from the HALE (Bogers et al., 2006) longitudinal study developed in Europe in 17 countries, which indicated that elderly from 70 to 99 years old who where engaged in physical activity showed about a 35% lower mortality risk.

Following the Latin proverb *"Mens sana in corpore sano,"* physical activity seems to have positive effects not only for physical health but for mental functioning (Callaghan, 2004; Podewils & Guallar, 2006). The effects of physical training not only benefit physical functioning but also have a positive effect on the CNS, supporting benefits in cognitive functioning and risk of dementia. A meta-analysis conducted by Colcombe and Kramer (2003) with 18 intervention studies examining effects of physical fitness training in cognitive functions yielded robust effects on several measures of cognitive functioning.

These benefits on cognitive functioning seem to be mediated by the well-established relationships between cardiovascular fitness and cortical activation. Thus, Colcombe, Erickson, Raz et al. (2003, Colcombe, Erickson, Scalf, Kim et al., 2006), performing both cross-sectional and experimental studies, found significant increases in brain volume in both gray and white matter regions as a function of fitness training for older adults who participated in aerobic fitness. The authors suggested a strong biological basis for the role of aerobic fitness in maintaining and enhancing CNS health and cognitive functioning in older adults. In Chapter 5 (see Figure 18) the benefits of physical exercise on cognition will be emphasized.

Moreover, mental functioning in old age can be impaired because of Alzheimer's disease or any other neurodegenerative type of dementia. As will be examined to some extent in the next section, recently important behavioral protective factors for dementia have been discovered, among them, physical exercise.

Fratiglione, Paillard-Borg, and Winbland (2004) systematically reviewed longitudinal studies exploring the effect of physical activity (among others) in dementia. They concluded that physical exercise is inversely associated with risk for all causes of dementia (including Alzheimer's disease). These results are very similar to those yielded by Laurin, Verreault, Lindsay, MacPherson, and Rockwood (2001) when assessing participants in 1991–92 Canadian Study of Health and Aging, a prospective cohort study of dementia. Similar results were found in the FINE study reported by Van Gelder et al. (2004). Finally, Podewils et al. (2005) conducted a prospective study to determine the association between physical activity and risk of Alzheimer's disease and vascular dementia, as well as to what extent apolipoprotein E genotype, 4 allele (APOE- e4) could be a moderator factor. Finally, Podewils and Guallar (2006) reviewed several experimental studies concluding (similar to Colcombe et al., 2006) that physical activity has a protective role in brain structure and function, thus, exercise could provide a simple means to maintain brain function and brain plasticity.

This important benefit of physical exercise of a behavioral habits requires four brief comments:

1. Although most of the studies reviewed by several authors yielded similar results, Verghese et al. (2003) and Wilson et al. (2002) were not consistent with the results presented here.
2. As has been emphasized by Podewils and Guallar (2006), all these studies have a potential limitation: the reverse causation bias. Since the onset of any neurodegenerative illness runs very slowly, reverse causation is a threat even in prospective cohort studies.
3. All these studies used different empirical definitions of physical exercise and in some studies the method used for assessing conditions involved was self-report. As is well-known, self-reports have noncontrolled sources of errors and bias (Fernández-Ballesteros, 2004, Fernández-Ballesteros & Botella, 2007).
4. Beyond our knowledge about the effect of physical exercise on brain tissues, it is still unknown what pathway, mechanism, or explanatory hypothesis is behind the benefit of physical exercise in cognitive impairment and dementia. Fratiglioni et al. (2004) suggest three major etiological hypotheses for dementia and Alzheimer's disease: the cognitive reserve hypothesis, the vascular hypothesis, and the stress hypothesis. Much more research is required but, at the moment, it can be concluded that regular physical activity seems to be an important and potent protective factor for cognitive decline, impairment, and

dementia. To those people who want to protect their physical and mental health, and their well-being: Do exercise!

Unfortunately, at this point, it is important to remember that although regular physical activity produces these positive outcomes, only a small group of elderly regularly follow this healthy lifestyle in the USA and European countries with high level of life expectancy but with a relatively high years-with-disability life expectancy (Marcus et al., 2000; Díez-Nicolás, 1996).

Therefore, since lifelong regular physical exercise is a healthy habit and should be promoted, a relevant issue is predictors for how to enhance physical activity involvement and adherence. Results from the MacArthur Foundation Successful Aging study indicated that people influenced by prior exercise behaviors and social-network emotional support reached and maintained a better and longer physical performance (Seeman et al., 1995). Also, other studies have pointed out that how subjects perceive exercising and/or their efficacy seem to be predictors for long-term exercise (McAuley, Elavsky, Jerome, Konopack, & Marquez, 2005). In addition, when subjects are exposed to positive stereotypes of aging physical performance standards increase significantly (Hausdorff, Levy, & Wei, 1999). In conclusion, sociodemographic and psychological factors (such as self-efficacy, self-stereotyping, and perceived emotional support when exercising) influence physical exercise outcomes. Much more attention should be paid to those intervening factors on the benefit of physical exercise, as has been noted by Conn, Minor, Burks, Rantz, and Pomeroy (2003).

Table 4. Benefits of physical exercise (adapted from WHO, 1997, p. 3)

Physical	Psychosocial	Society
• Reduction in risk of coronary heart disease and stroke • Prevention or control of high blood pressure • Prevention of osteoporosis • Improvement of mobility and muscle strength • Weight control • Reduction in accidental falls • Improving general cardiovascular fitness and function • Reduction in risk of diabetes • Help to reduce the risk of cancer of the colon	• Improvement of self-esteem and confidence • Increased opportunities for socializing and reducing isolation and loneliness • Increased capacity to remain independent • Enhance feeling of worth of older people	• Reduction in demand on health and social services • More positive images of older people and their value to society • Increased contribution to society and the economy of older people

Table 4 shows a summary of the positive influences of physical exercise emphasized by the WHO (1997), regular physical exercise has physical, psychosocial, and societal benefits. Physical activity is a protective factor of health (physical and mental), prevents and/or postpones disability, enhances physical, psychological (cognitive and emotional-motivational), and social functioning. Physical exercise is a protective factor of cognitive impairment and dementia and prolongs life and well-being in old age.

In other words, physical activity not only gives more years to life but more life to years as well. Finally, it is important to emphasize that the promotion of physical exercise among the elderly is a strong recommendation for active aging made both by international organizations, such as *The Heidelberg Guidelines for Promoting Physical Activity Among Older Persons* (WHO,1997, 1999, 2004) and the *Global Strategy*, or the HEPA, European Network for *Health-Enhancing Physical Activity*, and national organizations (e.g., the US Centers for Disease Control Prevention, 2004; the Canadian Fitness and Life Style Institute, 2001).

Diet and Nutrition

The aging process depends on the interaction between biogenetic and environmental factors; therefore, effects of environmental factors on the processes of aging are well established. Most of these factors are related to lifestyles that include nutrition, smoking, and alcohol consumption (Roberts & hays, 1998; WHO, 1990a; Sulander, Helakorpi, Tahkonen, Nissinen, & Uutela, 2003).

Among the more influential environmental factors generating individual differences during the aging process (because of its importance in genetic expression) are energy intake and the contribution of macronutrients to the total intake, physical activity, and other factors related to the energetic balance such as emotional stress, infections, etc. Epidemiological, physiological, and interventive studies have shown the effectiveness of controlling these environmental factors for promoting healthy aging, and increasing the lifespan (Bernis, 2007).

From a global perspective, food is a problematic issues: In some regions lack of food is the biggest problem throughout the lifecycle and in others overweight and obesity are becoming one of the biggest public health problems.

Being overweight has been defined as having a body mass index (BMI) of 25 or greater. An overview of the US situation can be found from Centers for Disease Control (2004; www.cdc.gov/nchs/hus.htm). Only 25% of women and 22% of men older than 65 have a BMI lower than 25 (1999–2002); in other words, three quarters of the elderly in the US are overweight or obese. Obesity is risk factor for a variety of acute and chronic illness in late life including cardiovascular disease, diabetes, and arthritis (Ausman & Russells, 1994, Steen, 2000). Therefore, obesity increases mortality and disability.

However, it should be emphasize again that, not only is overweight a risk factor in old age, but there are also risks of undernutrition, especially for those who are isolated, chronically ill or depressed, or simply poor. As Aldwin et al. (2006) pointed out, weigh loss in later life is a serious factor: Both under- and very overweight people have the highest mortality rates, whereas those who are slightly overweight have the lowest rates.

Regarding Europe, the proportion of the population that is overweight is lower. The SENECA (seven European countries; Haveman-Nies et al., 2003) study indicated that about 40% of older than 65 (men and women) have a BMI lower than 25. This is similar to the results from the FINE (five European countries; Van Gelder et al., 2004) study (43% BMI lower than 25 in men).

The HALE study (Bogers et al., 2006) combines longitudinal data collected in the period 1959–2000 (one from the Seven Countries Study, and other from the FINE study and the SENECA study) in a total of 13 European countries. Both studies had, respectively, 7,047 men aged 40–90 (Finland, Greece, Italy, the Netherlands, and Serbia) and 3,805 men and women aged 70–99 (Belgium, Denmark, Finland, France, Greece, Hungary, Italy, the Netherlands, Poland, Portugal, Spain, and Switzerland). Although HALE had a very broad scope (healthy aging), both constituent studies were mainly designed for assessing diet and nutrition in Europe, taking into consideration Northern and Southern European regions with different cultural and behavioral habits. From these studies, results indicated that the combination of low-risk factors including a Mediterranean diet, moderate consumption of alcohol, not smoking, and being physically active is associated with a more than 50% lower rate of all-causes and cause-specific mortality risks.

Important evidence supports agreement with a Mediterranean type of diet (low intake of saturated and trans fats and high consumption of fruit and vege-

Table 5. Benefits of the Mediterranean diet (adapted from Serra-Majem, Bertmomeu, & Bach, 2007)

Nutrient	Component	Benefits
Olive oil	AGMI, Polyphenol	Improve lipid profile (+HDL, −LDL) Hypertensive, Antiaggregant, Antithrombogenic, Vasodilatator
Fish	AGPI	Improve lipid profile (+ HDL, −TG)
Dry fruit	AGI	Improve lipid profile
Fruit and greens	Fiber, vitamins, minerals	Antioxidants Improve intestinal transit
Fruit and greens, pulses, integral cereal	Fiber	Reduce hyperglycemia postprandial, intestinal transit time, and energetic density

tables; Knoops et al., 2004). Table 5 shows basic nutrients of a Mediterranean diet, their components and benefits.

A Mediterranean diet is stronger related to survival and life expectancy (see Life expectancy in those Mediterranean countries, Figure 8). This type of diet decreases coronary mortality by about 40% and all causes of mortality by about 20%. Moderate alcohol consumption and coffee consumption (about 3 cups a day) is inversely related to cognitive decline. Not smoking compared with smoking decreases the mortality risk by 35%. Dietary patterns identified by factor analysis confirmed the persistence of geographical disparities but also the strong influence of socioeconomic status, which may modulate the cultural influence in the population of European elderly people.

The traditional Mediterranean Diet was defined by Keys (1980, 1995) as an alimentary pattern characterized by an energetic balanced (< 50% carbohydrates, 25% fat, and 10–15% proteins) with high intake of vegetables, legumes, fruits and nuts, cereals, and olive oil, a low intake of saturated lipids, a moderately high intake of fish, a low-to-moderate intake of dairy products (mainly in the form of cheese or yogurt), a low intake of meat and poultry, and a regular but moderate intake of wine during meals (Trichopoulou, Costacou, Barnia, & Trichopoulos, 2003).

Several studies have shown that adherence to the traditional Mediterranean diet is associated with a significant reduction in total mortality, low risk of coronary heart disease and cancer, and longer life expectancy (Renaud et al., 1995; Trichopoulou et al., 1995).

Recent attention has focused on the fact that the consumption of fruits and vegetables, rich in antioxidants, is also important for the maintenance of cognitive function in older age (e.g., Joseph et al., 1998; Kang et al., 2005). In a recent review of environmental influences on cognitive decline in old age, Elias and Wagster (2007) emphasize that even late in life the consumption of fruits and vegetables rich in antioxidants is important for the maintenance of cognitive function in older age. Moreover, when food rich in antioxidants is introduced later in life, cognitive decline might reverse and a combination of antioxidants and cognitive interventions seems to improve cognitive performance.

Kang et al.'s (2005) study in Brinham and Women's Hospital is a good example of the long-term effects of diet on aging and health. A total of 13,388 nurses were followed over 10 years. The diets of women in their 60s were assessed with special attention given to their intake of vegetables. When they were measured in their 70s, those who regularly ate vegetables showed slower overall decline on tests of memory, verbal ability, and attention than those women who did not.

Finally, it must be mentioned that several health organizations such as WHO, the Food and Nutrition Board of the US National Academy of Science, and the European Research Council recommend specific dietary allowances, particularly for older people. This information has been disseminated by newspapers generalizing that "Eating green improves not only your body but your mind" ("From Green and Leafy," Kang, 2004).

Smoking and Drinking

Smoking is one of the most unhealthy behavioral habits and risk factors. During the last 30 years, interventions through TV campaigns, legislation, and other health promotion and illness prevention programs have had important effects on stopping smoking, mainly in developed countries.

Across the lifespan, cigarette smoking is decreasing. Only about 10% of those older than 65 smoke in the US, and the HALE study in 17 European countries showed that 88% of women and about 50% of men from 70 to 99 years do not smoke or have stopped smoking more than 15 years ago. Most important, stopping smoking in old age still has beneficial effects on coronary artery disease and lung function (Hermanson et al., 1988; Higgins et al. 1993). It can be concluded that is never late to stop smoking.

Also, the elderly drink less than younger people, but metabolic changes across the lifecycle make drinking too much an unhealthy habit in older persons, making them more susceptible to alcohol-related diseases (liver, gastric, and pancreatic diseases) as well as to alcohol-related fall and injuries.

According to a recent WHO review of the literature, there is evidence that alcohol use at very low levels (up to one drink a day) may offer some form of protection against coronary heart disease and stroke for people age 45 and over (Jernigan, Monteiro, Room, & Saxena, 2000; WHO, 2002, p. 25). Therefore, moderate use of alcohol is one the ingredients of a Mediterranean type of diet. For example, in the HALE study, results were that moderate alcohol consumption, compared with non-drinking, decreases mortality risk by about 20%. There is even evidence that red wine is a protective factor of beta-related oxidative stress (Savaskan, 2003).

To summarize, not smoking and moderate alcohol consumption (about two glasses of wine a day) seem to be healthy behaviors.

Concluding Remarks

Aging well is strongly associated with what people do, and there is massive evidence about the importance of behavioral health and physical fitness in the process of aging. Although healthy aging is strongly dependent on the public health protection system, the individual is also responsible for his/her healthy behaviors and, therefore, responsible in some way for their process of aging.

Regular physical activity, a balanced Mediterranean type of diet, moderated drinking, and not smoking are very well-known, healthy aging habits. Most important, introducing these habits in old age still has positive results for the individual, therefore, it is never too late for improving health behaviors and physical fitness.

Finally, it must also be concluded that the extent to which an individual is committed to programs for healthy aging depends, also, on psychological motivational factors (see Chapter 6).

5
Cognitive Functioning

Introduction

Perhaps the most important threat people feel when approaching old age is an expected decline of cognitive functioning or, even worse, to be mentally impaired or demented. What can be done for maintaining cognitive skills and how cognitive decline and impairment can even be prevented is an important concern. In other words, what can be done to optimize and promote high cognitive functioning throughout the life cycle and to compensate declines are important issues not only for the scientific community but at the individual, family, community, and population levels as well.

Baltes and Schaie (1974, 1976) were the first authors to combat the false idea that age necessarily means losses, and cognitive decline and impairment. They emphasized that reserve capacity and plasticity of cognitive functioning in adulthood is evidenced in large interindividual differences, and in the multidimensionality and multidirectionality of cognitive change during adulthood. Finally, they introduced strong support for the modifiability of cognitive functioning throughout the lifespan, including old age. As was stated in the Introduction, these two papers were the starting point for a new positive view of cognitive functioning within the psychology of aging.

During recent decades, this positive view has been supported from multiple sources of data. As Schaie (1996, 2005a,b) underlines, there has been a shift in the study of aging: the combination of traditional cross-sectional studies with several types of large longitudinal studies, new methods for assessing change and for organizing the domain of variables (exploratory to confirmatory factor analysis), and finally, the conceptualization of age not only as an independent variable but as a dependent variable as well. All these changes have advanced our knowledge about aging and cognition in the predicted direction. As Schaie (2005b) stated: "we have begun to recognize that the passage of time and getting older cannot have any causal property for any observed behavior change" (p. 139).

To these shifts described by Schaie, two other advances should be added:
1. The continuation of multidisciplinary research on cognitive plasticity and modifiability of intellectual functioning (both usual and impaired) as well as the psychobiology of this plasticity (e.g., Rosenzweig & Bennett, 1996) and

2. The study of risk and protective factors for cognitive impairment and dementia (e.g., Schaie, 2005a,b). All these topics have been important concerns of research programs during the last 30 years (see Brenes, 2003; Fernández-Ballesteros, Zamarrón, Calero, & Tárraga, 2007, for a review).

In sum, at the beginning of this century important progress was made in the field of cognitive aging. Intelligence tests, used since the beginning of the twentieth century in educational and workplace settings, have been introduces within longitudinal designs in the field of cognitive epidemiology; results showed that those people with high cognitive or intelligence scores have a lower risk of mortality for any cause. Moreover, these advances support not only a more complex view of cognitive functioning across the lifespan but a new comprehensive panorama in which effective cognitive training and interventions can optimize cognitive functioning, compensate for intellectual losses and declines, or even palliate cognitive impairment. Here is an overview of the most recent advances regarding cognitive functioning across the lifespan.

1. Intelligence can be considered as one of the most valuable cognitive constructs. Large epidemiological studies show that intelligence scores, at any time on life, predict not only academic and professional success but also health outcomes and any cause of mortality (e.g., Batty & Deary, 2004; Gottfredson & Deary, 2004). As Deary and Der (2005) emphasize, cognitive epidemiology provides the strongest evidence for the importance of psychological (cognitive) factors in physical health and human survival. These predictions remain significant after adjusting for education and social class.
2. As cross-sectional, longitudinal, and experimental studies show, cognitive functioning experiences change throughout the life cycle: a strong development from birth to the late teens, more or less stable functioning during adulthood, and decline until death starting at different points in adulthood (e.g., Cattell, 1971; Schaie, 1990a,b).
3. Many authors such as Cattell (1971), Horn (1989), Baltes (1987), and Schaie (1990a,b, 2005a,b), show that cognitive functioning across adulthood presents several profiles depending on cognitive skills and aptitudes; In fact, two main trajectories can be identified:
    a) *Fluid, biological or mechanical intelligence*, linked with the speed of neural processing (e.g., inductive reasoning, visual-spatial ability, verbal fluency), which shows a strong and constant decline starting at the beginning of the thirties, and
    b) *Crystallized or cultural intelligence* (e.g., knowledge, vocabulary), which continues developing throughout the lifespan, at least until the seventies (for a meta-analysis see Verhaeghen, 2003). Moreover, from the eighth decade, most cognitive skills decline although individual differences continue to be present, making for very high variability among very old people (e.g., Lindenberger & Reischies, 1999; Baltes & Smith, 1999).

4. There are three main hypotheses explaining differential patterns in cognitive functioning across old age; as Schaie (2005b) stated: "The substantial age differences observed at a given point in time that often, *but not always* [emphasis added.], favor young adults over the elderly can perhaps be best accounted for by three co-occurring phenomena: neuropathology, disuse, and obsolescence" (134). Neuropathology is expressed through changes in the brain structures being understood as precursors of cognitive impairment but disuse and obsolescence refer to changes in the adjustment between a person's cognitive skills and social requirements and both can be reversible.
5. *Cognitive decline* (a "normal" component of aging), as usual cognitive functioning, should be distinguished from *cognitive impairment* caused by neuropathology from any type of dementia (vascular, Alzheimer's disease (AD), mixed, or from other causes). Alzheimer's disease is a major public health problem around the world (mainly in developed countries with high rates of people older than 65), it is associated with age, but not caused by age. Prevalence is doubling every 5 years from 60 years old (approximately 3%) to a prevalence of 45% at 90 (e.g., Martínez-Lage & Khachaturian, 2001; Petersen, 2001). The most important long-term consequence of dementia is severe disability. A set of risk factors has been established for dementia: age, family history, and presence of the APOE- e4. However, a set of behavioral risk and protective factors such as education, aerobic physical exercise, cognitive activity, etc., have been investigated in the last decade with promising results as will be presented in this chapter.
6. Intervention studies provide broad evidence supporting *plasticity, modifiability,* or *reserve capacity* of cognitive functioning throughout the lifespan. Although they have optimal periods of increase, they are dynamic. Experimental studies demonstrate that old people can learn and reserve capacities can be activated through exercise, training, or environmental interventions (e.g., Baltes & Baltes, 1990b; Fernández-Ballesteros et al., 2007; Schaie, 2005a,b) It can be concluded that a cognitively active lifestyle (emphasizing mental activity) across the lifespan can have a positive impact on cognitive functioning in old age (e.g., Fritsch et al, 2007)

This is not the right place to introduce theoretical approaches supporting cognitive plasticity across the lifespan (both usual: e.g., Schaie, 2005a; and impaired: e.g., Martínez-Lage & Katchaturian, 2001) and its neurobiological bases (for a short review see Kramer, Bherer, Colcombe, Dong, & Greenough, 2004). Nor will we elaborate those new bio-psychological concepts, such as cognitive or brain reserve capacity and/or plasticity (e.g., Fernández-Ballesteros, Zamarrón, Calero, & Tárraga, 2007; Stern, 2003) or those mechanisms (e.g., compensation) behind empirical data on the environmental and behavioral influences on cognitive functioning (for a review see Special Issue of the Journal of Clinical and Experimental Neuropsychology, 2003, see Yaakov, 2003). Our purpose in this section is

Table 6. Environmental and behavioral influences in cognitive functioning through aging

Time	Cognitive Functioning	
	Usual	*Impaired*
Distal	Educational attainment SES Childhood cognition	Educational attainment SES

Proximal	Physical exercise
	Daily life activities:
	  Physically demanding
	  Cognitively stimulating
	  Social/leisure activities
	Cognitive interventions and trainings
		Physical exercise
		Daily life activities:
		  Physically demanding
		  Social/leisure activities
		  Cognitive activities
		Reality orientation programs
		Psychostimulation programs

to review the evidence about environmental influences on cognitive functioning that promote, optimize, compensate, or palliate cognitive decline and cognitive impairment as factors building active aging.

In order to organize those factors (on the basis of our active aging model, Figure 16), let us take into consideration whether they have distal or proximal influences and whether they act on cognitive decline and/or cognitive impairment (risk for dementia). Table 6 shows those environmental and/or behavioral factors acting in usual and in impaired cognitive functioning. Among distal factors the most powerful are education and SES. Education and SES are long-term determinants of usual and impaired cognitive aging that emerge from early and subsequent family environment. Physical exercise, cognitive activity in daily life, social or leisure activities, and finally, cognitive training programs are influential proximal factors in both usual and impaired cognition.

Education and Socioeconomic Status

Among distal factors, educational attainment is a well-known factor influencing both usual and impaired cognitive functioning. This link is well established through epidemiological, cross-sectional, and longitudinal research (Carnero-Pardo, 2000).

Learning to read and write is one of the first operations in the regular education system. Reis and Castro-Caldas (1997) consider that reading and writing generate so-called (by Staats, 1971) basic behavioral repertoires that act as synergic principles constructing cognitive-language systems and, therefore, they are essential for cognitive development. As Stine-Morrow, Parisi, Morrow, Greene, and Park (2007) emphasize, "literate show strong effects on both cognitive functioning and brain structure suggesting that the literate brain was one with the relatively greater (coordinated) hemispheric specialization" (p. 63). Illiteracy and low educational attainment are the sources of cognitive decline, and cognitive impairment and dementia. As Stine-Morrow et al. speculate, both could be to the result of intellectual disengagement more than of aging, per se.

Moving to educational attainment, in a recent review, Anstey and Christensen (2000) analyzed 14 longitudinal studies examining the effects of educational level on cognitive change. Educational attainment had a protective effect on both usual and impaired cognitive functioning as assessed for mental state, memory measures, verbal abilities, and for general crystallized intelligence measures but less influence for fluid intelligence and speed.

In a typical study of the effect of education on cognitive functioning, Richards and Sacker (2003) used path analysis on data from the British 1946 cohort to model lifetime antecedents of cognitive functioning – as assessed in verbal memory and timed visual search – at 53 years old. Childhood cognition, educational attainment, and adult occupation (in this order) showed independent paths to cognitive reserve. It should be noted that education and profession are the two most important components of SES during adulthood, and, at the same time, that childhood cognition predicts professional success in adulthood as well.

The protective effect of education on cognitive decline and impairment has been shown in developed and developing countries, and in rural and urban contexts, as well as through epidemiological, longitudinal, and cross-sectional studies and has been explained using the brain reserve capacity concept (for a review, see Carnero-Pardo, 2000). For example, Lyketsos, Chen, and Antony (1999) assessed people aged 18 to 70 years at three occasions over 11 years, reporting that more than 8 years of education was associated with maintenance of cognitive function.

In longitudinal studies with older participants aged 70 to 79 at the initial assessment, Albert et al. (1995) predicted that cognitive change over a period of 2.0 to 2.5 years would be accounted for by education (among other variables). After reviewing this field, the authors said: "educational background was the strongest direct predictor of cognitive change" (p. 585). It should be emphasized that cognitive change is used as a very broad concept that includes from minimal decline to severe cognitive impairment; most important, education acts on both types of change and is considered one of the most important protective factors for dementia.

As is well known and has already been mentioned in Chapter 2, socioeconomic status (SES) is one of the most important predictors of life expectancy, survival, longevity, mortality, and health as well as being highly associated with intelligence and, therefore, with any measure of cognitive functioning during the life cycle. Since SES is a combined social indicator it is difficult to disentangle from other social conditions such as education or income.

A good example of longitudinal research on the effect of SES on cognitive functioning is given by Osler et al. (2003). They followed 7,493 males born in 1953 from April 1968 to January 2002. Participants completed a questionnaire with various cognitive measures in school at the age of 12 years and data on birth and parental characteristics were collected. The most important result was that the father's social class was associated with childhood cognitive functioning and was inversely correlated with all causes of mortality. Perhaps most important, from a general perspective of longevity, is that this inverse association between the father's social class at the time of birth and adult mortality remained after adjustment for birth weight and cognitive functioning.

Influence of SES on mental functioning has been tested in older people living in their homes and in residential settings. For example, Fernández-Ballesteros, Zamarrón, and Maciá (1996) studied a representative sample of the Spanish population older than 65 ($N = 1003$) living in their own homes ($N = 502$) and in residences ($N = 501$). Mental status was examined through the Short Mental Portable Status Questionnaire (SPSMQ; Pfeiffer & Pfeiffer, 1975). Results indicated that SES was more important than age for mental status; none of those people with high and medium-high SES met the cut-off for cognitive impairment in the SPSMQ while 17% of those with low SES scores did.

Among several potential explanations for the effect of distal education and SES on cognitive functioning, the reserve capacity construct described by social cognitive theories has the most plausible hypothesis: Across the life cycle, education and SES act directly on brain structures optimizing cognitive functioning, compensating declines, or even reducing or delaying clinical symptoms.

But intelligence is not only a product of the interaction between the biological organism and environmental factors but, also, as several authors claim (e.g., Bandura, 1986; Staats, 1971, 1975), intelligence is also a cause for further person-environment transactions through the entire life cycle. As Staats (1975) states, individual cognitive-language basic behavioral repertoires are both prerequisite for new learning as well as multipliers for all types of enriched experiences, influencing not only other cognitive events and experiences, but also other health, physical, mental, and socioemotional conditions, which are mediated by those repertoires.

Nevertheless, from the perspective of cognitive epidemiology, Batty and Deary (2004) stated: "high intelligence in childhood is likely to lead to educational success, placement into well-paid employment, enhanced social status, and the accompanying benefits to health that the latter has repeatedly been shown confer. Other investigators have argued that this causal pathway is only one possibility, no more plausible than the converse – measures of social position might be indicators of cognitive differences, which themselves affect health outcomes" (p. 586). That is, reverse causation can be also possible without longitudinal data.

It should be emphasized that any hypothesis or pathway trying to convert transactive and reciprocal relationships between the individual and his/her environment into unidirectional pathways between the individual and his/her environment (individual-environment or environment-individual) can be considered against empirical evidence (e.g., Bandura, 1997). Our position here states that education, SES, and cognition maintain reciprocal transactions throughout the lifecycle.

We will now move on to those proximal factors that contribute to cognitive functioning: physical exercise, daily living activities, and cognitive training in both healthy and cognitively impaired elderly.

Physical Exercise

As was emphasized in Chapter 4, physical exercise could be considered as one of the most powerful healthy habits throughout the lifespan, and in old age, contributing not only to longevity, healthy aging, and well-being but, also, to cognitive functioning.

Usual Cognitive Functioning

Regarding usual cognitive functioning, the meta-analysis conducted by Colcombe and Kramer (2003) examined 18 fitness intervention studies (conducted from 1966 through 2001). Physical fitness training had robust effects on measures of executive function, cognitive control, visual-spatial information processing, and speed.

These results, arising from experimental studies, are in accordance with theoretical assumptions (e.g., Rowe & Khan, 1997; Baltes & Schaie, 1974, 1976); with cross-sectional studies on aging, health, and competence (e.g., Fernández-Ballesteros, Zamarrón, Rudinger et al., 2004), with longitudinal studies on active aging conducted by the McArthur Foundation (e.g., Seeman et al., 1995), the FINE study (participating countries Finland, Italy, and The Netherlands, see Van Gelder et al., 2004), and from HALE (Bogers et al., 2006), and with other evidence on the relationships between physical exercise and biological systems functioning.

The positive effect of physical exercise in cognitive function not only concerns young elderly but also also refers to very old people. As we have already described, in the FINE study Van Gelder et al. (2004) followed participants aged from 70 through 90 years old (from Finland, Italy, and The Netherlands) for 10 years. The conclusions were that even the oldest group who participated in physical activities (at least medium-low intensity) postponed cognitive decline.

In summary, the already cited meta-analysis conducted by Colcombe & Kramer (2003), yielded the following conclusions regarding the effect of physical exercise and cognition:

1. Fitness (aerobic) training has positive effects on cognitive functioning in old people;
2. Although effects have been observed on a variety of cognitive tasks, its major effect is in executive control (e.g., planning, programming, task coordination, etc.), which is one of the most age-related functions;
3. Fitness training combined with strength and flexibility had more positive effects on cognitive functioning.

Without doubt, observed effects of aerobic exercise on cognitive functioning must have a biological basis in the CNS (e.g., Park, Polk, Mikels, Taylor, & Marzhuetz, 2001; Kramer, Hahn, & Cohen, 1999); similar to other physical training such as juggling (Draganski et al., 2004). Therefore, the authors consider that the

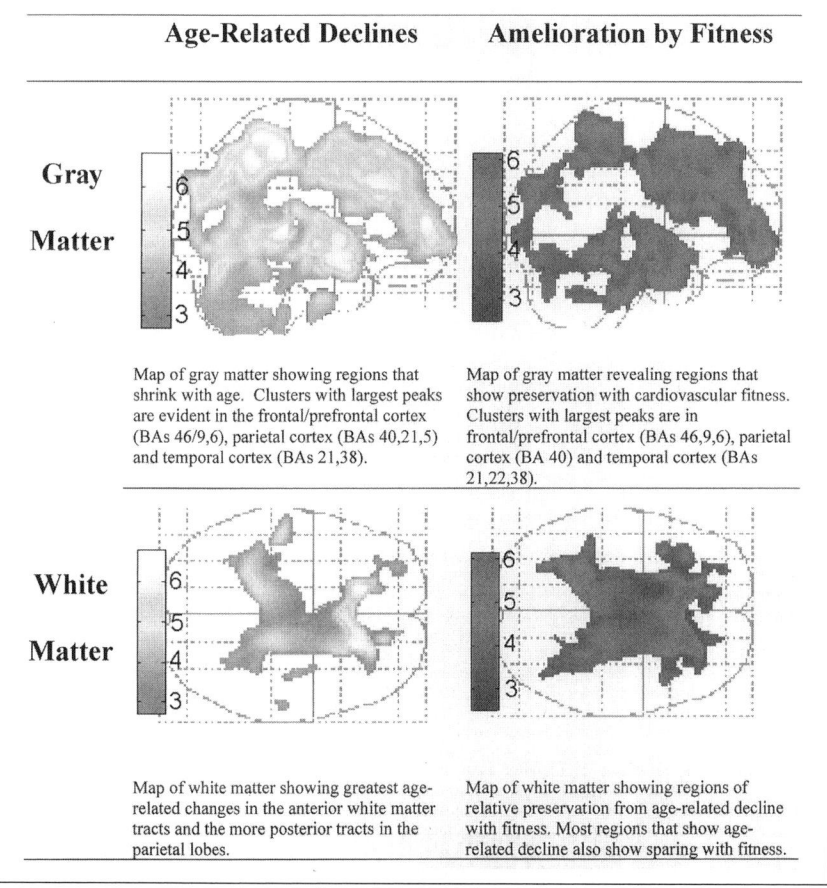

Figure 18. Statistical maps derived from multiple regressions of age and cardiovascular fitness on gray and white matter density (Colcombe et al., 2003, p. 178, reproduced with permission).

benefits of fitness training in cognitive function are to the result of the well-established relationships between cardiovascular fitness and cortical activation, which produce also changes in brain tissues. Nevertheless, very little is known about the effect of aerobic exercise on structural brain changes in humans.

Trying to improve this knowledge, on basis of the usual observation that the human brain gradually loses tissue, with a parallel decline in cognitive functioning, Colcombe and his group (Colcombe et al., 2003, 2006) performed two studies trying to assess brain changes attributed to aerobic exercise through magnetic resonance imaging (MRI). The first study (Colcombe et al., 2003) found that those older persons who had a long history of cardiovascular exercise had better preserved brains than did sedentary older individuals matched on age. Figure 18 shows (two images on the left) substantial deterioration in gray and white tissue densities as a function of age. Also, on the right of the figure, those regions most affected by aging show the advantage of aerobic fitness both in gray and white tissues.

In the second study, Colcombe et al. (2006) found significant increases in brain volume, in both gray and white matter, as a function of fitness training in older adults who participated in 6 months aerobic fitness training but not for those involved in other physical training (nonaerobic). In both studies, results support a strong biological basis for the role of aerobic fitness in maintaining and enhancing CNS health and cognitive functioning. In their last study, the authors suggest that "brain volume loss is not an inevitable effect of advancing age and that relatively minor interventions (only 6 months of regular aerobic exercising!) can go a long way toward offsetting and minimizing brain loss" (p. 1170).

Although new studies should replicate the existing results, as has been concluded by Raz & Rodriguez (2006), after reviewing the existing evidence about patterns of brain aging and cognitive decline and stability as well as effects of aerobic fitness on the brain, fitness exercise may influence the course of usual aging in a positive fashion. Although much more research should be done in order to test whether aerobic exercise improves not only brain tissue but, also, cognitive functioning, the results are highly promising.

Thus far, the effects of physical exercise on healthy elderly have been summarized but there is also evidence about the influence of physical fitness in impaired cognitive functioning resulting from Alzheimer's disease or any other neurodegenerative type of dementia.

Impaired Cognitive Functioning

Risk factors for cognitive impairment and dementia have been one of the most extensive research programs (age, family history of dementia, low education, and presence of the APOE- e4). However, in recent decades, researchers have focused on behavioral protective factors for Alzheimer's disease (and related illness), among them, physical exercise. In fact, physical activity seems to have a protective effect for cognitive impairment and dementia. This assumption is also supported by cross-sectional and longitudinal studies.

Fratiglione et al. (2004) systematically reviewed longitudinal studies exploring the effect of physical activity (among others) in dementia. They concluded that physical activity is inversely associated with risk for all causes of dementia (including Alzheimer's disease). Six of the nine studies reviewed showed a reduced incidence of dementia among persons performing regular physical exercise compared with those who were less active.

Larson et al. (2006) conducted a prospective cohort study ($N = 1,740$ older than 65 participants). During a follow-up of 6.2 years, the incidence rate of dementia was 13.0 per thousand person/years for participants who exercised three or more times per week compared with 19.7 per thousand for those who exercised fewer than three times per week.

These results are very similar to those yielded by Laurin et al. (2001) assessing participants in the 1991–1992 Canadian Study of Health and Aging, a prospective cohort study of dementia. Of the 6,434 subjects who were cognitively normal at baseline, 4,615 were assessed 5 years later. Screening and clinical evaluation were done at both waves of the study. Compared with no-exercise, physical exercise was associated with lower risks of cognitive impairment, Alzheimer's disease, and any other type of dementia. High levels of physical exercise were associated with the absence of cognitive impairment, Alzheimer's disease, or any other type of dementia.

Similar results were found in the FINE study reported by Van Gelder et al. (2004), from data from 295 healthy survivors, born between 1900 and 1929 in Finland, Italy, and The Netherlands. Although cognitive decline did not differ among men with high or low duration of activity at baseline, a decrease in activity duration of 60 minutes/day over 10 years resulted in a decline of 1.7 points in mental functioning. This decline was 2.6 times greater than the decline of men who maintained their activity level. A decrease in intensity of physical activity of at least a half a standard deviation was associated with 3.6 times greater decline than those maintaining their level of intense activity.

A last study examining the association between physical exercise, cognitive impairment, and bioneurological risk factors for dementia was performed by Podewils et al. (2005). They conducted a prospective study to determine the association between physical activity and risk of Alzheimer's disease and vascular dementia, as well as to what extent APOE- e4 could be a moderator factor in this association. Participants were 3,375 men and women, older than 65, free of dementia at baseline (also, participants in the Cardiovascular Health Cognition Study in 1992–2000). Participants in the highest quartile of physical energy expenditure had significantly lower risk of dementia in comparison with those in the lowest quartile. These associations were stronger in noncarriers of APOE-e4 and were absent in carriers in both Alzheimer's disease and vascular dementia.

The authors concluded that results support the hypothesis that being engaged in physical activity protects against subsequent risk of all-cause dementia (Alzheimer's disease and vascular dementia) over an average of 5.4 years follow-up but that the potential benefit of exercising may be limited to APOE-e4 noncarriers.

Also, Podewils and Guallar (2006) reviewed experimental studies on the effect of physical exercise on cognitive impairment and concluded that physical exercise has a protective role in brain structure and function. For example, Adlard, Perreau, Pop, and Cotman (2005) reported that 5 months of voluntary exercise resulted in a decrease in extracellular ß-amyloid plaques. Rardak et al. (2001) showed that swimming training improved some cognitive functions in rats with parallel attenuation of the accumulation of oxidative-damaged proteins.

Finally, Cotman and Berchtold (2002), using animal models, have been focused on understanding the neurobiological basis of these benefits. They conclude: "it is now clear that voluntary exercise can increase levels of brain-derived neurotrophic factor (BDNF) and other growth factors, stimulate neurogenesis, increase resistance to brain insult, and improve learning and mental performance ... Thus, exercise could provide a simple means to maintain brain function and promote brain plasticity" (p. 295).

After discussing this evidence about the strong association between physical exercise and cognitive functioning, it can be concluded that:

1. Regular physical exercise, from moderate to high fitness training has a positive effect on cognitive functioning in healthy elderly.
2. Physical exercise is also a protective factor for cognitive impairment and dementia.
3. Physical aerobic exercise seems to have both cardiovascular and brain effects.

Let us conclude with the wise Latin sentence "mens sana in corpore sano;" as Podewils et al. (2006) reminds us, this old proverb seems to be an empirically based recommendation.

Activity

Some of the studies reviewed above include not only physical activity but other types of daily-life activities (physically demanding, cognitive, or social activities) in their search for protective factors for cognitive impairment and risk of dementia. Most of these studies came from observational epidemiology and were conducted through prospective designs. Usually, they have a baseline where several cognitive and activity measures are collected and one of several follow-ups where cognitive decline is examined.

In these studies three types of activities can be distinguished: physically demanding, cognitively stimulating, and social and leisure activities (see Sturman et al., 2005). Although the effects of social activity, social networks, and social participation on psychological functioning will be addressed in Chapter 7, we will examine some of these studies in this section as well.

After a review of the literature supporting the effect of lifestyles on cognitive impairment, Fratiglioni et al. (2004) concluded that "active and socially integrated lifestyles in late life protect against dementia and Alzheimer's disease" (p. 343). We will give some examples about what these authors call "lifestyles" and how they are operationalized by type of activities and their effect on cognitive functioning (stable, declined, or impaired)

Regarding *physically demanding activities*, Albert et al. (1995) in the MacArthur Studies of Successful Aging examined longitudinal data for 1,192 persons from a community-based population aged 70–79 and followed for a 2.0 to 2.5 year period. They found that "strenuous activities" (together with education, peak pulmonary-flow rate, and self-efficacy) were direct predictors of cognitive change. The authors considered that these activities, which are "primary measures of physical activity" (defined as current energy expended in daily activities around the house, such as yard work, cleaning, etc.), predict cognitive decline. It should be emphasized that it is difficult to distinguish between "physically demanding activities" and regular physical exercise as already described (e.g., Podewils et al., 2005); this is one of the problematic issues in this type of research.

With respect to *cognitively stimulating and social activities,* Stine-Morrow et al. (2007) propose the "engagement hypothesis," suggesting that social and intellectual engagement may buffer age-related declines in intellectual functioning. Positive effects of stimulating engagement come from the effect of very demanding, complex work. For example, Schooler & Mulatu (2001), analyzing data from a representative longitudinal survey, showed that even in old age carrying out complex tasks has a positive effect on intellectual functioning. In the same line, Bosma et al. (2003) re-examined data from the Maastricht Longitudinal Study and showed that, after 3 years, those people (age range = 50–80) with very mentally demanding jobs developed almost three times less cognitive impairment than those with less demanding jobs.

Wilson et al, (2003) interviewed 4,000 older residents of the Chicago area at approximately 3 year intervals for an average of 5.3 years. Each interview included the administration of four cognitive tests. At baseline, each person rated frequency of participation in cognitively stimulating activities (e.g., reading a magazine) and from this list a previously established composite measure of cognitive activity was derived ranging from 1 to 5 (higher scores, more frequent participation). More frequent cognitive activity was associated with an approximately 19% decrease in the annual rate of cognitive decline ($p < .001$). The effect remained when depressive symptoms and chronic mental conditions were controlled and when persons with evidence of memory impairment at the baseline were excluded.

Cognitively demanding activities seem to also prevent cognitive impairment. Wang et al. (2006) assessed 5,437 persons older than 55 years randomly selected from nine communities in China; they were followed for nearly 5 years. Sociodemographics, lifestyles, and medical conditions and use of medication were assessed. Mental status was evaluated through the MMSE (Mini-Mental State Examination; Folstein, Folstein, & Mchugh, 1975). People were also asked how often they participated in social and leisure activities, for how long, and the type of activity performed (playing games, reading, writing, painting, playing music, dancing, watching TV, listening radio, walking, fishing, visiting friends, etc.). After adjusting for educational level, analysis showed that cognitive activities in both the individual item (playing board games, reading) and the composite measure were associated with a reduced risk of cognitive impairment. At the same time, watching TV was associated with an increased risk of developing cognitive impairment. After reviewing Wang et al.'s paper, Knoefel & Jankowiak (2006), in the *Patient Page* of *Neurology* advised: "Some of the same things that are good for maintaining good physical health also help your brain stay healthy. These include what you eat, how physically active you are, and probably how you use your brain (both avoiding risky behaviors and staying mentally active)" (p. E23).

Trying to distinguish between classes of mental stimulating or cognitively demanding activities, Fritsch, Smyth, Debanne, Petot, & Friedland (2005) examined the association between different types of mentally stimulating leisure activities and mental status in Alzheimer's disease cases or in normal controls. The authors used a case-control design comparing participation in activities across the lifespan in persons with AD ($N = 264$) (recruited from clinical settings and from the community) and controls ($N = 545$) (recruited from friends and neighbors of the cases or randomly drawn from the community). Three activity factors were identified: novelty seeking, exchange of ideas, and social activities. After adjusting for control variables, logistic regression analysis showed that greater participation in novelty-seeking and exchange-of-ideas activities were significantly associated with decrease of AD. The odds of AD were lower among those who participated in both types of activities.

Recently, Salthouse (2006) published critical and contradictory evidence (including of his own study, Salthouse, Babcock, & Miles, 2002) about the relationships between mental stimulation and cognitive decline. Nevertheless, he concluded that "despite the current lack of empirical evidence for the idea that the rate of mental aging is moderated by amount of mental activity, there may be personal benefit to assuming that mental exercise is true" (p. 68).

However, not only is being involved in cognitively stimulating activities associated with cognitive functioning, but, *leisure and social activities* seem to be associated with cognitive decline and risk of dementia. Although it is very well, known in the gerontological literature that everyday leisure activity is highly associated with well-being, mental health, and even with survival (e.g., Menec,

2003), research into potential relationships between this type of activity and cognitive functioning and dementia is relatively new. A first problematic issue refers to the empirical definition of "leisure" activity and to what extent social-leisure activity could be separated from physical, cognitively demanding, or social activity.

Verghese et al. (2003) examined the relation between leisure activities and the risk of dementia in a prospective cohort of 469 subjects older than 75 years of age who lived in the community and did not have dementia at the baseline. Participants were followed over a median of 5.1 years. Frequency of participation in leisure activities at enrollment was examined and, also, cognitive-activity and physical-activity scores were calculated with the unit of measure as activity-days per week. Risk for dementia was calculated according to the baseline level of participation in leisure activities, adjusting for age, sex, educational level, presence or absence of chronic medical illness, and cognitive status at the baseline. In the follow-up, 124 subjects developed dementia (Alzheimer's disease, 61 cases; vascular dementia, 30 cases; mixed dementia, 25 cases; and other type of dementia, 8 cases). The authors reported that reading, playing board games, playing musical instruments, and dancing were associated with a reduced risk of dementia. A one-point increment in the cognitive-activity score was significantly associated with a reduced risk of dementia (hazard ratio, 0.93 95% confidence interval: 0.90 to 0.97), but a one-point increment in physical-activity was not. The association with cognitive-activity and risk of dementia persisted after the exclusion of those participants with possible preclinical dementia at baseline.

Scarmeas, Levy, Tang, Manly, and Stern (2001), tried to determine whether leisure activities modified the risk of dementia, 1,772 nondemented participants older than 65 years (living in northern Manhattan), were followed in a community-based cohort study. Subjects' leisure activities were assessed at the baseline and for up to 7 years (mean 2.9); annual examinations with standard neurological and neuropsychological measures were performed. Results suggested that engagement in leisure activities reduced risk of incident dementia and the authors suggest that possibly these activities provide a cognitive reserve that delays onset of clinical manifestation of the disease.

Also, Crowe, Andel, Pedersen, Johansson, and Gatz. (2003) assessed 107 same-sex twin pairs discordant for dementia and from whom information on leisure activities were self-reported more than 20 years prior to clinical evaluation. Response about the 11 activities (reading, listening to radio, watching TV, social visit, cultural activities, home and family, clubs and organizations, studies, house and gardening, outdoor activities, and playing sports) were classified in three factors (through a factor analysis): intellectual-cultural, self-improvement, and domestic activities. Matched-pair analyses compared activities within the discordant twin pairs while controlling for level of education. For the total sample, participation in a greater overall number of leisure activities was associated with lower risk of cognitive impairment (both in Alzheimer's patients and, generally, in dementia). Greater participation in intellectual-cultural activities was associated with lower risk of Alzheimer's disease for women but not for men.

Although these studies seem to be intriguing and stimulating to continue searching, it is important to emphasize three major flaws in the scientific study of the association between activity with cognitive functioning:

1. The first one has been emphasized by Kramer et al. (2004), referring to the hypothetical link between cognitive functioning and activity; that is, whether the last is the cause or the consequence of the former. In other words, physical, cognitive, or social activity require good cognitive functioning and, therefore, those subjects with good cognitive functioning performed more activities (physical, cognitive, or social activities). Moreover, most leisure activities are social in nature (dancing, playing cards, etc.), and some authors emphasize the leisure aspect of the activity and others the social aspect. In sum, the nature of the activity should be disentangled.
2. The second criticism comes from the nature of activity itself; Gallacher, Bayer and Ben Shlomo, (2005) – commenting the Glei et al. (2005) paper – emphasize the difficulty in classifying a given activity as "social" or "intellectual" or even "physically demanding" because most activities are multidimensional. The authors consider that although a factor analysis gives a mathematical solution, it can never be considered as a functional classification.
3. The third problematic issue is methodological and has been pointed out by Salthouse (2006). Self-reports are the method used for reporting activities, moreover, a high proportion of studies are retrospective and both facts introduce an important source of bias (see Fernández-Ballesteros, 2004; Fernández-Ballesteros & Marquez, 2003; Fernández-Ballesteros & Botella, 2007). It should be emphasized that the goodness of a prospective study refers not only to the assessment of the dependent variable (that is, cognitive impairment) but, most importantly, to how independent variables are measured (that is, physically demanding, cognitive, or social activities). Without doubt, level and type of activity performed must be much more carefully studied and described and other methods and designs should be used.

Cognitive Training and Interventions

A last research program supporting the importance of environmental effects on cognitive functioning and cognitive decline or impairment comes from those experimental studies where cognitive functioning is manipulated under the assumption that cognitive skills can be trained or taught. Depending on the length of cognitive intervention, two approaches can be considered: cognitive training (also-called: dynamic assessment, cognitive plasticity, or testing-the-limits) and cognitive interventions.

Usual Cognitive Functioning

At the beginning of the 1980s, Denney (1982) was one of the first authors to review the effect of cognitive training and learning in old age. During the last 25 years, across a large number of studies, cognitive plasticity, reserve capacity, or learning potential of older persons has been tested through *cognitive training* using experimental pretest-training-posttest designs. Briefly, the methodological paradigm is as follows:
1. A baseline is established in the performance of a cognitive task (usually intelligence fluid tasks such as perceptual relationships, inductive reasoning, memory, or motor tasks),
2. The cognitive task is trained during a short period of time (a few hours), and
3. After training, a new posttest is taken. Gains (posttest minus pretest) after training, or post-test scores (or within-person variability) of a given person are considered his/her learning potential, cognitive plasticity level, or cognitive reserve capacity (for a methodological review see Fernández-Ballesteros & Calero, 2000).

Cognitive training studies with healthy elderly have yielded very homogeneous results:
1. After training, elderly improve their scores in the trained task at almost the same rate as young people do; differences between young and older individuals are in the baseline performance and depend on the task trained and the training performed (e.g., Baltes & Kliegl, 1992; Noice et al., 2004).
2. When cognitive training is performed in those elderly who had shown cognitive decline, training was more effective than for those who had not shown decline (e.g., Willis & Schaie, 1986; Schaie, 2005b). Improvements are quite stable through time, after 3 to 6 months.
3. Most important, after several years, although the trained group, even at the oldest age, still maintained some gains above the initial level, the nontrained group dropped out (e.g., Saczynski & Willis, 2002).
4. The factorial structure of the ability trained does not change (e.g., Fernández-Ballesteros & Calero, 1995).
5. Cognitive plasticity in the very old (75–101) was very modest, suggesting that biological conditions create a ceiling for cognitive plasticity (Singer, Lindenberger, & Baltes, 2003; Lindenberger & Reischies, 1999).
6. Finally, there is empirical evidence that cognitive decline associated with age can be compensated through cognitive training in healthy elderly (Nyberg, 2005; Schaie & Willis, 1986; Willis & Nesselroade, 1990; Schaie, 2005a, 2005b).

As an example of this research program in cognitive training, we will briefly describe the Schaie and Willis study conducted inside the Seattle Longitudinal

Study. Participants were classified by their cognitive decline (small or large) over 14 years. Depending on the ability declined, they received 5 h of inductive reasoning or spatial orientation training. Some 40% of subjects improved the trained ability and they compensated for their decline. Training benefits were maintained 7 years later (Saczynski, Willis, & Schaie, 2002).

Although these and other studies have shown important results about the modifiability and plasticity of human cognition, there was no data about whether, or to what extent, improvements of cognitive abilities through experimental training have repercussions for elderly in their daily life.

Also, conclusive results come from those *long-term intervention studies* where cognitive functions (attention, perceptual speed, memory, etc.) are trained during several sessions per week conducted over a long period of time.

As has been already mentioned, reaction time is a basic process for cognitive functioning and intelligence; reaction time may even explain IQ's association with death and survival (Deary & Der, 2005). Since reaction time declines very early in life (from the third decade), cognitive-intervention training parameters related to time are important for improving cognitive functioning.

Therefore, the first cognitive intervention we are going to present refers to speed of processing. There is abundant evidence that, as part of the usual and normal aging process, most individuals experience a decline in the speed with which they process information (e.g., Salthouse, 1996). Also, it is well established that this decline in speed of processing accounts for cognitive decline in other complex cognitive abilities, as well as in daily-life performance. For example, Ball, Edwards, and Ross (2007) summarized the effect of speed of processing in competence for driving, risk for falls, common mobility tasks, or instrumental activities such as looking up phone numbers, counting, finding an item on a crowded shelf, reading food and medication labels, etc. The authors concluded that speed of processing is important not only for everyday performance but for maintaining health status.

Ball et al. (2007) combined data from six studies on training speed of processing and its impact on cognitive and everyday functioning. Across studies, participants were 2,039 community-dwelling older adults ranging in age from 55 to 95 years (Mean age = 73.94; SD = 5.96). Speed of processing training varied across the studies but each study used "visual awareness" as a standardized method for enhancing abilities through practice. Results showed that training in speed of processing produced improvements in the selected instrument "useful field of view" test. The effects were higher in those individuals with processing deficits. These benefits were generalized to everyday activities and were maintained for at least 2 years.

Also, on the field of attention, Scalf et al. (2007) examined the impact of functional field of view (FFOV) practice in adults' attentional functions and correlates in brain regions. A total of 45 individuals (age range = 55–85) participated in this study; they were randomly assigned to practice and control groups. Results showed that practice tended to improve performance on processes of visual attention and perception. Neuroimaging data revealed increased recruitment in those neural correlates of these improvements (right ventral precentral gyrus and right inferior frontal gyrus). These practice-related changes in brain activation were correlated with improvements in task performance in the expected way.

Since older persons are highly concerned with memory problems, memory interventions are the most frequently developed cognitive interventions for old people. Using meta-analysis, Verhaeghen, Marcoen, and Gossens (1993), after reviewing 33 studies with data from 1,539 older persons, reported that memory intervention programs, in comparison with control groups and/or placebo group, had significant effects (size effects 0.75 SD in comparison with 0.40 as effect of practice). These improvements were assessed both by objective memory tests as well as by subjective memory reports. Verhaeghen et al. (1993) concluded that memory functioning retained its plasticity in old age using various objective measures (words, number, pictures, etc.) of memory functions (primary memory, working memory, episodic memory, etc.).

Also, Floyd and Scogin (1997) found that memory training (over no training) had positive effects on subjective memory; however, differences in effectiveness were found among mnemonic training, expectancy modification, or placebo procedures such as unstructured practice. Also, Hohaus (2007) found that a memory program incorporating the principle of successful aging significantly improved memory performance and subjective perceptions of everyday memory.

Recently, Rebok, Carlson, and Langbaum (2007) reviewed traditional and novel approaches for training and maintaining memory abilities in older adults. In order to examine the empirical basis for classifying memory training methods, they preformed a meta-analytic review. They reviewed 300 memory training studies for relevancy in previous-quality criteria. From those studies considered ($N = 218$), 39 gave preliminary support for 16 treatments to be considered evidence-based. These studies included multiple mnemonic techniques but also specific training techniques such as restructuring and visual memory support. The authors concluded that "... there are potentially several evidence-based options for older adults who wish to improve their memory and reduce memory problems. However, to what extent evidence-based treatments work under daily life conditions, where strict adherence to treatment protocols may be unrealistic, is an open question" (p. 55). After emphasizing the constraints of traditional memory training platforms – which require very restricted administration conditions – they review other platforms and approaches for memory training such as: collaborative training, videotape and audiotape training, and online and CD-ROM training programs. They conclude that these new approaches may enhance the accessibility, affordability, and applicability of memory training and cognitive stimulation programs.

Finally, let us examine effects from other "nonstandard" (cognitive-tasks-based) intervention procedures, such as self-monitoring, in improving memory. Dunlosky et al. (2007) reviewed evidence from the outcomes of two studies relevant to the efficacy of this behavioral approach. The hypothesis was that older adults can improve the effectiveness of learning by monitoring their progress toward a learning goal and by using the output from such monitoring to allocate study time and to inform strategy selection. Both interventions demonstrated performance gains in memory performance after self-monitoring training, although these training gains did not exceed gains obtained through standard mnemonic training.

Thus far, training and intervention programs for speed, attention, and memory have been presented but multimodal or multifunctions interventions for enhancing cognitive functioning can also be found.

Ball et al. (2002), addressed the question whether improving cognitive functions through four cognitive interventions might improve mental abilities and daily functioning in older, independent-living adults. The design used was a random controlled trial (RCT). Participants were 2,832 volunteers aged 65 to 94 years, recruited in six metropolitan areas in the US, and randomly assigned to one of four groups: 10-session group memory training (verbal episodic = 711), reasoning (ability to solve problems, $N = 705$), speed of processing (visual search and identification, $N = 712$), or a control group ($N = 704$). Eleven months after the training, a four-session booster training was offered to a random sample of the treatment groups. Immediately after the intervention, trained participants demonstrated reliable improvements of 87%, 74%, and 26%, respectively, in speed, reasoning, and memory. Booster sessions enhanced training gains in speed and reasoning ($p < .001$) interventions (speed booster, 92%, no booster, 68%; reasoning booster, 72%; no booster, 49%). Improvement were maintained at 2 years but no maintenance on everyday functioning was found. The authors concluded that training effects were of a magnitude equivalent to the decline expected in the elderly without dementia over a 7- to 14-year interval but, also, that longer follow-up was required.

There is important evidence from animal models that differential experience induces neurochemical changes in cerebral cortex of the rat and regional changes in cortex weight, changes in cortical thickness, size if synaptic contacts, number of dendritic spines, and dendritic branching. As Rosensweig and Bennett (1996) support, enriched experience and training appear to evoke the same cascade of neurochemical events causing plastic changes in brain. This evidence is being applied to promote both child development and successful aging. A last example of the biological plasticity produced by cognitive intervention programs is a study performed with young participants by Draganski et al. (2006). They tried to test whether extensive learning induced functional plasticity as assessed through brain changes. Magnetic resonance images were obtained at three different time points while medical students studied for their medical examinations. Results showed that learning of abstract information may be related to specific patterns of structural matter changes in concrete brain areas according to the information processed. The authors concluded that "plasticity is a characteristic of the nervous system that evolved for coping with changes in the environment. Understanding changes in brain structure as a result of learning and adaptation is pivotal in understanding the characteristic flexibility of our brain to adapt" (p. 6317).

In summary, during the last decades, empirical evidence has been reported coming from experimental studies supporting cognitive plasticity and reserve capacity of cognitive functioning in healthy elderly. We also have empirical data about the role of cognitive interventions in compensating usual cognitive decline. The question now is to what extent cognitive activity, cognitive training, and cognitive interventions have a role in cognitive impairment (dementia and Alzheimer's disease).

Impaired Cognitive Functioning

Although bioneurological signs of dementia seem to start very early in a patient's life, early clinical symptoms usually appear when he or she starts to have memory problems: "Alzheimer's disease patients learn very slow and forget very rapidly new learned material" (Martínez-Lage, 2002, p. 111; Petersen, 2001). Some authors have even claimed that AD subjects are essentially unable to learn at all when higher-order learning principles (in contrast to classical or operant conditioning) are required (Verhaeghen, 2000).

First of all, as has been stated above, there is empirical evidence that cognitive activity is a protective factor for dementia and cognitive decline as well as that educational attainment is a protective factor of all types of dementia. *Cognitive training* (learning potential or cognitive plasticity) has also been expanded for demented people with two main research questions: to what extent do people with more or less severe cognitive impairment have cognitive plasticity and to what extent can the plasticity measured be more useful for diagnosis than other more frequently used cognitive-impairment assessment exams.

Although the diagnosis of dementia (and its several subtypes) is multifactorial it is difficult to distinguish between normal and pathological aging with only cognitive instruments (Snowdon, 2003). Christensen et al. (1991) performed a meta-analysis of 77 studies in an attempt to identify the best measure for differentiating between the two states. Their results showed that memory scales are better instruments for diagnosis than any other mental examination.

Nevertheless, Welsh et al. (1992) pointed out that the use of combined measures of delayed verbal recall, verbal fluency, and executive control were the best predictors for AD. In fact, most of the neuropsychological batteries for dementia combine several neuropsychological tests.

M.M. Baltes and associates suggested that cognitive plasticity may be an early indicator or predictor for dementia. They posed the question of whether healthy people and those at risk for dementia would show significant differences in cognitive modifiability (Baltes & Baltes, 1997, p. 91). Their results supported the hypothesis that people assessed as having, or being at risk for, dementia display fewer after-training gains – and, therefore, less cognitive plasticity – than healthy people, and that plasticity measures were better methods for assessing cognitive impairment than the commonly used static measures of mental examination, digit-backward and forward, recognition, and free recall. In sum, cognitive plasticity measures accounted for additional variance in the prediction of mental health status (Baltes, Kuhl, & Sowarka, 1992, Baltes Kuhl, Gutzmann, & Sowarka, 1995).

In the same line, Fernández-Ballesteros and her group tested the extent to which healthy, cognitively impaired, and demented elderly show learning potential (or cognitive plasticity) or, in other words, they can benefit from cognitive training; to what extent learning potential can discriminate healthy people from those diagnosed with mild cognitive impairment (MCI) and with Alzheimer's Disease (AD); and whether cognitive plasticity can be improved through psycho-stimulation programs.

In a first study, Fernández-Ballesteros, Zamarrón, Tárraga, Moya, and Iñiguez (2003) tested the extent to which cognitively impaired subjects can show cognitive plasticity in comparison with healthy elderly. A total of 200 subjects participated in the study: 100 healthy elderly, 50 with MCI, and 50 diagnosed with AD. The Learning Potential Assessment Battery for Dementia (BEPAD) was developed; BEPAD is formed by four dynamic subtests assessing learning potential with the following tasks: visual memory (position learning test), verbal learning (verbal learning test), executive function (Hanoi learning test), and verbal fluency (verbal fluency learning test). For all the four tasks very short trainings were developed; participants were trained through several trials throughout the pre- and posttest phases. Results were the following:

1. Healthy, MCI individuals, and AD patients significantly improved their scores in the posttest phase.
2. Healthy subjects significantly differed from MCI and AD both in the pretest and in the posttraining scores.
3. MCI subjects benefited more from training than AD patients did. The most important conclusion is that, although MCI subjects and AD patients can learn significantly less than healthy subjects, both impaired groups benefited from a very short cognitive training in those cognitive functions very sensitive to neuropathology such as visual memory, verbal learning, executive function, and verbal fluency strategies. Moreover, as shown in the position learning test, they can learn not only through practice and reinforcement, but also through cognitive strategies training.

In a second study, these authors tested whether learning scores could correctly classify healthy elderly, MCI individuals, and AD patients. Results showed that all "dynamic" or plasticity scores (posttest) discriminate these three groups better than pretest scores or mental exams. A total of 89% of cases are correctly classified by the BEPAD: 95.7% of the healthy subjects, 90.6% of AD patients, and 71.1% of the MCI individuals (Fernández-Ballesteros, Zamarrón, & Tárraga, 2005).

Finally, when AD patients received a psychostimulation training program they increase their cognitive plasticity; on the other hand, control patients do not decrease in their learning potential (Zamarrón et al., 2008).

Although much more research must be done, all of these results support the hypothesis that while there are significant differences in learning potential between healthy elderly and subjects with cognitive impairment, even those with Alzheimer's disease can also learn. These findings stand behind and can support the benefits of the so-called "nonpharmaceutical" or "soft" interventions for dementia that we will review next.

Cognitive stimulation programs are a relatively new type of psychological intervention developed in order to maintain or palliate cognitive impairment in dementia patients. Prospective studies have shown that physical, mental, and cognitive activities are considered protective factors for cognitive impairment and dementia. Also, animal models support the idea that environmental enrichment can improve cognition (e.g., Adlard et al., 2005). Therefore, it can be stated that physical, mental, and social stimulation must be an avenue of development for maintaining, or even palliating, negative effects in the individual and his/her family who suffer from dementia from any cause.

Cognitive stimulation or rehabilitation is a comprehensive term that includes a broad set of cognitive and behavioral training programs such as motor stimulation in combination with cognitive cues (Olazarán, Muñiz, & Reisberg, 2004), behavioral training in ADL (Zanetti, Binetti, & Magnini, 1997), memory training programs (Clare, Wilson, & Carter, 2003; Cahn-Weiner, Malay, & Rebok, 2003), cognitive rehabilitation and counseling (Quayhagen, Quayhagen, & Czaja, 2000), or, the most extensive, reality orientation programs. All of them have the objective to delay symptoms of dementia. Most of them do not have standardized procedures, and there is not enough data about their efficacy. We will briefly consider reality orientation and integrated psychostimulation programs as examples.

Reality orientation (RO) is the most extensive and well-known training program. RO is an archetypical training for improving orientation in demented patients (see Spector, Orrell, Davies, & Woods, 2001) and it is currently implemented all over the world in day care centers, nursing homes, or psychogeriatrics wards for elderly with dementia or AD.

Until recently, most evaluations of RO have had minor results (e.g., Woods, 1996). Nevertheless, Spector et al. (2003) introduced several changes into the standard RO program by incorporating some of the tasks common to psychostimulation treatments. We next introduce two of the studies that have been published in the last 5 years.

A single-blind, multicenter, randomized, controlled trial was performed by Spector at al. (2003). A total of 115 elderly with dementia were randomized within centers to the intervention group and 86 to the control group. A 14-session program was run twice a week for 45 minutes per session over 7 weeks. At the follow-up, between groups comparisons yielded results showing improvement in mental status (measured by MMSE), in the Alzheimer's Disease Assessment Schedule ADAS-Cog (Rosen et al., 1984), and in rated quality of life. Patients' communication improved but no differences were found in functional abilities, anxiety, and depression. Comparing this nonpharmaceutical program with the currently used drugs, the authors reported that "it was not quite effective as rivastigmine, donepezil, and galantamine. For greater improvements, cognitive stimulation treatment did as well as galantamine and tacrine and substantially better than rivastigmine the lower dosage of donepezil" (p. 252).

The integrated psychostimulation program (PPI) was developed by Tárraga and associates (Tárraga, 1994; Tárraga et al., 2006). The PPI is a daily program that includes a set of sessions implemented in a day care center. Cognitive tasks, psychomotor activities, and reinforcement of instrumental activities of daily living are implemented during the training sessions. The PPI is a tailored program adjusted to the level of each patient. The PPI has been evaluated through several studies conducted with mild AD-diagnosed patients (Tárraga, 1994), and the authors report the delay of cognitive impairment as measured by the MMSE (Folstein et al., 1975) and, also, some positive results in a quality of life measure.

An interactive multimedia internet-based system (IMIS) was developed from this psychostimulation program. In short, the IMIS consists of 19 sets of stimulation exercises dealing with the following cognitive functions: attention, calculation, gnosis, language, memory, and orientation. Each set starts by assessing a baseline for each patient. A randomized study for testing the relative efficacy of each program (PPI, IMIS & medication) with mild AD patients was conducted (Tárraga et al., 2006). Forty-six patients participated in this study (all patients were treated pharmacologically for at least one year before starting the study). At random, 16 received IMIS, PPI, and ChEIs (mean age: 75.8), 15 received IPP and ChEIs (mean age: 77.4), and 12 in the control group received ChEI medication only (mean age: 76.9). A battery of neuropsychological assessment tests were administered at baseline and at 12 and 24 months. Briefly, patients with both PPI training and IMIS had improved outcome measures; after 12 weeks of training they showed improved scores in MMSE and and ADAS-Co and these improvements were maintained in the follow-up after 24 weeks. Patients treated with PPI alone showed better results than the control group but positive effects were attenuated in the follow-up at 24 months.

In summary, there is some evidence than psychostimulation programs have incipient positive but modest results for maintaining or palliating cognitive impairment in dementia (including Alzheimer's disease) patients. Nevertheless, much more evidence is required in order to improve these results and transform psychostimulation treatments into effective empirically based treatments for dementia.

Concluding Remarks

During the past decade, relevant progress has been made in the study of cognitive aging, which is important for the optimization and compensation of cognitive functioning in old age. The most important conclusions to emerge have been:

First of all, distal factors coming from the socialization process (education attainment, family SES, and childhood cognition) and current environment such as lifelong education and social position have a major influence in cognitive functioning, both usual and impaired.

Secondly, aerobic training, from moderate to high fitness training, has a positive effect on cognitive and brain function in healthy elderly. Physical exercise also seems to be a protective factor for cognitive impairment and dementia.

Research supports that there is broad cognitive plasticity and reserve capacity throughout the life cycle including in old age. Cognitive training can compensate cognitive decline in healthy elderly. Even individuals with mild cognitive impairment as well as mild Alzheimer's disease patients show cognitive plasticity to some extent. Most important, cognitive plasticity measures are good predictors for cognitive impairment and for modifiability of psychostimulation training programs in demented people.

Also, there is evidence that daily cognitive activity and social or leisure activities have a beneficial effect in cognitive functioning and they are protective factors for cognitive impairment. Nevertheless, new studies with more sound methodology should be conducted.

There is empirical evidence that long-term cognitive-intervention programs improve cognitive functioning in healthy elderly.

There are some empirical data about beneficial effects of psychostimulation programs. Nevertheless, much more effort ais required to standardize and evaluate psychostimulation program as empirically based psychological treatments.

In sum, all this progress supports not only a more complex view of cognitive functioning across the lifespan but a new comprehensive view in which effective cognitive training and interventions can optimize cognitive functioning, compensate intellectual losses, and decrease or even palliate cognitive impairment.

6

Emotional and Motivational Functioning: Affect, Control, and Coping

Introduction

Emotions are adaptive mechanisms that prepare the organism for action; they are also central to human motivation for attachment and social functioning, and for the individual value system. Also, affective experience is central to personality, influences cognitive functioning and appraisal, and plays an important role in coping with stressful events.

As Caprara and Cervone (2000) emphasize, "through their capacity to set goals, develop strategies, reflect on themselves, and evaluate their performance, people are able to self-regulate their behavior and emotional states ... People's reflections on their past actions, their future prospects, and their personal qualities underlie individual differences and intraindividual coherence in motivated action" (p. 339). Most definitions of successful aging include self-evaluation, subjective health appraisal, and life satisfaction as emotional outcomes of positive aging. High subjective well-being has been understood as the hallmark of successful aging, but a positive view of life depends on self-regulatory processes and coping styles that can integrate positive and negative events, as well as positive and negative feelings; as Lazarus states, the importance of coping in orchestrating the balance between positive and negative emotions should be emphasized (Lazarus, 2003; see Chapter 3).

It is well established in the general literature on health that positive emotions (positive thinking and attitudes) are psychological conditions linked with longevity and healthy life (e.g., Leventhal & Patrick-Miller, 2000; Mayne, 2001). As Anderson and Anderson (2003) pointed out, beyond healthy life styles (such as diet and physical exercise) and genetic dispositions, emotional functioning must be highly ranked as a determinant of health and longevity.

In the field of developmental psychology, it is an important consensus that, across the lifespan, age is associated with positive emotional development. Moreover, emotional functioning is inseparable from situational appraisal, as well as within the broader domain of coping (e.g., Carstensen et al., 1999, Carstensen, Mayr, Pasupathi, & Nesselroade, 2000; Labouvie-Vief, DeVoe, & Bulka, 1989; Labouvie-Vief & DeVoe, 1991; Lazarus, 1991; Lazarus & Folkman, 1984, Ryff & Singer, 2003).

Also, during recent decades several theoretical and methodological advances have been produced both from a theoretical perspective (e.g., Fredrickson, 2000, 2001) as well as from an applied scope (Seligman et al., 2005). Positive emotions not only have a central role but they can be trained; that is, several interventions for promoting positive emotions, positive thinking, and optimism have been developed in recent years (e.g., Seligman, Steen, Park, & Peterson, 2005). In other words, positive emotional functioning can be improved through psychological intervention.

It is also well-known that negative emotional conditions such as depression, pessimistic explanatory style, feelings of loneliness, etc. are psychological characteristics strongly associated with mortality, illness, and even with suicide and dementia in old age (Pennix, et al., 1998; Peterson, Seligman, & Vaillant, 1988; Whooley, & Browners, 1998, Stek et al., 2005). Negative emotions have been central in gerontology; as has been pointed out by Pressman & Cohen (2005), a recent search in PsycINFO revealed that there are over 20 times more studies on depression and health than on happiness and health. In fact, as emphasized by Cartensen and Turk-Charles (1994), not until the end of 20th century did we focus on the development of emotions through old age and the benefit of positive emotions, thinking, and attitudes on the process of aging.

Why have emotions been neglected within the study of aging? Perhaps because clinical geropsychology and psychogeriatrics have been more interested in cognitive decline and impairment and in negative emotions (depression and anxiety) in old age than in other feelings or emotional states. It is only in the last 20 years that emotional functioning in old age has been converted into a field of research. Cartensen et al. (2000) tried to explained why research on affect across lifespan and, especially in old age, was neglected for so long:

> "Part of the reason emotional development was not studied in adulthood until relatively recently relates to long held presumptions that emotional functioning in later life parallels biological and cognitive functioning in adulthood and old age, namely levelling in adolescence and early adulthood, remaining reasonably stable in midlife, and becoming dysregulated and rigid in old age ... On the contrary a small but growing literature on the adulthood course of emotion paints a distinctly positive picture and suggests that improvements in emotional functioning may continue well into middle-age and perhaps old age" (p. 644).

Before examining the role of positive emotions in active aging it is important to summarize some empirical results about aging and emotions from the last 20 years:
1. Older adults, as compared with younger, show an increase in emotional complexity and heterogeneity (e.g., Carstensen et al., 2000; Labouvie-Vief et al., 1989; Labouvie-Vief & DeVoe, 1991; Turk & Turk, 2005).

2. There is strong evidence supporting the idea that age is unrelated to the frequency of reported positive emotional experience (Carstensen et al., 2000; Fernández-Ballesteros, 1992; Fernández-Ballesteros et al., 1996; Gross et al., 1997; Magai, Consedine, Krivoshekova, Kudadjie-Gyamfi, & McPherson, 2006), the salience of emotion increases linearly with age (Carstensen & Turk-Charles, 1994), at least until the seventies (Staudinger, Freund, Linden, & Maas, 1999), although it is controversial whether intensity declines both in positive and negative feelings (Turk & Piazza, 2007).
3. Older people, in comparison with younger and middle-aged, reported less negative emotional experience and greater emotional control and age is associated with more differential experience (Carstensen et al., 2000; Mroczek & Kolarz, 1998). Also, more positivity than negativity is shown in discrete emotions and negative emotions are associated with poor health throughout old age (Chipperfield, Perry, & Weiner, 2003; Taylor et al., 2000),
4. Elder adults report better emotional self- regulation than younger adults (e.g., Gross et al., 1997, Labouvie-Vief et al., 1989). In other words, emotions and their regulation become more salient as people age (e.g., Isaacowitz, 2005), this is important because, as Higgins, Grant, and Shah (1999) pointed out, emotional self-regulation is a source of adaptation and well-being in old age (Labouvie-Vief & Marquez, 2004; Higgins, 1997; Higgins et al., 1999). Therefore, old people having a more articulate emotional system might be considered a substantial characteristic for successful aging.
5. Although several losses and stressful events usually happen during the aging process, there are minor changes throughout old age in happiness, well-being, and life satisfaction (Diener & Diener, 1996; Fernández-Ballesteros, 1996).
6. Several emotional theories assume these key points for successful aging:
    a. The emotional system represents a set of articulated dispositions that facilitate responses for a better adaptation (including emotional regulation) of promoting survival and fitness (e.g., Fredrickson, 2001; Magai et al., 2006);
    b. Emotional functioning is on the basis of cognitive appraisal and evaluation, and coping (Blanchard-Fields, Camp, & Casper-Jahnke, 1995; Lazarus, 1991; Lazarus & Folkman, 1984; Labouvie-Vief et al., 1989); and
    c. The importance of emotions increases with age because, as people approach endings, the emotional quality of social relationships becomes central for the individual (Carstensen, 1991; Carstensen et al., 2000).

On the other hand, as already mentioned, one of the characteristics of pathological aging is poor mental health and negative emotional functioning. Aldwin et al. (2006), emphasized that depression, anxiety, or hostility are risk factors for health and, therefore, for optimal aging. For example, Murphy, Monson, Olivier, Sobol, & Leighton (1987), in a 16-year prospective study of a general population sample, indicated that those people with depression or anxiety disorders at the baseline experienced 1.5 times the number of deaths expected on the basis of rates for a large reference population. Also, Stek et al. (2005), from a prospective population-based study of 85-year-olds, showed that those subjects who suffered from depression and feelings of loneliness had a mortality risk two times greater. Finally, it is assumed that positive affect is a protective factor for physical and mental health throughout aging.

In sum, results in the study of emotions across the aging process show an increase in emotional control, complexity, and competent emotion regulation and a decrease of negative emotions. Emotional functioning also seems to be strongly associated with other determinants and outcomes of positive aging, positive affect is behind most of the psychological concepts that are considered personal determinants for active aging such as control, self-efficacy for aging, coping styles (WHO, 2002) and are always present as outcomes of successful aging. Therefore, we are considering here that emotional functioning and motivation are central conditions for aging well. In this section we discuss the effects of positive emotions on aging, but before that, we should clarify some conceptual issues.

First we notice that, here, affect and emotion are used interchangeably, as similar concepts. Following Fredrickson (2001), affect is a general subjective concept referring to accessible, long-lasting feelings. It is linked to subjective perceptions and is centrally embedded in a variety of psychological constructs such as attitude, mood, and emotions. In fact, emotions are generally understood as a strong and momentary, affective, multicomponent (physiological, motor, and cognitive) response triggered by a specific stimulus or situation (see also Diener, 1999; Ekman & Davidson, 1994). Both affects and emotions can vary along a broad dimension from positive to negative poles. Since there is only a response parameter to distinguish between affect and emotion, we will continue to use both terms as interchangeable.

Second, although emotions and affects refers to states of the organism, positive affect supports personality constructs such as extroversion, purpose in life, self-efficacy, optimism, sociability, activity and energy, and effective coping as well as negative affect lie behind depressive mood, anxiety and stress, among other constructs. Usually, authors distinguish among those molar personality and psychopathological conditions and more pure and simple measures of positive emotions (Lyubomirsky, King, & Diener, 2005).

Finally, a last aspect that should be taken into consideration is the extent to which positive and negative affect are bipolar extremes of the same dimension or orthogonal factor. As Pressman & Cohen (2005) discussed, this methodological issue depends on the type of measures and scales, and the stimulus used by researchers. Also, when we are dealing with positive or negative emotions, it is important to consider their generalizability across time and situations in order to establish its effects on health. That is, to what extent is a *state* or a more stable *trait* or a set of dispositions, such as optimism, positive thinking, or depression.

Positive Emotions and Positive Aging

Our key question is: Why are positive emotions postulated as constituent for optimal aging? We will next present four, nonmutually exclusive, but complementary, arguments.

The first reason, as has been already stated, assumes that positive emotions are related to success in life, and as Lyubomirsky, et al. (2005) pointed out, those people who feel positive emotions tend to be successful and accomplished in multiple life domains. These authors analyzed sectional, longitudinal, and experimental evidence about the repercussion of positive affect in success throughout life and their effect sizes were meta-analytically examined. They concluded that positive affect produces success in several domains across life and it is linked to, or it determines, many positive characteristics or human resources associated with adaptive results in life. Therefore, aging is also a context where positive emotions should have a determinant role.

Second, as is emphasized by several authors, it is also assumed that positive affect triggers adaptive behaviors. Fredrickson (2001) formulates a theoretical model for a better understanding of the role of positive emotions: the *broaden-and-build theory* of positive emotions (see also Fredrickson & Losada, 2005). This theory states that:

> "Certain discrete positive emotions – including joy, interest, contentment, pride, and love – although phenomenologically distinct, all share the ability to broaden people's momentary thought-action repertoires and build their enduring personal resources, ranging from physical and intellectual resources to social and psychological resources. In contrast to negative emotions, which carry direct and immediate adaptive benefits in situations that threaten survival, the broadened thought-action repertoires triggered by positive emotions are beneficial in other ways. Specially, these broadened mindsets carry indirect and long term adaptive benefits because broadening builds enduring personal resources, which function as reserves to be drawn on later to manage future threats" (p. 219).

As has been stated throughout this chapter, optimal aging requires a broad set of thought-action adaptive repertoires; these repertoires could be triggered by positive emotions elicited by healthy food, physical, and cognitive fitness; by coping with adversity in a proper manner; and by increasing social relationships, social productivity, and social participation (Aspinwall et al., 2001; Lyubomirsky, et al., 2005; Salovey, Rothman, Detweiler, & Steward, 2000). In other words, positive affect seems to be a condition for a broad set of protective physical, cognitive, and psychosocial behaviors.

Our third argument regards the role of positive affect (as well as other positive psychological constructs such as optimism, personal control, etc.) in survival and longevity (for a review, see Vázquez, Hernangómez, & Hervás, 2003) in all biological systems and as a protective factor for psychopathology and mental health.

Pressman and Cohen (2005) reviewed the literature on the association of positive affect (PA) and biomedical events such as mortality, morbidity, survival, disease severity, and physical functioning of biological systems associated with health (cardiovascular, endocrine, and immunologic functions). From this review, it can be summarized that empirical evidence supports the following conclusions:

a. There is a strong association between positive affect and traditional causes of mortality (also in older individuals).
b. Positive affect benefits health problems as diverse as stroke, rehospitalization for coronary diseases, the common cold, and accidents.
c. Highly activated positive emotions were associated with increases in cardiovascular response.
d. There are associations between positive affect with "more quiescent and sometimes lower levels of stress hormones and higher levels of other hormones whose rises are thought to play a positive role in health" (p. 953).
e. Positive-affect inductions in the laboratory were generally associated with acute quantitative and qualitative positive changes in the immune response.

Positive emotions seem to have be long-term protective factors both in physical and mental health. For example, in the Nun Study, Danner, Snow, and Friesen (2001) reported that those sisters who wrote essays with positive emotional contents at a young age (on average, 22 years old) had a higher life expectancy, by about 6.9 years, than those with less positive emotional expression.

Also, positive emotions seem to have effects in a broad age range. For example, Ostir, Markides, Black, and Goodwin (2002) followed 2000 individuals, from 65 to 99 years old, over 2 years. Positive affect and well-being seemed to be a protective factor for disability and recovery of physical illness. Even unrealistically optimistic beliefs about the future might be health-protective factors (Taylor et al., 2000; Salovey et al., 2000).

Authors have tried to reach a better understanding of the role of positive affect in health conditions (e.g., Pressman & Cohen, 2005). Two general models have been posited showing two pathways: The first posits direct effects of positive affect on behavior and physiological systems; the second proposes that positive affect influence health as a mechanism for coping with stress. These two models are also related to the two issues already mentioned: the first one links affect, directly, to the onset and progression of physical and mental disease, and the second considers affect as a buffer for the effect of stress (and, therefore, adaptive coping mechanisms play an essential role). This is not the right place to discuss both models, we will only conclude that there is broad empirical evidence supporting that positive affect is highly related to behavioral and biomedical functioning and that it is not only related to health but also to psychosocial functions, which have already been tested as components of optimal aging, including coping styles and their repercussion on health and well-being.

Our last argument for including emotional functioning in active aging deals with the fact that positive emotions can, potentially, be promoted and improved and, therefore, that this determinant of successful aging can be manipulated. Since the year 2000, empirical research has been conducted in order to collect evidence about the efficacy of psychological intervention on positive affect. Fredrickson (2000), on the basis of her broaden-and-build model, developed a range of intervention and coping strategies for optimizing health and well-being to the extent that they cultivate positive emotions counteracting negatives ones, broaden habitual modes of thinking, and build personal resources.

Recently, Seligman et al. (2005) reported on the evaluation of internet-based interventions for enhancing emotional states (www.authentichappiness.org). They recruited a sample from visitors to the Web who were tested before and after interventions in happiness and depression and to whom a set of exercises designed to increase happiness were administered. A total of 577 adults were recruited and participated in the study. After they accepted the study conditions and reported a set of sociodemographic data, baseline tests in happiness and depression were administered. Then they received a randomly assigned exercise developed for increasing happiness. Participants were instructed that, when completing their assigned exercise, they must return filled out questionnaires to the Web site. Also, several follow-ups were performed: after 1 week, 1 month, 3 months, and 6 months. Training in happiness embraced the following modules: Placebo control exercise (early memories), Gratitude visit, Three good things in life, You at your best, Using signature strengths in a new way, and Identifying signature strengths.

"Using signature strengths in a new way" and "three good things" increased happiness and decreased depression for 6 months after treatment. "Gratitude visit" produced positive changes in 1 month. All the other exercises (including the placebo task) produce positive but momentary effects. Long-term benefits depend on the adherence to treatment. Even though the design was a randomized controlled trial (RCT), results can only be generalized to those subjects looking for happiness through the web. Nevertheless, this study allows us to consider that positive emotion can be trained, at least, in those subjects who are highly motivated.

Positive Emotions and Other Personality Concepts

A first issue that we should briefly discuss is the overlap of positive emotions with personality constructs such as extroversion, neuroticism, or optimism; because we should remember that positive affect is associated with several personality characteristics. This is not the right place to review this conceptual and epistemological issue in detail, but it is important to answer the question: Do personality conditions predict successful aging?

A first important issue regarding personality and emotions is that extroversion is highly associated with life satisfaction and well-being whereas neuroticism is highly associated with psychopathology and negative emotions. Therefore, extroversion and stability are two predictors of well-being and life satisfaction across the lifespan (e.g., Neugarten, 1977)

Common stereotypes of aging say that the elderly are rigid, disagreeable, and hostile (see Fernández-Ballesteros, 1992) in other words, stereotypes assume that personality changes through age. Nevertheless, most authors studying personality, based on results from cross-sectional as well as longitudinal studies covering long period of time, assume that personality is quite stable from the thirties on (e.g., Caprara, Caprara, & Steca, 2003; Costa & McCrae, 1997; McCrae, 2002). Nevertheless, there are tendencies of both stability and change in the sense that neuroticism is quite stable across age, but extroversion and openness decline.

For example, studying elderly with health problems, Weiss et al. (2005) assessed the Big Five in 1,000 medicare recipients older than 65 (age range 65–100). Based on age (from 65 to 79 and 80 to 100) and gender, they were assigned to four groups. Both men and women significantly increased in scores on Agreeableness. In this same line, Roberts, Walton, and Bogg (2005) reviewed relationships between consciousness and health and aging. Two interesting results were noted: first, that conscious people are more likely to engage in healthy and protective behaviors and to resist highly risky ones, and they more likely to be involved in and to conserve their social relationships; second, that consciousness is related to age.

These results are about changes in personality characteristics across the lifespan but most studies show that there is a strong stability in most personality characteristics. Recently, Roberts and Del Vecchio (2000) conducted a meta-analysis on the relative stability of the personality from childhood to old age. Results showed that stability coefficients increase from childhood (.31), to young age (.54), to adulthood (.64), to old age (.71). These results support that personality reaches its highest stability after the fifties and not in the thirties (Costa & McCrae, 1997; McCrae, 2002).

A second question regards whether personality predict mortality. Wilson et al. (2005) studied the association of the personality traits of Neuroticism and Extroversion with risk of death in old age in 6,158 individuals. A high level of Extroversion, compared with a low level, was associated with a 21% decrease in risk of death. Adjustment for medical conditions and health-related variables did not substantially affect results. Moreover, results suggested that higher extroversion and lower neuroticism are associated with reduced mortality in old age and that these associations are mediated, in part, by behavioral patterns of cognitive, social, and physical activity (see Weiss & Costa, 2005).

Optimism has also been shown to be protective for health whereas pessimism is linked to poor health (e.g., Giltay et al., 2004; Peterson et al., 1988; Segestran, 2001; Schulz et al., 1996). Kubzansky, Sparrow, Voconas, and Kawachi (2001) prospectively examined, through the MMPI the relationship of an optimistic or pessimistic explanatory style with coronary heart disease incidence in an ongoing cohort of 1,306 men. During an average of 10 years of follow-up, those reporting a high level of optimism (compared to those with high level of pessimism) at the baseline had multivariate-adjusted relative risks of 0.44 and 0.45 for combined risk of coronary heart disease, fatal and not fatal, respectively. The authors concluded that optimistic styles may protect against coronary heart disease in older men.

Scheider, Weintraub, and Carver (1986) considered dispositional optimism as a protective predictor of successful adaptation to stressful encounters. Results from two different studies showed associations between optimism and problem-focused coping, seeking social support, and emphasizing positive aspects of the stressful situation. On the contrary, pessimism was associated with denial and distancing, focusing on stressful feelings, and disengagement from the goal. Important for our subject, they found a positive association between optimism and acceptance/resignation, but only when the event was uncontrollable (and this situation is very common for the elderly).

In a Dutch longitudinal study of aging (Bijnen et al., 1999), 545 men, aged 64–84, were followed over 15 years in order to assess their expectancy on physical health; those most optimistic ("I am still full of plans") had a 50% lower risk of death from cardiovascular disease over the 15 years than the least optimistic.

After the review of those studies, again two main issues, one methodological and the other theoretical, emerge:
1. Are there differences between optimism and positive emotions? Optimism is considered as a trait and positive affect is considered as a state but both are highly associated.
2. Is optimism an intervening variable that triggers other positive conditions (such as healthy basic-behavioral repertoires)? or is optimism (or positive emotions) a buffer against stress? or is it directly acting through biological systems (such as immune or cardiovascular systems)? Much more research should be conducted in this area as it is an important domain for positive aging.

Our conclusions regarding positive emotion and personality are:
1. Personality is highly stable across the lifespan and through old age;
2. Extroversion is a second-order personality factor associated with positive emotions (life satisfaction and well-being);
3. Neuroticism is a basic trait related with psychopathology and negative emotions and, therefore, with pathological aging; and finally

4. Optimism – as a stable trait of positive emotional functioning – can be considered as one of the components or predictors of successful aging.

A last issue that we should deal with refers to the overlap of positive emotions with other psychological components of successful aging such as personal control (and related concepts such as self-stereotypes and self-efficacy) and coping styles. On the basis of the broaden-and-build theory by Fredrickson (Fredrickson & Losada, 2005), positive emotions could be considered as having the property of broadening thought-action repertoires and building enduring personal resources. Also, Pressman and Cohen's (2005) stress-buffering model shows behavioral resources (such as coping styles) linking stress to disease.

Before examining these psychological components of successful aging, it is important to emphasize a methodological threat: Positive emotion, as well as any other human subjective condition, is assessed through verbal reports, therefore, all of them share method variance (Fernández-Ballesteros, 2003; Fernández-Ballesteros & Botella, 2007; Fernández-Ballesteros & Marquez, 2003). Moreover, from a conceptual point of view, positive verbalizations are behind personal control, self-determination, self-efficacy or self-images, optimism, or even coping styles. In other words, positive affect can be considered to involve all the other psychological conditions of optimal aging, which we are going to deal with next.

Personal Control

There is a long tradition in the study of aging to consider the sense of control as an adaptive psychological mechanism within the aging process (see Baltes & Baltes, 1986). Personal control is a broad comprehensive concept that refers to a person's perceived competence and potentially controllable outcomes (e.g., Rodin, Timko, & Harris, 1977; Moos, 1981; Skinner, 1995; Zautra et al., 1995). This concept integrates others constructs such as "self-determination," "locus of control," "sense of coherence," or "self-efficacy" and, therefore, affects and self-regulation processes are behind all of them.

Affect and motivation are regulated by individual appraisal about the extent to which external events can be controlled. As Caprara and Cervone (2000) state, self-evaluation and perceived control are elements of the self-regulatory system.

Also, sense of control is considered a consequence of social "empowerment" and, therefore, it can be considered a political objective (*II International Plan of Action on Aging, Priority Direction III*; UN, 2002). Finally, as already described in Chapter 3, according to Heckhausen and Schulz (1995), two modes of control can be distinguished, primary and secondary, and both can be considered important for successful aging.

Perceiving oneself as controlling the environment has been understood by authors as the hallmark of successful aging (Eizenman, Nesselroade, Featherman, & Rowe, 1997; Lachman, 1986; Lachman & Leff, 1989; Rowe & Khan, 1998); in other words, perceived control of environmental circumstances is one of the psychological conditions for active aging.

Peterson (1999) defined personal control as "the individual's belief that he or she behave in ways that maximize good outcomes and/or minimize bad outcomes. A belief in personal control may or may not be veridical, but what makes the notion intriguing is its self-fulfilling nature. Because personal control leads the individual to engage the world in a vigorous fashion, outcomes that originally elude control may eventually become controllable" (p. 288).

Personal control across the lifespan is one of the conditions for good performance and health (both physical and mental health) and is one of the explanatory factors for objective health and physical fitness, as well as for quality of life and well-being both in the elderly living in the community (e.g., Burns & Seligman, 1989) or living in institutions (e.g., Rodin, 1986; Timko & Moos, 1989). Also, personal internal control is an explanatory factor of subjective capacity and competence and has an indirect effect on objective, cognitive, and physical competence (Fernández-Ballesteros et al., 2004). On the contrary, lack of control is related to passivity, poor performance, depression, and illness as well as being predictor of mortality (Peterson et al., 1998).

Personal control is not only correlated with illness (physical and mental) but with duration of reported symptoms, results of physician exams, medical tests, longevity, and survival time; most of these predictors have been obtained through longitudinal studies. The biological link between sense of control and health has been well-established through the immunological system in animal and human experimental research (Kamen-Siegel, Rodin, Seligman, & Dwyer, 1991; Maier, Watkins, & Fieshner, 1994).

Finally, perceived control is an indispensable condition for other key issues relevant for active aging such as being involved or following health promotion and illness prevention programs (Peterson & Stunkard, 1989), adherence to physical exercise, and physical competence (Fernández-Ballesteros et al, 2003), even though it is a good predictor of mortality (Eizenman et al., 1997).

Among those control concepts listed by Peterson, *self-efficacy* is perhaps the best well-known construct in the successful-aging literature. Perceived self-efficacy is conceptualized as "beliefs in one's capabilities to organize and execute the courses of action required to produce given attainments" (Bandura, 1997, p. 3). Self-efficacy is also understood as a consequence of regulatory anticipation; based on past experiences of success and failure, people anticipate future outcomes (Higgins, et al., 1999). Following Bandura, perceived self-efficacy is a domain-based psychological concept and it should be referred to a concrete situation including, in our case, the process of aging. Self-efficacy, as a situational variable, predicts (in a given situation) the effort spent in coping, thoughts and emotional patterns experienced, and reached outcomes. In the last 25 years self-efficacy has been searched through cross-sectional, longitudinal, and experimental designs. Effects of self-efficacy have been studied in several life domains trying to assess individual differences across age. Also, several studies have been conducted in order to examine the extent to which self-efficacy predicts healthy and successful aging. Finally self-efficacy for aging has been studied in active aging promotion programs.

Bandura (1997) pointed out that since many physical, psychological, and social capacities decrease when people become older, age differences in personal efficacy might be expected throughout life (p. 198). Fernández-Ballesteros, Díez Nicolás, Caprara, Barbaranelli, & Bandura (2002) assessed personal self-efficacy for four domains (family and couple relationships, work, finances, and health) in a representative sample of people ($N = 1200$) older than 18 years. They found that only on the health domain did the older group report significantly lower feelings of self-efficacy (for solving problems related with health) than the younger groups.

Self-efficacy has been one of the predictors of positive aging in the MacArthur Longitudinal Studies of Successful Aging. The better independent predictors of good cognitive functioning were sense of efficacy for everyday situations, physically active habits, and pulmonary capacity. Consistent with prediction, self-efficacy was a good predictor for cognitive performance (Seeman et al., 1996a; Chodosh, Reuben, Albert, & Seeman, 2002).

There are also several experimental studies in which self-efficacy has been studied as a mediator of memory functioning (e.g., Valentijn et al., 2006), memory training (e.g., Lachman, Weaver, Bandura, Elliot, & Lewkowicz, 1992; Rebok & Balcerak, 1989); health functioning (Carroll, 1995; De Vellis & De Vellis, 2001; Ruiz, Dibble, Gillis, & Gortner, 1992); mental health functioning in depression (Holahan & Holahan, 1987, Davis-Berman, 1989), and also for its implication in the adherence to physical training or any other intervention program.

Finally, very few studies have been conducted in order to examine to what extent self-efficacy for aging can be trained and improved. Fernández-Ballesteros and her group examined whether self-efficacy for aging can be promoted (Fernández-Ballesteros, Caprara, et al., 2004; Fernández-Ballesteros, Caprara, García, & Iñiguez, 2005). After a training program on active aging (see Chapter 8), all measures of self-efficacy for aging significantly improved.

In sum, self-efficacy beliefs are strongly related to successful aging, first because they contribute to perceiving age-related situations not as threats but as challenges; second, because they support individuals to remain committed to selected goals, and finally, because self-efficacy perceptions have a synergic effect with other factors for enhancing outcomes. Therefore, the perception of self-efficacy is not only related to the process of active aging but with active aging promotion (see Chapter 8).

A last construct depending on the self-regulatory system as central to emotional-motivational functioning is *self-perception of aging*. Aging self-perception, self-stereotypes of aging, aging-related cognitions, all these concepts require self-evaluation throughout the process of aging or the representation of oneself in present or future situations. Self-perception of aging has being operationalized as the images people have about themselves getting older (e.g., "things keep getting worse as I get older").

Levy and associates have developed a research program on self-stereotypes (assessed both implicitly and explicitly). Implicit self-stereotypes trigger negative outcomes in several tasks such as memory performance, handwriting, walking, and physiological activation. Even though self-perception of aging predicts health and mortality. Levy and associates (Levy, Slade, & Kasl, 2002; Levy, Slade, Kunkel, & Kasl, 2002), on the basis of the Ohio Longitudinal Study of Aging and Retirement (OLSAR), analyzed relationships between mortality and self-perception of aging. The final cohort of OLSAR is composed of 338 men and 322 women ranging from 50 to 94 years (Mean = 63.00 years, SD = 9.23). At the baseline self-perceptions about aging or self-stereotypes were measured by four items from the Philadelphia Geriatric Center Moral Scale (PGCMS, Lawton, 1975), data about health and psychological conditions were examined in several waves, and the study also contains data about the course of survival over the 22.6 year period. The results were impressive: Those with more positive aging self-perceptions at the baseline lived 7.6 years longer (after relevant factors were controlled). The risk ratio of .87 ($p < .001$) suggests that positive self-perceptions of aging reduce the risk of mortality. For each change of one point in the positive self-perception of aging measure, the risk of dying decreased by 13%. When it was analyzed in what extent Will-to-Life (operationalized through three Semantic Differential Scales applicable to in the base-line to "your life in retirement": "Empty-Full," "Hopeless-Hopeful" and "Worthless-Worthy") mediate survival; as expected – although self-stereotypes had a direct influence on survival – will-to-live was an indirect predictor for self-stereotype (Levy, Slade, Kunkel, & Kasl, 2002. Naturally, semantic labels also have emotional (evaluative) meaning and positive adjectives attributed to oneself are associated with positive self-stereotypes.

Wurm, Tesch-Römer, and Tomasik (2007) examined the influence of views of aging – both control belief and aging-related cognitions – on health changes in old age. The authors based their analyses on data from the longitudinal part of the German Aging Survey carried out in 1996 and in 2002 (N = 1,286; age range at baseline: 40–85 years). Results indicated that positive and negative aging-related cognitions had an impact on health changes but not *vice versa*.

A last interesting study comes from the opposite of positive images about aging, that is, dissatisfaction with aging. Maier and Smith (1999), on the basis of the Berlin Aging Study, assessed 516 individuals from 70 to 103 years old, between 1990 and 1993. By 1996, 50% had died. Among 11 indicators, only low perceptual speed and dissatisfaction with aging were the uniquely significant controls for age, SES, health, and the other 16 indicators. Therefore, a cognitive (such as perceptual speed with a strong neurological base) and an affective psychological conditions were the two main risk factors for mortality.

As has been already stated, self-perception, self-efficacy, self-stereotypes, and other self-regulatory constructs have behind them emotional self-regulatory processes that determine a positive/negative appraisal about the past, the present, or the future referring to oneself.

In this same line of inquiry, Ostir, Ottenbacher, and Markides (2004) tested whether a positive attitude or affect toward life may help people to avoid becoming frail. Participants were 1,558 Mexican-Americans, with a mean age of 72 at the onset of the study, in reasonably good health. At the baseline, participants were assessed with standardized tests on physical performance and daily life activities as well as positive affect reports ("I feel just as good as other people," "I enjoy life"). After 7 years they were retested when the average age was 79; 10% of the sample were frail and after 7 years the incidence of frailty increased 7.9%. For each unit of positive affect reported 7 years before, the chance of becoming frail decreased by 3%, in addition there was an increased chance for better health outcomes, greater functional independence, lower morbidity, and high survival. The authors conclude that these findings support that positive affect is a protective factor against functional and physical decline in old age.

Although all of these results open a promising panorama for research (and also for psychological interventions), none of the theories from the field of emotions can explain the multilevel, individual, and social implications in these emotional-motivational constructs. There is no comprehensive theory that can explain the relationships between self-stereotypes and social stereotypes. From social psychology, "stereotype threat" is the most extended theoretical explanation (Levy, 2003) for accounting for results from aging self-stereotypes. Nevertheless, it can be assumed that positive images about aging can belong to the so-called "affective style" (Davidson, 2000) and, as positive emotions do, they could act as buffers for responses to stress or, perhaps, as has been hypothesized by Pressman and Cohen (2005), positive emotion and positive images could be direct protective factors for health.

In sum, the emotional-motivational system regulation embraces personal control and any other construct requiring personal appraisal and coping.

Coping with Stress

According to several theoretical frameworks of successful aging (see Chapter 3), successful aging can be considered as a coping process. Old age is associated with bio-psycho-social changes; these changes require adaptation and resilience. Following Rutter (1987), resilience "is the positive pole of individual differences in people's response to stress and adversity" (p. 316) or, in other terms, resilience is the ability to maintain stable equilibrium and a high level of psychological and physical functioning in spite of losses or negative circumstances (Bonanno, 2004). In the context of the MacArthur Foundation Network on Successful Aging, "resilience" has been defined as the ability to recover swiftly from any misfortune or challenge.

As was emphasized in Chapter 3, several authors have considered that successful aging, as a process of adaptation and resilience that implies internal resources or dispositions of coping with stress (see, for example, Kahana & Kahana, 2001, 2003, Kahana et al., 2005; Kane, 2003). The way people cope with life crises or stressful life events is one of the well-known behavioral conditions linked with health and well-being over the aging process.

Coping strategies are those sets of behaviors (motor, emotional, and/or cognitive) considered as self-regulation processes for adapting or overcoming biological, environmental and social, or personal stressful situations when those situations are appraised as exceeding the individual's resources (Lazarus & Folkman, 1984). As Moos (1986) conceptualized, coping can be situated in the interplay between environmental contexts and personal resources and their impact on how individuals cope with life transitions and crises (p. IX). In other words, ways of coping with stress can be placed within the stressful situation (and its parameters: predictability, novelty, etc.) and the person's appraisal or personal significance of the situation.

Perhaps, the broadest conceptualization for understanding successful aging as a process of coping is Brandstädter's model of assimilative and accommodative coping (Brandstädter & Renner, 1990). Highly associated to the SOC, Baltes' and Heckhausen and Schulz' models of successful aging (see Chapter 3), Brandstädter and collaborators proposed two different but complementary strategies of coping. *Assimilative* strategies imply that the individual tries to modify the environment (primary control) for managing and overcoming stressful events, *accommodation* coping refers to the individual's flexible adjustment to the stressful event, trying to adjust his/her needs to the circumstances. Although these two types of coping strategies are complementary, they usually act successively when stressful events arrive. The individual starts coping with assimilative strategies, actively counteracting conflictive situations, but when there is increasing difficultly and/or they become chronic, accommodative strategies could be required in order to preserve well-being and self-esteem. These two broad coping styles are a high-order category for classifying other types of coping.

Authors from the lifespan approach not only introduce a broad conceptual framework helpful in old age but also emphasize an important issue: the predictability of stressful events. Neugarten (1977) pointed out that people have a very accurate prediction about the events occurring across the life cycle; although this calendar could change from generation to generation, most of the stressful situations in old age can be predicted and, therefore, individuals can cope by anticipating the situation.

The cornerstone of Kahana and Kahana's (2003) model of successful aging (see

Chapter 3) is, precisely, proactive coping strategies (preventive and corrective). Older successful agers are viewed as "active agents who engaged in preventive and corrective behaviors to maximize their quality of life in the face of stressors" (Kahana et al., 2005).

Along the same line, as has been stated, the Baltes and Baltes' (1990b) SOC model introduced three mechanisms that can be considered as proactive (preventive and corrective) ways of coping: selection, optimization, and compensation.

On the basis of research on social cognition, social interaction, and stress and coping, Aspinwall and Shelley (1997) proposed proactive coping as the process through which people anticipate or detect potential stressors and act in advance to prevent them or to mute their impact. Proactive coping has five steps:
1. Resource accumulation,
2. Recognition of potential stressors,
3. Initial appraisal,
4. Preliminary coping efforts, and
5. Elicitation and use of feedback concerning initial efforts.

Taking into consideration that aging (indeed life in general) is a process with potential stressors, and taking into account the importance of promoting positive aging, proactive coping has a potential value for us. Three most important conclusions emerge from the coping and aging literature:
1. There is a broad evidence about the stability of coping behavior across the lifespan (e.g., Aldwin, Sutton, & Lachman, 1996);
2. Although authors distinguish broad and general coping skills (e.g., Brandstädter & Renner, 1990), they also consider some specific coping styles in old age (e.g., Staudinger et al., 1999);
3. Stressful situations, such as bereavement, retirement, chronic illness, etc., have different incidence through life and can be considered as major stressful situations in old age (Fernández-Ballesteros, Díaz, Izal, & Hernández, 1988).

We will next discuss three main issues: types of coping styles, more common stressors in old age, and relationships between stress and health.

Major Types of Coping Styles

As Moos and Schaffer (1986) have emphasized, it is difficult to distinguish the effectiveness of a given type of coping because it could be adaptive for one situation and not for another. Nevertheless, the most accepted, broad classification is the following:
1. Logical analysis and mental preparation,
2. Cognitive redefinition,

3. Cognitive avoidance or denial,
4. Seeking information and support,
5. Taking problem-solving action,
6. Identifying alternative rewards,
7. Affective regulation,
8. Emotional discharge, and
9. Resigned acceptance.

This set of coping skills can be divided into active and passive ways of coping. Passive coping would be cognitive avoidance or denial, emotional discharge, and resigned acceptance. Active coping skills would be all the rest. We will next introduce some studies regarding this broad classification.

In the Bonn Longitudinal Study of Aging (BOLSA), Rudinger and Thomae (Thomae, 1975; Rudinger & Thomae, 1990) classified the ways of coping as active (activities for improvement health conditions) and passive (accepting the situation) but both ways of coping influenced perceived health and none of them were related to objective health or any other objective conditions (such as SES).

Staudinger et al. (1999), in the Berlin Study on Aging (70 to 100 years old) included 13 coping styles: comparison with the past, wish for information, comparison with others, keep going, adaptation to the given, ups and downs, faith, humor, distraction, social support, someone else to take over, life loses meaning, and giving up. After a factorial analysis of these 13 coping styles they found three factors (low intercorrelations, covering 42% variance): the first factor set was termed regressive styles (e.g., someone else to take over), active styles (e.g., wish for information), and passive (e.g., faith). Independently with this classification, several of these ways of coping were not related to age (such as social support), others decreased with age (such as giving up and wish for information), and others (such as keep going or life loses meaning) increased with age. Results showed that six coping styles (e.g., humor, keep going, and wish for information) were positively related with resilience as assessed through an aging-satisfaction score but seven coping styles (such as life loses meaning and someone else to take over) were negatively related. Finally, coping styles explained 20% of the variance in resilience. In the Berlin study, coping styles were not only related to subjective factors (such as resilience, life satisfaction) but, also, the relationships between aging satisfaction and somatic risk (objectively assessed) changed when controlling for coping styles. In sum, the use of certain ways of coping (such as wish for information and social support) are protective in dealing with physical impairment.

Results from the Lund 80+ reported by Svensson, Dhlin, Hagberg, and Samuelsson, (1993) showed that active coping styles relate to life satisfaction while passive coping relates to low life-satisfaction, and that emotional and avoidance coping strategies mainly relate to high life-satisfaction in healthy individuals. Most important, these four types of coping styles were related to personality and control as well as to three types of stressful situations: change in health, change in marital status, and cognitive change.

In sum, there is no consensus about ways of coping; a broad classification of active and passive coping styles seems to be more efficient, and the ways of coping are highly related with the type of stressful situation, therefore, we will next consider the more common stressful situations in old age.

Stressful Situations in Old Age

Although the most common image about old people is that they must cope with a high number of stressful situations, older persons report fewer life events and rate these events as being less stressful than do younger people (Orrell & Davis, 1994); as McLeod (1996) stated, these differences could be attributed to age differences in resilience but, also, to emotions self-regulation.

Death of partner, retirement, chronic illness and subsequent disability, and financial difficulties are the most frequent and conflictive stressful life events reported by several samples of people older than 65 (Fernández-Ballesteros et al., 1988; Murrell, Norris, & Grote, 1988). However, the appraisal of these events as predictable could make them less stressful or, as Lazarus (2003) sates, from negative life experiences some people extract positive psychological growth after adaptive coping in grieving over major loss, which commonly requires considerable psychological struggle.

Authors have considered that adaptive coping for those events are different and even that life events could give an opportunity for development. We will discuss, as an example, of one of most relevant stressful situations: death of partner.

The loss of husband or wife is one of the most stressful situations in life since it requires high level of readjustment, and it is also very common in old age (see Holmes & Rahe, 1967). Moreover, there is strong empirical support that losing the partner in old age is associated with higher mortality risk and with greater cognitive decline (e.g., Bogers et al., 2006). Nevertheless, for some people, death of the partner – also death of close family members or friends – can be a trauma with effects on health (mental of physical) or, by contrary, a stimulus for personal development.

Tedeschi and Calhoun (2004) studied very carefully the results of trauma over the loss of the spouse and they focus on five domains of potential growth: a greater appreciation of life and changed sense of priorities; increasing more intimate relationships with others; stronger sense of personal strength; more recognition of new possibilities for one's life and, finally, spiritual development. The authors suggest that people whose personalities tend to be socially extroverted and open to new experiences are especially likely to gain from the aftermath of a traumatic situation. Interestingly, posttraumatic growth does not always go hand-in-hand with happiness, lack of distress, or intrusive thoughts. Often, over time, distress is lessened but not necessarily all the time or immediately. This is not the road to long-term recovery but, likely it is the road of optimal elderly.

Also, Moore and Stratton (2002) interviewed 51 widowed men aged 58–104 some 2 years after the death of their wives; the authors found men who were coping rather well. The outcome of grief for these men was a type of adaptive responsivity that helped them to create new lives for themselves.

Our last example of the ways of coping with losing the partner come from another way to lose a tight relationship that is very unusual in old age: divorce. King, Baker, Burton, and Velazquez (2004) studied older women whose marriages ended in divorce. They labeled a new mature coping style: "to investigate and discover new possible selves." To be able to discover new scripts and scenarios for satisfying their own needs differentiated those women with high and low life satisfaction. In sum, a very common situation in old age – the loss of a partner – is managed in multiple ways of coping ending in positive outcomes.

There are other common stressful situations coming from the fact that age and chronic illness is strongly associated (see Segerstrom & Miller, 2004). Fernández-Ballesteros et al. (1988) studied the most frequent stressful situations among the elderly (in a sample of elderly from 62 to 89 years old). The more frequent and highly conflictive situation was "to be chronically ill." In this same line, Chovan and Chovan (1985) found that health-related concerns were the most frequently reported by older adults (older than 60), more than any other stressful event (reported by a 51% of their sample). McLeod (1996) also reported that the prevalence of chronic health problems and related events ran from 30% to 55%. More important, to be chronically ill is highly associated with disability; therefore, a stressful situation for any individual and more likely for an elder person it is the loss of one or various of his/her capacities as the consequence of a chronic disease.

There are individual differences in coping with physical deficits. As has been noted, it is difficult to generalize which are adaptive or healthy coping strategies, as Aldwin & Park (2004) emphasized, the effect of coping on physical-health outcomes appears to vary by the type of illness and also, ways of coping are very diverse.

Rothermund and Brandstadter (2003) investigated the process of coping with health-related stressful events in a 4-year longitudinal study of 762 participants (initial age range: 58–81 years). Active coping behavior, compensating for functional impairments, increased up to 70 years. Above that age, a decrease of active coping styles was found and, at the same time, there was a substitution of feelings of acceptance of deficits and losses. These results are quite similar to those yielded by Staudinger et al. (1999).

Benyamini and Lomranz (2004) also looked at how the elderly cope with losses in capacity. They conducted a study with 423 older adults whose physical condition required them to give up various physical activities such as soccer, volleyball, etc. As was predicted, in one group of participants results were strong feelings of depression but in other participants this association was not found. Those participants not depressed were shown to have developed alternative activities to replace those lost, and they retained the same morale than those who were healthy.

Most important, not only are there differences between different coping styles across the aging process but it is also important to test whether some of these styles predict mortality. For example, Murberg, Furze, and Brus (2003) assessed the effect of avoidance coping styles on mortality risk among 119 patients (mean age 66.0 ± 9.1 years) who were recruited from an outpatient cardiology practice. Results showed that avoidance-oriented coping style was significantly associated with increase of mortality.

In sum, although to some extent coping styles depend on the type of stressful events, the variability in the ways of coping – even for the same situation – make it difficult to draw any conclusion referring to this crossroad, apart from highlighting strong individual differences in coping with stress mechanisms.

Coping Styles and Health

Ways of coping has been understood as a moderator variable on the effect of stressful events on health but, as Aldwin and Park (2004) pointed out, relatively few published studies have actually examined this hypothesis. Research on coping styles can be divided in two types of effects of coping:
1. Empirical results devoted to test the effect of coping skills on cognitive and emotional conditions such as cognitive impairment, subjective health, life satisfaction, or well-being, and
2. The use of differential coping strategies is related to concurrent and even subsequent psychological adjustment with a variety of health-related stressors such as cancer (e.g., Stanton et al., 2000), heart disease (Van Elderen, Maes, & Dusseldorp, 1999), cardiovascular outcomes and cholesterol (Vitaliano, Russo, & Niaura, 1995; Vitaliano, Russo, Paulsen, & Bailey, 2005), and rheumatoid arthritis (Newth & DeLongis, 2004), among other health problems.

Penley, Tomaka, and Wiebe (2002) performed a series of meta-analytic studies on the association of coping and physical and psychological health outcomes in nonclinical adult samples. Results showed that problem-focused coping was positively correlated with health outcomes. Also, among the elderly, population research show that active (vs. passive) coping styles are associated with physical symptoms, better mental health and better health-related quality of life, better immune function (Stowell, Kieklot Glaser, & Glaser, 2001), and better cardiovascular risk factors (Vitaliano et al., 1995a,b).

In sum, active coping styles are related to a set of positive subjective events such as life satisfaction, subjective well-being, and quality of life but also with several objective health indicators such as better cognitive functioning, better objective health indicators, and more vigorous immune response to stress.

Nevertheless, the importance of coping styles in individuals' subjective and objective health conditions could be understood from the main-effect or from the stress-buffering models. In any case, as has already been mentioned, coping styles must be considered as the subject's resources determining health practices and/or mediating the effect of stress in the immune and cardiovascular systems (Pressman & Cohen, 2005). As Folkman and Moskowitz (2000) emphasize, the positive affect can be considered "the other side of coping." They arrived at this conclusion when they reviewed findings about the co-occurrence of positive affect with negative affect during stressful situations as well as the adaptive function of positive affect during stress. In sum, since positive affect has significant adaptive functions in the coping process, it becomes important to understand how positive affect influences active ways of coping.

An important caution already emphasized is that both positive affect and ways of coping are assessed through self-reports that share the same method variance. In sum, personal control and positive self-images, adaptive coping styles, and positive affect are threatened by the same method bias. Research both in coping and in affect should pay attention to this methodologically problematic issue.

A final interesting and new research program linked to coping styles arises from the concept of *allostatic load,* defined as cumulative biological dysregulation very related to stress. Allostatic load is examined through physiological parameters and it is considered a biomarker of biological decline (including cognitive impairment). As an example, in one of the scientific reports from the MacArthur Foundation Studies on Successful Aging, Seeman et al. (1995) tested the effect of stress on cognitive and physical decline. Results indicated that older women who had high levels of stress for a period of more than 2 years showed decline in memory and physical performance (Seeman, McEwen, Singer, Albert, & Rowe, 1997a, Seeman, Singer et al., 1997b). These results have been examined from the perspective of the allostatic theory. Ten parameters of allostatic load were examined (e.g., cortisol levels, cholesterol level, blood pressure, etc.). High allostatic load was associated with poorer cognitive and physical functioning (Seeman, McEwen, Rowe, & Singer, 2001).

These results support the hypothesis that stress is a major risk-factor for pathological aging but also that allostatic load could be a line of research allowing the use of multimethods in the study of stress and coping and, finally, that coping with stress is a central issue for successful aging.

Concluding Remarks

A general conclusion emerges from the study of emotions and motivational functioning across the aging process. In short, there is an increase in emotional control, complexity, and emotion-motivation regulation. Also, emotional-motivational functioning is behind most of the psychological concepts considered as personal conditions for optimal aging such as control, self-efficacy, and coping styles. Finally, positive emotions (life satisfaction and well-being) are outcomes of successful aging. Therefore, emotional and motivational functioning are central aspects for aging well.

Individual appraisal of the extent to which external events can be controlled and any other appraisal about him/herself, on the field of health, self-esteem, and self-images about the future are consequences of emotional-motivational regulation.

Finally, coping strategies are considered self-regulation processes for adapting or overcoming biological, environmental and social, or personal stressful situations when those situations are appraised as exceeding the individual's resources. These strategies are considered an adaptive mechanism across the life cycle for successful aging.

Perhaps the most important issue is the evidence supporting that idea that positive emotions can be promoted; self-regulation mechanisms can be enhanced; control, self-efficacy, and self-appraisal can be trained; and adaptive coping styles can be improved.

7
Social Functioning and Social Participation

Introduction

One of the basic needs of human beings is social contact; throughout the history of gerontology, social interaction and social support has been central issues. In sum, social functioning is associated with survival and longevity, physical and mental health, healthy cognitive functioning, and life satisfaction and well-being (e.g., Antonucci, Okorodudu, & Akiyama, 2002; Cohen & Syme, 1985a).

Chapter 3 shows that social functioning (social participation, integration, and/or engagement) is included in all definitions (lay, working, and empirical) of successful aging and is considered one of its more important domains (e.g., Baltes & Baltes, 1990b; Rowe & Khan, 1998; Fries, 1989; Mendes de Leon, 2005). As Mendes de Leon said: "A solid scientific foundation will sustain our understanding of the importance of social engagement for successful aging and will guide the development of programs or interventions that will make meaningful difference in the health and well-being of older adults" (p. 64).

In short, there is extensive evidence about the impact of social functioning in physical and mental health, in positive emotions and well-being, and in cognitive functioning (e.g., Cohen, 1988; Krause, 1987; Siegrist et al., 2004). The lack of social integration and/or the existence of social isolation are important risk factors for physical and mental health and they are also determinants of dissatisfaction and depression.

Before introducing supporting arguments about the relationships between social functioning and several domains of successful aging we must distinguish briefly some of the concepts implied.

As has been emphasized by several authors, there is little consistency in the frequency of use and meaning of the concepts implied in the broad field of social functioning: social relationships, social activity, social support and social networks, social engagement, social integration, social participation, among others. Antonucci et al. (1996) distinguish the following concepts: *social relations* as an umbrella concept involving all type of interpersonal interactions and transactions; *social network* as the structural characteristics of an individual's social relationship (number, age, etc.); *social support* as the exchange of resources, goods, or services between or among social network members; and *social integration* as the degree to which an individual is blended into a group, organization, or community. Also, social integration could be considered as an umbrella concept, as the outcome of social networks and social support covers other terms such as social *engagement* (involvement within the social network) or social *participation* (involvement in social activities), and other social activities and performances such as *volunteering* or *social productivity*.

In sum, social functioning refers to an undefined set of concepts, with functional power for successful aging, highly associated to biomedical and psychological outcomes from survival to health, from physical to cognitive and emotional functioning in old age. Next, we will introduce some supporting evidence for the association between main outcomes of successful aging to social functioning.

Social Functioning and Positive Emotions Across the Life Span

We start by describing the most common pattern on social functioning across the aging process and its relationships with positive emotion and well-being. The most extensive finding, supported in this field from cross-sectional and longitudinal studies, is that rates of social interaction decline slowly from middle age to old age, and more rapidly after the seventies (e.g., Antonucci, Sherman, & Akiyama, 1996; Carstensen, 1993).

This pattern has been explained by several theories of aging. Disengagement theory predicts that decline in social contacts expresses an adaptive mechanism of social separation and retreat. Activity theory proposes that, although in old age human beings continue to have a similar need of social contacts, it is the social system that establishes barriers for such contact. Finally, interchange theory explains that the decline in social contact is caused by the unbalance of help needed and received. All these theories predict that the individual's responses to this decline in social contact are embedded in dissatisfaction.

Nevertheless, this pattern in social functioning has several nuances coming from well documented empirical research:

1. Across life span, when people – rather early in life, during the third decade – reduce social contacts positive feelings, life satisfaction, and well-being do not decrease.
2. During adulthood there is an increase in satisfaction with standing social relationships (e.g., Antonucci et al., 1996) and with social activities, in comparison with younger ages (Willigen, 2000).
3. There is cross-cultural evidence for the stability across age of positive interactions but there is a general decline in negative interactions in close relationships (Akiyama, Antonucci, Takahashi, & Langfahl, 2003).
4. The reduction of social contact occurs in peripheral relationships and, at the

same time, closer relationships increase during the life span (e.g., Cartensen, 1993; Carstensen, Mayr, Pasupathi, & Nesselroade, 2000).
5. Although very old people receive more social support than they give, some very old people still support others and continue participating in social and productive activities (e.g., Wagner, Schütze, & Land, 1999; Bukov, Maas, & Lampert, 2002).
6. Work is a source of social interaction, but retirement is one of the markers of old age. Although retirement began as a conquest and as a social right, mandatory retirement is considered as a mandatory "disengagement" for social participation, a source of inequality and ageism, and, at the individual level, a loss of control, power, and financial resources. In sum, retirement is a transition and could be a constriction for aging well (e.g., Hardy, 2002; Solinge & Henkens, 2007).
7. There are cultural differences in social participation in voluntary work; in general there is decline across aging (in some countries the decline is only in time devoted to voluntary work, in other countries the decline is also in frequency), but this decline could be attributed more to health problems than to age (Maier & Klumb, 2005; Börsch-Supan & Jurges, 2005; Bukov et al., 2002).

On the basis of these findings, Carstensen and her group (1991, 1993; Carstensen, Isaacowitz, & Charles, 1999) formulated the socioemotional selectivity theory (SST). In brief, this theory assumes that the perception of time is the basis for the selection and pursuit of social goals. The perception of time has important implications for socioemotional and motivational functioning. It is postulated that:
1. Social interaction is essential for survival;
2. Human being is inherently agentic planning future goals; and
3. Since he/she has multiple goals, selection is a basic process for adaptation.

SST "maintains that the view of time as expansive or limited influences the appraisal process that precedes goal selection" (Carstensen et al., 1999, p. 166). Therefore, social interaction is motivated not only by fundamental human needs but also by the modulator role of socioemotional functioning. In addition to serving basic survival functions, social interaction allows people to acquire information, develop and maintain a self-concept, and regulate emotional states.

The core of the SST stated that the elderly are highly selective in their social interactions for a better emotional regulation and the outcome is higher well-being. When time is considered in expansion, contact with new partners is the priority but, when time is perceived as limited, close relationships are the priority and, therefore, emotional regulation assumes the highest priority, increasing life satisfaction and well-being.

Social Functioning and Health

Health is one of the core outcomes of successful aging, throughout the history of behavioral health and health psychology, and public health, one of the most consistent findings is that social functioning is not only essential for psychological well-being across the life span but, also, it has an essential role in longevity and survival.

The Alameda County study is one of the pioneer longitudinal research programs for analyzing the predictive power of the social network for longevity and survival. For 9 years, Berkman and Syme (1979) followed-up a community database sample of people between the ages of 30 to 69, living in Alameda County (USA). In brief, social participation (e.g., membership of a church) and the overall *social network index* (based on four measures of social contact) predicted mortality independently of physical health, healthy lifestyle, or the use of preventive services. This study was extended to 17 years in a sample of more than 4,000 individuals from age 38 through more than 70 years old. After adjusting for age, sex, race, and baseline health status, people with the high social network index had a 50% lower risk of mortality than people with the lowest (Seeman, Kaplan, Knudsen, Cohen, & Guralnik, 1987).

A replication of the Alameda County study was conducted by Schoenbach, Kaplan, Fredman, and Kleinbaum (1986). A modified version of the social network index was included in a 13-year follow-up in a sample of more than 2000 community participants living in Georgia (USA) aged 15 and over. This index was comprised of marital status, number of relatives, close friends living nearby, number of close neighbors, number of frequently visiting, church attendance, and membership of a church group, and also predicted survival. More recent studies have yielded the same results about the association between social participation and survival and mortality (for a review, see Bath & Deeg, 2005; Kaplan et al., 1988; Minkler, 1985; Seeman et al., 1996b; Harris & Thoresen, 2005).

Following Berkman's conceptual framework, Litwin (2007) tried to identify the salient network correlates of 7-year all-causes of mortality among a Jewish sample, aged 70 and over, in Israel ($N = 1,811$). The analysis included age, income, education, gender, and current work status. The social network variable included respondent's marital status, the number of children in close proximity, and frequency of contact with children, friends, and neighbors. The social engagement measures included visitation at a senior club and synagogue attendance. Also, measures of heath-promotion, risk behaviors, emotional state, and physiological pathway were collected. Summarizing, at the end of the study 38% of the sample had died and two main network-related components were found to be predictive of survival: contact with friends, a social network interaction variable, and a social engagement variable (synagogue attendance).

Most of the studies searching for social functioning and participation effects have considered survival and mortality as well as well-being and life satisfaction. Nevertheless, effects of social functioning in morbidity and other biomedical parameters and health outcomes are confused (Cohen, 1988; Bath & Gardiner, 2005; Lennartsson, 1999; Willis et al., 1997). For example, Lum and Lightfoot (2005) examined longitudinal data from 1,993 and 2,000 panels of the Asset and Health Dynamics among the Oldest Old Study (AHEAD). Their findings provide empirical support to earlier claims that volunteering slowed the decline in self-reported health and physical functioning levels, slowed the increase in depression levels, and improved mortality rates for those who were involved in volunteer work (see Morrow-Howel et al., 2003).

Also, Bennet (2005) investigated whether social engagement longitudinally predicted objective and subjective physical health in a sample of 359 (older than 65 years) followed-up at three points in time. Although social engagement predicted subjective health, none of the objective measures of health were predicted by social engagement.

Nevertheless, there is empirical support for the link between social participation and two relevant health problems for the elderly: disability and cognitive impairment and dementia. The association between social relationships and disability prevalence, incidence, and recovery has been well established. For example, Zunzunegui et al. (2005) examined data from longitudinal studies conducted in Finland, the Netherlands, and Spain. Participants at baseline were 3,648 individuals between 65 and 85 years old. Disability was determined at baseline and at follow-up. Social participation, number of family ties, and the presence of friends constituted an index of social ties. For every country, this index, having friends, and social participation were negatively associated with the prevalence of ADL disability prevalence. ADL disability incidence was negatively related to the number of family ties. The authors concluded that social ties had a beneficial effect on the maintenance and restoration of functional activities and had a protective effect from disability incidence.

Mendes de Leon, Glass, & Berkman (2003) examined the effect of social engagement on disability in a representative sample of 1,169 men and 1,643 women in noninstitutionalized population from New Haven, CT (USA) assessed at baseline and several follow-ups (three in-home and four telephone interviews during 9 years). Eleven types of social, productive, and religious activities were included (e.g., sporting events, shopping, paid and unpaid community work, etc.). Disability status was assessed through three self-reported measures. A summary score was formed adding the three items. Three set of covariates related with disability outcomes were also assessed: SES (education and income), health, and overall number and extent of social relationships. Results showed a strong and robust cross-sectional association between social engagement and disability; more socially active persons reported lower levels of disability than their counterparts. Also, results showed that the protective effects of social engagement diminished slowly over time. The authors concluded that their findings were not consistent with a direct or causal affect of social engagement on disability.

In an attempt to examine different effects caused by social participation in volunteering, religious involvement or social support, Oman, Thorensen, & McMahon (1999), studied a sample of 1,972 older residents in California (USA) with 31% of respondents as volunteers. High volunteers has a 63% lower mortality than nonvolunteers. Multivariate adjustment moderately reduced differences to 44%, mostly from physical functioning, health habits, and social support but, more interesting, and unexpectedly, volunteering was more protective for those with religious involvement and perceived social support.

The association between social functioning (and social network and any other set of social relationships) and health in old age requires some theoretical assumptions. Throughout the history of the study of the relationships between social networks and health, two general models have been discussed:

1. Whether social support enhances health and well-being, irrespective of stress level (that is, directly) or
2. Social integration protects people from the pathogenic effects of stressful events (indirectly or, "buffering hypothesis"). Both hypotheses have been tested in several studies and have been considered compatible (e.g., Cohen, Teresi, & Holmes, 1985,1986; Rozanski, Blumenthal, & Kaplan, 1999).

More recently, several authors have emphasized that social networks seem to be related to disease in a nonspecific way three hypotheses have emerged.

A first potential assumption, which has been emphasized by several authors, is that the potential direction of causality may possibly be reversed. That is, that the observed relations among high social interactions and health outcomes (from survival to morbidity) are because healthier people have more social relationships and not the inverse (e.g., Bath & Gardiner, 2005; Lennartsson, 1999). Those longitudinal studies where cross-sectional relationships between social participation and health or psychological benefits have been dissipated across time provide support to this potential explanation. Nevertheless, those long-term longitudinal studies where social participation predicted survival (controlling for other potential independent variables) support the rejection of this hypothesis.

A second argument could be that social contacts provide not only emotional but instrumental support, that is advice, contact, health services, etc.; individuals with broad social relationships may obtain better and more medical care and support than others (Berkman, 1985). However, this theoretical explanation has not been tested because there is no empirical evidence that people with higher social engagement attend more significantly to health resources (e.g., Bath & Gardiner, 2005).

A last explanatory argument is that the relationship between social integration and health is mediated by psychological mechanisms. Since social relationships are a potent source of reinforcement and have been highly associated with well-being, the effect of social relationships could be mediated by positive emotions and, therefore revert back to the direct *versus* "buffering" hypotheses discussed by Pressman and Cohen (2005) (see Chapter 6). Nevertheless, research does not allow us to conclude in favor of any of the above listed explanatory hypotheses.

As Mendes de Leon (2005) states, if we speculate that social relationships (social networks, social support, social, activity, social engagement, social integration, or social participation) is causally involved in the disease process we should test differential rates of progression over time in this process as a function of social relationships. A pattern should also be found between illness processes and social interactions but this pattern has not yet been found. Nevertheless, a second way to test for a direct relationship between social interactions and successful aging could come from the evaluation of social interventions. As Menes de Leon pointed out "... change in social engagement is potentially modifiable, and that change in social engagement may hold promise as a method to promote successful aging" (p. 66). Although we are going to consider this strategy in Chapter 8, we must take into consideration that we can increase successful aging through increasing the quality of social interaction but that this outcome could have no relationships with health but with life satisfaction or any other positive aging outcome.

Although the discussion between theoretical explanations is not finished we must take into consideration a conceptual and methodological flaw emphasized by Bath and Deeg (2005). Social participation is operationalized by a set of heterogeneous elements; that is, interactions with others refer to a high range of familiarity and closeness (family members, friends, neighbors, club memberships, etc.), performed activities differ in their nature (physical, cultural, or spiritual, etc.), integration contexts are plural (elder's home, children's house, church, day care center, etc.). Therefore, a basic question is how social integration can be decomposed into its constituents and to what extent each one of the elements implied produces different positive effects on health and well-being.

In sum, much more conceptual clarification and methodological sophistication is required (Fernández-Ballesteros, 2007). New research must take into consideration all these theoretical assumptions about the relationships between social functioning and health, survival and longevity.

Social Functioning and Cognitive Impairment

It is very well established that social disengagement is a risk factor for cognitive impairment as well as that social engagement decreases the risk of cognitive impairment and dementia (see Chapter 4). In fact, disengagement theory explains cognitive impairment as a disengagement phenomenon. Next we will review some empirical support for the connection between social relationships and cognitive functioning.

Bassuk, Glass, and Berkman (1999) followed-up 2,812 individuals older than 65 years from 1982 through 1994; social contacts (e.g., presence of spouse, monthly visual contact with three or more relatives or friends, etc.) and cognitive function (assessed with the Short Portable Mental Status Questionnaire, SPMSQ, Pfeiffer & Pfeiffer, 1975) were both assessed. After adjustment for age, initial cognitive performance, sex, ethnicity, education, income, housing type, physical disability, cardiovascular profile, sensory impairment, depression, smoking, alcohol use, and level of physical activity, those people who had no social ties at baseline, in comparison with those persons who had five to six social ties, increased the incidence of cognitive decline (hazard ratios were: 2.24 at 3 years, 1.91 at 6 years, and 2.37 at 12 years).

Also, Saczynski et al. (2006) examined whether low level of social participation predicted the risk of incident dementia in 2,513 Japanese-American men involved in the Honolulu Heart Program and the Honolulu-Asia Aging Study beginning in 1965. Social engagement was assessed in midlife (1968) and late life (1991). Although the former was not associated with dementia, in late life, compared with participants in the highest quartile of social engagement, those participants with lower level of social participation had a significantly increased risk of dementia (hazard ratio = 2.34).

Similar results were obtained by Wang, Karp, Winbland, and Fratiglioni (2002) analyzing data from the longitudinal Kungsholmen Project (Sweden) from 1987–1996. Social engagement in different social activities performed 6.4 years before the diagnosis of dementia was related to a significant decrease in the incidence of dementia.

From the MacArthur Studies of Successful Aging, Seeman, Lusignolo, Albert, and Merkman (2001) examined the association between social relationships and cognitive functioning in a cohort study of 1,189 initially high-functioning older adults. Data were collected at the baseline in addition to changes in cognitive performance over a 7.5 year period. Results revealed that:
1. Participants reporting more emotional support had better cognitive functioning at the base line, in comparison with those who were unmarried or reported problematic relationships;
2. At the follow-up, after 7.5 years, greater social support at base line predicted better cognitive functioning (controlling for baseline cognitive functioning, sociodemographic, behavioral, psychological, and health status). These results suggest that social environment could be a protective factor for cognitive impairment. As pointed out in Chapter 4, social activity seems to maintain and enhance cognitive functioning.

In summary, there is a large cross-sectional and longitudinal literature suggesting that older people who self-report greater engagement in social and leisure activities do not decline in mental status or decline less, and, more surprisingly, elderly participating in this type of activity, in comparison with those that do not, are less likely to be diagnosed with Alzheimer's disease or dementia. But do we have experimental evidence?

Park, Gutchess, Meade, and Stine-Morrow (2007), introduce social activities as nontraditional interventions for improving cognition. They review experimental evidence about the role of social activity and cognitive engagement in improving cognitive functioning. They suggest that social engagement in specific social activities produces effects by stimulating new neural pathways; for example, training older adults in theater acting may involve deep processing of character motives and interactions, and this deep engagement could extend more broadly to information processing. Also, the authors show empirical evidence that interpersonal aspects of acting contribute to reducing age differences in cognition.

Although this minimal experimental evidence could make a new step forward on the relationships between social interactions and cognitive functioning, as already stated, we should remember that there are several conceptual and methodological flaws in this field. Although there is some evidence in longitudinal studies, as Kramer et al. (2004) pointed out, the hypothetical causal link between social activity and cognitive functioning could be in the opposite direction; that is, the latter could be the cause and not the consequence of the former. Also, as emphasized by Bath and Deeg (2005) social activities or social interactions are described in very vague terms; much more task analysis must be done when causal relationships between two variables are going to be tested (Salthouse, 2006). Finally, self-reports are the most extensively used method for reporting the performance of social activities; this fact introduces an important source of bias (see Fernández-Ballesteros, 2004, 2007; Fernández-Ballesteros & Marquez, 2003; Fernández-Ballesteros & Botella, 2007). Without doubt, the level and type of activity performed must be much more carefully studied and described and experimental and longitudinal methods and designs should be used.

Concluding Remarks

It is extensively supported and widely recognized that social interaction (social activity, social participation, social integration, social engagement, etc.) is an important domain for healthy and successfully aging, as well as for well-being and quality of life in old age and throughout the life cycle.

Social activity is a broad domain including many aspects from family and friends relationships to work (paid and unpaid work) or any other social commitment. There is broad empirical evidence that social activity is associated with survival, longevity, morbidity as well as with optimal cognitive and emotional functioning. Nevertheless, several conceptual and methodological problems should be overcome in order to improve our understanding and clarification of the nature of the relations between social interaction and health and active aging.

PART III
PROMOTING ACTIVE AGING

8
Active Aging Promotion Programs

Introduction

As has been emphasized by Glass (2003), no one speaks of "successful infancy" or "optimal adolescence" because "infancy" or "adolescent" together with "successful" or "optimal" adjectives would be likely redundant. With the exception of environmental poor conditions, most children and adolescents experience growth and biophysical and psychosocial development and do not require any positive verbal alliance. But, "aging well" – or any other of the combinations of aging and a positive adjective – seems to be two opposite terms. As Freund and Baltes (2007) have said, the term "successful aging" can be considered as an oxymoron.

In the mind of people – not only lay people's thinking but also in the minds of scientists, clinicians, and even gerontologists – these two terms are in contradiction: one usually elicits negative emotions (aging); the other has a positive meaning ("successful," "optimal," "productive," "active," etc.). As has been pointed out in Chapter 1, stereotypes and social images as well as most scientific research hypothesize that aging is a negative phenomenon in which decline, pain, and suffering is a central characterization. As recognized in the *II International Plan of Action on Aging* (MIPAA: UN, 2002), stereotypes should be combated at the macro, meso, and micro system levels in order to promote enabling environments for enhancing the self-esteem of elder persons and quality of life and well-being throughout aging. MIPAA emphasizes that the promotion of a positive view of aging is an integral aspect for involving older persons in society and development. Therefore, any policy, program, or mass media campaign devoted to promoting a positive view of older persons is a first step toward promoting active aging.

However, as has been already stated in Chapter 1, during the last decades a positive conception of aging has emerged. There is empirical evidence supporting that across the life span, during the process of aging, declines and deficits occur in some physical, psychological, and social conditions but there is also a broad plasticity in human nature, compensation of these declines is possible, and positive changes take place as well. The balance between both positive and negative changes guide the diversity of the process of aging and that age can also be hopeful, satisfactory, and productive. After defining active aging, after introducing the most important predictors and determinants of this way of aging, we will now introduce those programs that can increase healthy, satisfactory, and productive aging.

Successful aging does not mean only long life (longevity or survival) but good life; as Glass (2003) said: "It refers to the capacity to function across many domains, including cognitive, social, and emotional ... envisioning exceptional functioning as possible" (p. 282). Nevertheless, as is clear in lay, working, or empirical definitions, and also from theoretical models of successful aging, health is the first and central condition for successful aging or, in other terms, as has been pointed out by Lupien & Wan (2004), "getting old with the minimum load of age-associated diseases is the biological definition of successful aging" (p. 1416). Also, illness prevention could be understood as central for successful aging, therefore healthy behaviors are also highly associated with successful aging (e.g., Li et al., 2001). Thus, behavioral health is a key issue for active-aging promotion. We will, next, introduce some relevant concepts for this central component.

Health promotion is a relatively new discipline overlapped considerably by the more consolidated discipline of prevention. As Noack (1987) pointed out, the most important difference between both concepts is that whereas prevention is a disease-related discipline, health promotion is a health-related one. Also, we must distinguish between primary, secondary, and tertiary prevention. Whereas primary prevention is defined as the promotion of health by personal and social efforts and, therefore, could be considered as synonymous with health promotion; the central effort in secondary prevention is early detection of diseases and, also, prompt and effective interventions. Finally, tertiary prevention is synonymous with rehabilitation consisting of interventions for reducing impairment and disabilities as consequences of illnesses. These three types of prevention are important for active aging but, since we are dealing with the contribution of psychology to active aging, in this chapter we are emphasizing health promotion and illness prevention; in other words, our interest is in those behavioral and psychological, risk and protective factors related to the most important sources of morbidity and disability in old age.

From a bio-psycho-social perspective of positive aging, it should also be taken into consideration that not only do health and illness have psychosocial and behavioral correlates (risk and protective) but, also, that aging well requires not only good health but other important psychological and psychosocial conditions such as good intellectual and mental functioning, positive mood, perceived control, active coping styles, as well as social relationships, participation, and engagement. Nevertheless, it must be pointed out again and again that a multidimensional concept of aging well is required; in no way can active aging be reduced either to health or to any of its ingredients (psychological or social) of individual functioning.

A last introductory issue regards the paradigm that active aging has anything to do with "anti-aging" movements (or anti-aging medicine). Active aging is not looking "younger"; in fact, anti-aging medicine has been the attempt to eliminate the effects of time in the human body. Positive aging, as has been already said, implies the optimization of all individual functioning (health as well as cognitive, emotional, and social functioning) and the compensation of declines and losses as well as the recognition of growth and development through old age. Therefore, the acceptance of physical traces from "time lived" is important because these traces enact, express, report, and teach something to the individual.

Lifelong Health Promotion

From a life course perspective, the process of aging well is the process of living well (or a "good life" as some authors claim), and it starts from birth. As was pointed out by Kalache and Kickbush (1997), disseminated by WHO (2002), and likely adopted by many authors, the process of aging is considered lifelong from childhood to old age, as shown in Figure 14 and described in Chapter 3.

Physical and functional capacity (vital capacity, muscular strength, and cardiovascular output), cognitive functioning (fluid intelligence), and social relationships (number of people in the network) increase in childhood and peak in early adulthood. On average, these peaks are followed by a slow decline. The rate of decline, however, depends on factors related to lifestyles (regular physical exercise, diet, no smoking, moderate alcohol consumption), schooling, selected profession, intellectual and cultural activities, coping with stressful situations, social participation, etc. All of these factors, provided by the environment (from a physical, cultural, and political point of view) and selected by the individual, can enlarge the quality of life across the aging process. This decline can be so strong that the individual can cross the disability threshold caused by different types of morbidity (stroke, diabetes, dementia, and/or social isolation, etc.). Through this adaption process, in order to age well, individuals must optimize their resources and compensate potential declines.

The acceleration or deceleration of this decline during the aging process is determined by the interaction between human agency and environmental conditions; that is, both by the individual and his/her behaviors and by the environment through political supportive or devastating actions. Therefore, from physical exercise to cognitive activity, across the life cycle, it should be emphasized that never it is late to introduce individual changes and public policies that increase human development and decrease the risks for decline and impairment.

It should be assumed that, from a population perspective of aging, all policies and intervention programs for human development (including health, education, employment, family protection, etc.) can be considered policies for promoting active aging. As WHO (2002) stated, those policies potentially can give the following results:

1. Fewer premature deaths in the highly productive stage of life;
2. Fewer disabilities associated with chronic diseases in older age;
3. More people enjoying a positive quality of life as they are growing older;
4. More people participating actively as they age in the social, cultural, economic, and political aspects of society, in paid and unpaid roles, and in domestic family and community life;
5. Lower costs related to medical treatment and care services.

This population lifecycle scope can be complemented from an individual perspective. As we already emphasized, individuals are not passive entities reacting to their physical and social contexts; individuals differ in their sensory-motor, emotional-motivational, and cognitive-language behavioral repertoires and, therefore, in the ways they act and adapt to the environment. Throughout the life cycle, a person's growth and decline are two trajectories that depend on the transactions among the environment, the individual, and his/her behavioral repertoires.

As has been emphasized by Freund (Freund, 2006; Freund & Baltes, 2002), the SOC theory of successful aging by Baltes and Baltes (1990b) allows us to contextualize motivational processes into a life span perspective. SOC theory predicts that a positive developmental trajectory might maximize growth (gains) and minimize decline (losses). As it is shown in Figure 14, selection, optimization, and compensation are processes behind the promotion of human growth and development; for example, through selecting physical activities the individual learns new sensory-motor repertoires, higher levels of linguistics skills are optimized through reading, or involvement in social contexts usually increases social skills, etc. The SOC theory also takes into consideration those processes counteracting losses when they occur, as is expected in old age when the risk of decline is higher or when losses are the result, not of age, but of illness or accident.

In the same line, when declines and losses appear, the way the individual copes is essential to accelerate or decelerate this process. As has been described in Chapter 6, he/she could cope with adversity adaptively by trying to modify the environment (assimilative strategy) and/or by trying to adjust or accommodate himself/herself to the new circumstances (Brandstädter & Renner, 1990; see Chapter 6). The balance of these broad and complementary strategies will lead the individual's vital trajectory to move above or below disability threshold.

Such loss-related processes are required when individuals cope with losses because one's plan should be restructured or changed (loss-based selection) or because individuals need to counteract declines (i.e., compensation). As Freund pointed out, "both processes of goal pursuit and accommodation comprise the same behaviors (e.g., investing time and effort). They differ regarding the focus on achieving higher levels of functioning (optimization) versus counteracting internal or external losses (compensation)... Optimization represents approaching desired outcomes . . . whereas compensation is geared toward avoiding negative outcomes" (Freund, 2006; pp. 240–41).

Therefore, promotion of human development (including health promotion and illness prevention) across the life cycle has long-term repercussions on aging well. All programs promoting sport and physical exercise, good nutrition, no smoking, etc., and creating healthy habits or healthy lifestyles throughout the life cycle can be considered as active-aging promotion programs (see Chapter 4).

Also, as has been emphasized in Chapter 5, schooling and education have an extraordinary influence on cognitive functioning in old age and intelligence (as a product of the interaction between the organism and the environment) also influences health and aging throughout the life course. The assumption from cognitive epidemiology is that high cognitive functioning individuals maintain and better protect their health against chronic diseases and accident (e.g., Batty & Deary, 2004; Deary & Der, 2005). Therefore, all policies and programs implemented for extending education, improving cognitive functioning, and reducing inequalities across the life cycle could be considered as active-aging promotion programs.

Also, those efforts to improve self-fulfillment, self-regulation, self-improvement, achievement motivation, etc. will be basic to the establishment of emotional-motivational repertoires supporting the selective optimization of human development. Weissberg, Kumpfer, & Seligman (2003), emphasized that the implementation of effective health-promotion programs for children and youth, promoting their physical, cognitive, and socioemotional competencies as well as their healthy habits, is an investment in society and is perhaps the most efficient way to promote active aging.

The complexity of all these potential active-aging programs make their follow-up and evaluation practically impossible. Moreover, unfortunately, most youth programs are mainly "secondary" prevention programs devoted to drug abuse, delinquency, youth violence, and other social problems more than to maximize physical, cognitive, emotional-motivational development, and social participation and engagement.

In sum, all positive developmental promotion actions implemented across the life span could be considered as a lifelong active-aging promotion program but, at the moment, the evaluation of these policies and programs, their effectiveness, efficacy, and efficiency are difficult (if not impossible) to establish.

Promoting Healthy Aging During Adulthood

Usually, only those policies and/or intervention programs devoted to elder adults (people older than 55 through 65 years) are considered healthy aging promotion programs. Several publications and internet pages (see References section) disseminate active-aging concepts, life styles, protective factors, and other related competencies (e.g., Bond, Culter, & Grams, 1995; Fernández-Ballesteros, 2003; Klein & Bloom, 1997; Roff & Atherton, 1990; Rowe & Khan, 1998; Wykle, Whitehouse, & Morris, 2005, among others). Also, several other secondary and tertiary prevention programs have been developed and implemented to improve medical and geriatric care in institutional health services (for example, internal medicine: Hazzard, 2000; geriatric services: Kane, 2003; health care: Landefeld, 2003).

Healthy-aging promotion programs are based on:
1. The prevalence of most common diseases in old age and their repercussions for mortality (life expectancy) and disability (disability life expectancy),
2. The risk or protective factors of those more prevalent diseases and negative conditions, and
3. Expenditure for and evaluation of health promotion and illness prevention programs.

Prevalence of Most Common Disease in Old Age and Their Repercussions for Life Expectancy, Healthy Life Expectancy, and Disability-Free Life Expectancy (DFLE)

Health promotion and illness prevention require the estimation of the attributable burden of specific illnesses on health. One of the first studies on the burden of disease in healthy life expectancy was conducted by Mathers, Vos, and Stevenson (1999) for the general population in Australia; identifying and ranking leading causes of loss of health for men and women such as ischemic heart diseases, cerebrovascular disease, vascular disease, chronic obstructive pulmonary disease, lung cancer, Alzheimer's disease, prostate cancer/breast/ovary cancer, osteoarthritis, colorectal cancer, diabetes, hearing loss, hypertensive disease, Parkinson's disease, lymphoma, falls, eye disorders, asthma, stomach cancer, pancreatic cancer, nephritis/nephrosis, traffic accidents, bladder cancer, skin cancer, and inflammatory heart disease. Also, the burden of each disease on healthy life expectancy was calculated; for example, the elimination of ischemic heart disease leads to the greatest gain in life expectancy for men (1.9 years) and women (1.1 years), followed by cerebrovascular disease disease for men (0.65 years), and osteoarthritis (0.85 years).

The increasing demand for active aging and quality of life in old age makes the role of prevalence of disease and its repercussions on disability a focus of inquiry. Jagger et al. (2007) researched the burden of disease on DFLE in old age. A longitudinal study with follow-up at 2, 6, and 10 years of a total of 13,004 individuals older than 65 years was preformed in the UK. Disability was assessed through the Basic Activity of Daily Living (B-ADL) and Instrumental Activity of Daily Living (I-ADL) at baseline and at the three follow-ups. Total life expec-

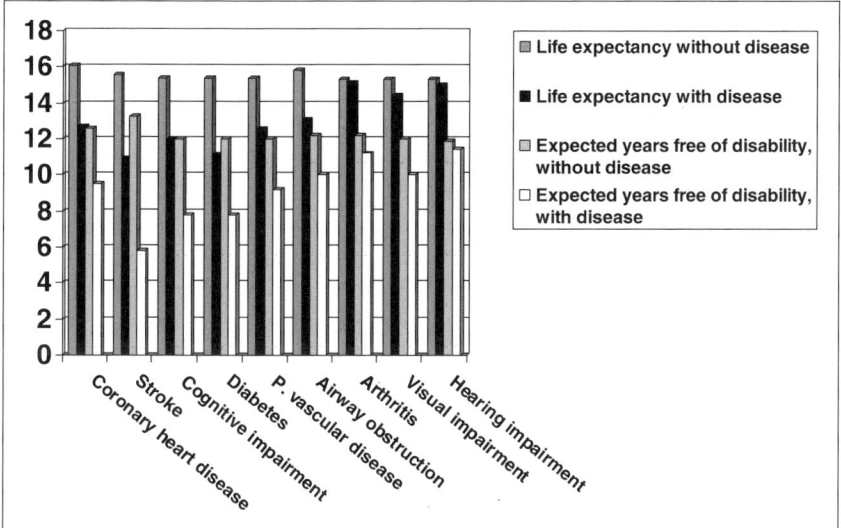

Figure 19. Life expectancy and expected years free of disability with and without disease at age 65 in men (adapted from Jagger et al., 2007).

tancy and DFLE were calculated for all disability conditions. Prevalence of chronic conditions at baseline were calculated for men and women; the most common conditions were: arthritis (more in women), hearing impairment (more in men), coronary diseases (more in men), chronic airway obstruction (no sex differences), visual impairment (more in women), cognitive impairment (more in women), stroke (more in men), diabetes (more in men), peripheral vascular disease (more in men).

This study yielded the following results: on average, at age of 65, men have 15.3 and women 19.4 years of total life expectancy and, respectively, 12.1 in men and 11.0 in women are years free of disability. Figure 19 shows life expectancy and expected years free of any disability, with and without disease, in men. Stroke is the disease with more impact both in total life expectancy (difference of 4.7 years between men with and without disease) and in expected years free of any disability (difference of 6.5 years between men with and without disability). Cognitive impairment has an impact on life expectancy of 3.4 years less in men (and 3.6 in women) and 4.2 years less in expected years free of any disability (4.4 in women).

In summary, highest number of disability-free years in comparison with total life expectancy are in persons free of stroke, cognitive impairment, arthritis, and/or visual impairment at baseline. The authors concluded that the elimination or reduction of these conditions in a given population would result in the compression of disability and in the increase of healthy aging. Therefore, prevention of these illnesses will have an important effect on DFLE and healthy life expectancy in old age.

Risk and Protective Factors of the More Prevalent Diseases and Negative Conditions in Old Age

Authors agree that expected increases in life expectancy and healthy life expectancy will be the result of improvements of lifestyles (reducing risk factors and increasing protective ones), from the use of preventive and screening services, and from biomedical advances.

Although Lubitz (2004) stated that the relative influence of these three factors is unclear, the Institute of Medicine Committee on Assuring the Health in the Public in the 21st Century (2002) considered that lifestyle, behavior, and environment are responsible for more than 70% of avoidable mortality. Lubitz concludes that there is strong empirical evidence that favorable health-risk profiles throughout the life span result in longer life, that is, both healthy longevity and active aging.

Although humans have observed regular relationships between their behavior and their health throughout history, "risk factor" is a relatively new term coming from empirical research developed by the collaboration between biomedical and behavioral researchers. Primary research on risk factors has a cross-sectional basis, but during recent decades longitudinal and experimental evidence from evaluation of intervention studies have also been collected and disseminated. Therefore, risk factors are becoming an important focus in public health and health psychology.

As the opposite of risk factors, in more recent times, "protective factors" have been also described. Protective factors can be considered a set of behaviors that empirically have a salutogenic influence on health and defend the individual against risk factors and diseases. It can be emphasized that there is not a comprehensive theory embracing those risk and protective factors.

In sum, risk factors and protective factors may increase or decrease an individual's chances for developing a given disease, health problem, or negative condition in old age. Since research on protective factors in old age is very recent, most of the studies in health prevention focus on risk factors.

Our interest in risk factors here has two main objectives: the population and the individual. Risk factors are those human behaviors or unhealthy habits linked with morbidity, mortality, disability life expectancy, or unhealthy life expectancy. At the individual level, the assumption is that reducing risk factors (and increasing protective ones) will produce in the individual a positive effect for survival, longevity, healthy and satisfactory life. At the population level, the assumption is that reducing risk factors in a given population will increase life expectancy, DFLE, and, thus, all these effects can improve the compression of morbidity for the population (see Chapter 2).

At the general population level, Figure 20 shows data from WHO (2000) for world deaths showing nine of the selected factors considered as mainly associated

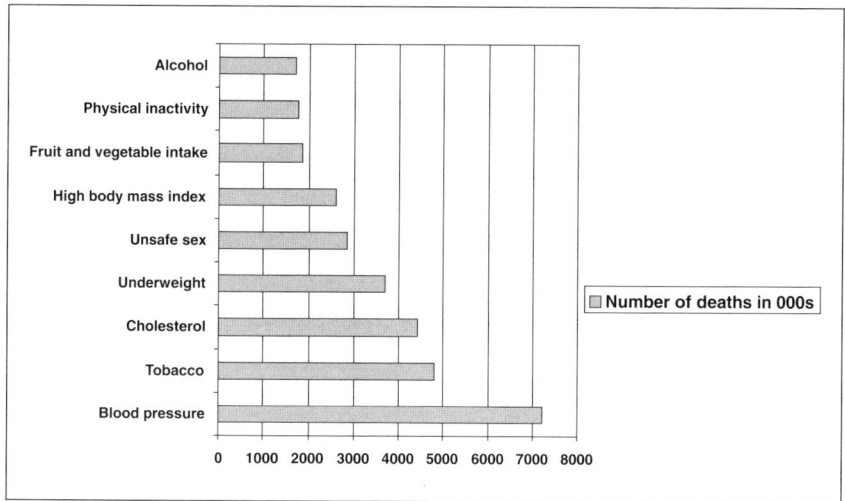

Figure 20. World deaths in 2000 attributable to selected behavioral risk factors (adapted from WHO, 2000).

with illness and disability. Blood pressure and cholesterol are two risk factors with high prevalence in old age, which can be controlled through behavioral strategies but inactivity and poor diet – two behavioral life styles – contribute to mortality and morbidity.

When the focus is a risk factor in an older population, Kamimoto, Easton, Maurice, Husten, and Macera (1999; see http://www.cdc.gov/aging/publications.htm), concluded that the five most important risk factors associated with the leading causes of morbidity and mortality among US older adults (65 years and older) were: overweight, drinking and driving, inadequate fruit and vegetable consumption, physical inactivity, and smoking.

As has been pointed out by Nusselder (2003), reduction in the exposure to risk factors results in compression of morbidity in the population depending on two different effects:

1. As a result of the reduction of exposure to a risk factor, lower disability rates produce an increase in life expectancy without disability and the correspondent decrease in life expectancy with disability, and
2. The reduction of exposure to a risk factor results in an increase in survival, which determines that people could be longer exposed to the (reduced or not) risk factors. On balance, life expectancy with disability decreases when the effect of the disability reduction on the number of years with disability exceeds that of increased survival. For example, the consequences of a hypothetical elimination of smoking for health expectancy in Holland produced a larger gain of 2.5 years in men and 1.9 years in women in DFLE than in total life expectancy (1.6 and 0.8 years, respectively, for men and women). Nusselder (2003) concludes that elimi-

Table 7. Negative conditions associated with aging, medical problems, and illnesses, and behavioral preventive or protective factors (modified from Fries, 1989)

Negative conditions	Examples of behavioral preventive or protective factors
Negative psychological conditions	
Low physical fitness	Aerobic exercise, weight control, not smoking
Low mobility, flexibility, balance	Stretching, flexibility & balance exercise
Low reaction time, speed	Training
Decline in intelligence and memory	Lifelong education, cognitive activities, cognitive and memory training, aerobic exercise
Low control, negative self-stereotypes	Improving control and self-efficacy for aging
Social isolation and sadness	Social skills training, promoting prosocial behaviors, social networks, pleasant events, coping training
Medical problems and illnesses	
Blood pressure, CVD, peripheral diseases	Exercise, diet, stress control, not smoking
Osteoarticular diseases	Exercise, diet, weight control
Dementia	Lifelong education, cognitive, sociocultural activities, aerobic exercise
Depression and anxiety	Pleasant activities Social skills training Cognitive restructuring training
Immuno-neuro-psychological system regulation	Stress control and coping Positive emotions
Cancer	Diet, not smoking

nating smoking would compress life expectancy with disability in absolute and relative numbers. In our terms, at population level, not smoking will bring an increase in healthy life expectancy and in longevity.

Fries (Fries & Crapo, 1981; Fries, 1989) was one of the first authors in the field of biomedicine to emphasize modifiability and plasticity in old age, particularly, in negative conditions associated with age, that is, more frequent illness, and negative psychological manifestations. Table 7 shows a synthesis of those negative conditions and risk and protective behavioral factors.

Health-promotion programs in old age must take into consideration not only the most well-known healthy lifestyles (physical exercise, diet and weight control, not smoking, moderate drinking of alcohol), but, also, new protective factors such as lifelong education, cognitive, cultural and social pleasant activities, feeling of control, coping with stress, training positive emotions, and social skills training.

As has been pointed out by the WHO (2001; see Table 2, Chapter 3) policies for active aging must take into consideration four types of components:

1. Reducing risk factors associated with major diseases and increasing factors that promote behavioral health and physical fitness
    a. Ensure adequate nutrition throughout the life course.
    b. Prevent the use of tobacco and determine the extent of the healthy use of alcohol.
    c. Policy for health monitoring and the use of medication and correct adherence to medical treatments.
    d. Promote physical activity throughout the aging process.
2. Promote protective factors of cognitive functioning
    a. Promote literacy programs throughout the life course and lifelong learning programs.
    b. Promote the use of cognitive exercises in old age.
    c. Promote engagement with cognitive demanding tasks.
    d. Exercise communication and verbal skills.
3. Promote positive affect, control, and coping
    a. Promote pleasant events in old age as preventive factors of depression and loneliness.
    b. Promote active and competent coping with stress, anxiety, and conflict.
    c. Promote self-efficacy beliefs.
    d. Promote positive thinking and sense of control.
4. Promote psychosocial functioning and participation
    a. Encourage empowerment in old age and combat negative images about age and aging.
    b. Enable people to build collective efficacy beliefs.
    c. Promote prosocial behaviors.
    d. Promote social participation.

These four domains have been proposed in Chapter 3 as domains of active aging and have been developed in Part II as constituting the experimental base for supporting active-aging promotion projects. In summary, we already know which are the most common actions and interventions for improving behavioral health and physical fitness, cognitive functioning, affect, control and coping, and social interactions and participation.

Expenditure and Evaluation of Health Promotion and Illness Prevention Programs

As has been emphasized by Fries (1989) and WHO (2002), after adolescence most leading causes of disease are noncommunicable diseases (NCD) and most causes of death in those people older than 60 years are NCD, therefore, as is well known, they are preventable or can be postponed. However, although health promotion and illness prevention programs are important components of health care, it is commonly accepted, all over the world, that they receive less support and attention than secondary prevention and illness care.

Callahan and McHorney (2003) pointed out that although lifestyles, behavior, and environmental factors are responsible for more than 70% of avoidable mortality (see Institute of Medicine Committee on Assuring the Health of the Public in the 21st Century, 2002; Steel, 1997), 95% of health-care expenditure goes to medical care and biomedical research. Therefore, most of what is spent on health care is going to "pathological" and, perhaps, "usual" aging but very little is being invested in positive aging.

Kaplan (2000), reviewed evidence supporting the efficiency of health promotion and primary prevention in comparison with secondary prevention programs, concluding that there is a relative and positive effect of health promotion programs based on life styles and behavioral habits compared to those prevention programs based on a disease model. Data from several program–evaluation studies supported that primary prevention has substantial benefits. Quality-adjusted life years (QALYs) has been used in evaluation research to conceptualize the relative benefits of prevention programs. QALYs is a measure of life expectancy adjusted for quality of life as an indicator of health status in terms of equivalent well-years of health. For example, a disease that reduces quality of life by one half will take away 0.5 QALYs over the course of one year. Most important, a given program for a given population with a given problematic situation can be evaluated through a cost-effectiveness analysis if the cost of care for the program is compared with the existing therapy or program, relative to the change in health measured in a standardized unit such as the QALY. This is an important step forward both for program evaluation research and also for the science of health promotion and illness prevention, and even for assessing the impact of health promotion programs in aging well.

Although this is not the right place to discuss the difficulties for evaluating health promotion programs, from this perspective, three more concrete questions arise:

1. Are health promotion interventions successful in changing behavioral habits or risk factors,
2. To what extent does promoting behavioral lifestyles relevant for NCD have an effect on the related disease and on quality of life in old age, and

3. What are the economic implications (cost and benefit) of the effect on healthy lifestyles?

Syme (2003) considered that, in fact, helping people change high-risk behavior would not only be the key to prevention but, also, the best answer to the important challenge of an aging society. Nevertheless, it is concluded that both individual and community interventions programs have had only modest impact in changing target behaviors. We will illustrate with some examples.

The Multiple Risk Factor Intervention Trial was a randomized, primary-prevention trial to test the effect of a multifactor intervention program on mortality from coronary disease (CHD) in 12,866 high-risk men aged 35 to 57 years. Over the follow-up period of 7 years, risk-factor levels declines but no differences in total mortality rates were found. After a series of post hoc explanations, the group concluded that preventive measures require much more research in order to document changes in target behaviors as well as changes in specific morbidity and mortality (Multiple Risk Factor Intervention Trial Research Group, 1982).

In order to answer our second question, we will look at a simulated example. Trying to examine the effect of physical exercise in years of life and quality of life, Hatziandreu, Koplan, Weinstein, Caspersen, and Warner (1988) developed a very helpful computerized model. Two hypothetical cohorts of 35-year-old men were followed to age 65. The model was based on 1,000 individuals who were jogging regularly in comparison with 1,000 inactive individuals. The results yielded were that jogging reduces heart disease, increase life expectancy, and, also, that the cost to produce a year of life is quite low relative to most medical and even secondary prevention programs.

Therefore, this simulation study gives us a positive answer to our third question: the economic implications of healthy life styles. As has been already pointed out, this is a tricky situation: Since healthy elderly live longer, they cannot cost less than those who are unhealthy or disabled. As Lubitz (2004; Lubitz et al., 2003) pointed out, elder people with better health had a longer life expectancy than those with disability or frail health, nevertheless, the expected health expenditures for healthier elderly persons, despite their greater longevity, are similar to those for less healthy persons. Lubitz et al. (2003) concluded that "health-promotion efforts aimed at persons under 65 years of age may improve the health and longevity of elderly without increasing health expenditure" (p. 1048).

Other programs identified for health promotion and illness prevention devoted to old people at the community level are CHAMPS I, CHAMPS II, and CHAMPS III (Community Healthy Activities Model Program for Seniors). The CHAMPS programs are comprehensive lifestyle interventions to increase physical activity in sedentary and underactive older adults. The program uses client-centered motivational, behavioral, and cognitive techniques to help participants overcome barriers, exercise safely, and develop a balanced and appropriate exercise program that includes endurance, flexibility, and strength training. Participants choose their own form of activity, and with guidance, build their own exercise regimens. Several instruments have been developed for evaluating these programs.

Although there are very many evaluation studies looking for the efficacy, effectiveness, and efficiency of health promotion and illness prevention programs in the areas of diet, physical activity, and other healthy habits, there are no conclusive results (e.g., Clark, Nigg, Greene, Riebe, & Saunders, 2002; Moe et al., 2002; Toobert, Strycker, Glasgow, Barrera, & Bagdale, 2002). For example, Stearns et al. (2000) show that lifestyles and functional adaption are associated with reduction in Medicare expenses. Although there are no clear conclusions about their efficiency and long-term effects, certain behaviors have significant implications for health costs as well as on the health and quality of life of the elderly.

Finally, it should be emphasized that health promotion and illness prevention programs, usually called "psychosocial interventions," are based on information about target behaviors to be changed and their relationships with the disease to be prevented. As Syme said, "to develop more effective prevention programs, we will have to train a new generation of active aging experts who cannot only provide people with risk information but also work with them as partners in achieving mutually agreed upon goals" (Syme, 2003, p. 400).

It should be underlined that most health promotion programs developed from a medical perspective are based mostly on information about the effect of a given unhealthy habits or risk behavior. However, healthy habits are difficult to change with only information, or by an act of will. As Bandura (2005) states, any health promotion program requires the exercise of motivational and self-regulatory skills. If health is the goal,... (and in NCD)... biomedical interventions are not the only means to solve the problem; a broadened perspective expands the range of health-promoting practices and enlists the collective efforts of researchers and practitioners from a variety of disciplines who have much to contribute to health from a population or individual perspective.

As a matter of fact, behavioral change is a key issue for active-aging promotion, not only because it is required for health promotion and illness prevention but because they carry on psychological conditions such as information dissemination, emotional reactions, and behavioral adherence. Therefore, psychologists – as experts on behavioral change–are called to be much more involved in effective health-promotion intervention programs.

Summarizing, health promotion and illness prevention are broad disciplines; it is extremely difficult to generalize and to arrive to a final conclusion about long term efficacy, effectiveness, and efficiency, perhaps because they are new scientific fields in evolution. During the last years several interesting proposals have been made. Glasgow, Vogt, and Boles (1999) claimed for a more comprehensive evaluation framework more appropriate to health promotion. They said: "multilevel interventions that incorporate policy, environmental, and individual components should be evaluated with measurements suited to their settings, goals, and purpose" (p. 1322). Also, Jackson and Waters (2005) claim for specific criteria for a systematic review of health promotion and public health interventions. Judd, Frankish, and Moulton (2001) set up standards for the evaluation of community-based health-promotion programs. Ory, Jordan and Bazzarre (2002) reported on the constitution of the Behavioral Change Consortium of 15 National Institutes funded behavior change projects with the goal of evaluating the efficacy and effectiveness of novel ways of intervening in diverse populations to reduce tobacco dependence, increase physical exercise, and improve nutrition. All of these initiatives constitute a new scenario for health behavior-change research evaluation.

Although there are a set of thorough recommendations for conducting evaluation research in health-promotion programs, the field seems to be (as Pirandello's peace) "looking for the best framework." In conclusion, much more effort is required to reach a comprehensive, and conclusive long term evaluations of healthy aging programs.

Active-Aging Promotion Projects

Since active aging is a multidimensional concept the promotion of positive aging cannot be reduced to health promotion and illness prevention. When the objective is promoting positive (successful, optimal, active) aging, several other domains must be promoted, taught, and trained.

At the same time that psychologists are involved in the implementation and evaluation of health promotion programs, they are also involved in evidence-based active-aging promotion interventions. As described in Chapters 4, 5, 6, and 7, behavioral and psychological treatments in controlled experimental situations have had positive results in the improvement of healthy lifestyles and fitness, in the optimization or/and compensation of cognitive functioning, in the enhancement of emotional functioning, perception of control, active coping styles, and in the improvement of social integration and social participation.

In order to identify active-aging promotion projects, two types of inquiries have been conducted: an internet search and a scientific literature database analysis (see Chapter 1).

1. The internet search, using the key words "active-aging promotion" (and related terms), gave more than 2 million results in Google. As expected, although most of these sites has the objective to promote active aging, there was a broad heterogeneity of contents (elements, actions, subprojects, etc.), and scopes (international, community, local, etc.), in addition, most of them did not provide information on the empirical effects of those active-aging promotion projects. Therefore, it is highly difficult to present any synthesis from them.
2. On the contrary, the search of scientific literature yielded very few references to active aging (and related terms excluding broad terms such as quality of life)

promotion actions, programs, or projects but few of them reported evaluation results.

It must be taken into consideration that any project or program for promoting positive aging would require a set of scientific conditions: basic theoretical assumptions, specific objectives, defined actions and components, comprehensive design, implementation procedures, follow-up and an evaluation framework in which multicomponents, assessed through multiple outcomes, using multiple data-analysis designs, in multiple settings and with multiple populations or groups are considered from a multiple perspective (Cook, 1985). Unfortunately, most of the promotional efforts on active aging have not met these requirements. It is for this reason that we are only introducing some examples of active-aging promotion projects or programs.

Trying to organize the selected projects we are going to distinguish between population and individual initiatives. In other words, some programs are tailored to the individual level (e.g., self-help programs) and some are addressed to a given population (e.g., at a macro, meso, or micro system level; see Chapter 3).

Here are some examples of the active-aging promotion projects found.

Individual Materials

Self-Help Books and Electronic Information

When a given person is highly motivated for active aging, electronic pages and books are an important source of information and, therefore, they are one of the most common ways to change behavior. During recent decades, not only scientific literature on active aging has been published but also paperback books and internet pages for promoting active aging devoted to lay people (for example: Bond et al., 1995; Fernández-Ballesteros, 2002a; Fries, 1989; Giampapa, Pero, & Zimmerman 2004; Klein & Bloom, 1997; Roff & Atherton, 1990; Rowe & Khan, 1998; Wykle et al., 2005; among others). Also, at the end of the Reference section, the reader can find a list of internet pages helpful for starting on active, aging promotion routines.

Counseling

Ponzo (1992), suggests that a strategy for promoting successful aging is counseling. The author suggests that before people reach old age, counselors should suggest and train cognitive and emotional conditions (e.g., consciousness, control, etc.); doing wellness work. Also, from a life span perspective, it is suggested that, linked with life events (e.g., retirement, widowed, etc.), counselors should help the individual with training cognitive and memory activities, adaptive coping styles, social skills, etc. (see Lopez, in press).

As an example of evaluation, while administering five counseling sessions promoting active aging for 2 weeks, Ramamurti, Jamuna, and Reddy (1992) evaluated 20 retired men compared with 20 controls (age range in both groups 62–76) through a pre-/posttest design. Results indicated significant improvement in self-acceptance of aging changes, as well as improvement in self-perception of health, activities of daily living, and familial and social relationships.

Vital Aging Project

- *Basic principles*. On the basis of all the empirical evidence discussed here, over the last 10 years, two projects for promoting optimal (successful, competent, productive, active) aging have been developed:
  - "*Vivir con Vitalidad*" is conceived as a 70-hour training course implemented at the Autonoma University of Madrid in those psychosocial domains involved in active aging (Fernández-Ballesteros, 2002a, 2005).
  - "*Vital Ageing-M*." On the basis of the Spanish program, "Vivir con Vitalidad" was transformed into "Vital Ageing-M," a multimedia course carried out under the auspices of the EU Socrates-Minerva Program ("VITALAGELL-C") and supported by a consortium made up of NETTUNO (Italy), the Autónoma University of Madrid, the Gerontology Institute of the University of Heidelberg, and with the cooperation of the Open University (UK). "Vital Ageing-M" has been developed in Spanish, Italian, and English, but the only complete version is in Spanish. "Vital Ageing-M" ("Vivere con Vitalitá" in Italian or "Vivir con Vitalidad-M" in Spanish) is a 50-hour video course with supporting materials on the internet. The course lessons were set up by European experts from Germany, Italy, and Spain in English, Italian, and Spanish, respectively.
- *The general objective:* "to promote well-being and quality of life among the elderly."
- *Specific objectives:*
  1. "To transmit basic knowledge on how to age actively and competently";
  2. "To promote healthy lifestyles";
  3. "To provide training in strategies for compensating cognitive, memory, and functional decline";
  4. "To provide training in strategies for optimizing affective/emotional, motivational, and social competencies";
  5. "To promote personal development and social participation," and
  6. "To promote the use of new technologies."
- *Contents*. "Vivir con Vitalidad" and "Vital Ageing-M" are both multidimen-

sional projects developed for promoting active aging and addressing four psychological domains:
- *Behavioral health* and *fitness* have five lessons: "Control life," "Nutrition and health," "Taking care of your body," "Regular exercise: the best lifestyle," and "Self-responsibility and self-management."
- *Cognitive functioning* is taught through the following five topics: "Train your mind: How to prevent brain aging," "Improve your memory," "Be an expert on your memory problems," "Wisdom: the expression of lifelong learning," and "The creative age."
- *Affect, control,* and *coping styles* are trained through the following five lessons: "Feeling self-efficacy," "Positive thinking," "Pleasant activities and well-being," "Coping with stress," and "Death is also part of life."
- *Social functioning and participation* is dealt with in the following four lessons: "Sexuality: beyond genitality," "How to improve relationships with family and friends," "Others need me," and "A new system of communication: internet."

– In addition to these four domains, "Vital Aging-M®" has three general lessons: "Aging well," "Presentation," and "Summary, conclusions, and evaluation."
– *Structure.* All lessons have a similar structure:
  1. The trainer makes a general presentation, and talks about supporting evidence for a given topic,
  2. A pretest of the particular behavioral or psychological characteristic (diet, physical exercise, self-efficacy, pleasant activities, etc.) is administered,
  3. Identified competencies are trained and the trainer suggests practice and exercises,
  4. A posttest is requested, and
  5. The trainer make some concluding remarks. All materials recommended can be found on the internet.
– *Standard Procedure.* The implementation of the course (for evaluation purposes) is as follows: Participants are all volunteers responding to a general announcement for "Vivir con Vitalidad®" and "Vital Ageing-M®" in selected senior citizen residences and clubs. Every group has approximately 20 participants. Each group is supported by a tutor who is responsible for equipment, distribution of materials, and collection of tests. Sessions last 2 h with a break of 15 minutes, and cover one topic each. The entire Vital Ageing-M course takes a total of around 3 months. In the sessions, written material is distributed to all participants (video-lesson transcription, tests, and exercises for the lesson), they watch the video-lesson, and, where required, they fill out the instruments proposed and distributed.
– *Evaluation.* Two types of evaluation studies were preformed of both active-aging projects: ex-post (or summative) evaluation and intermediate (or formative) evaluation.
  - Summative evaluation studies used quasiexperimental designs (pre-/post-

test with control group) to access impact of both programs. As reported by Fernández-Ballesteros, Caprara, García, & Iñiguez, 2004; Fernández-Ballesteros, Caprara, & García, 2005), experimental older individuals ($N = 137$; age range $= 55 - 82$), after receiving the program and in comparison with a control group, showed the following results: improved their diet, increased or started regular physical exercise, improved their self-efficacy for aging, increased their level of physical, pleasant, cultural, and social activity, and, after the training and in comparison with the control group, they reported higher life satisfaction and well-being.

- *Formative Evaluation.* Achievement tests were performed for all lessons; taking the scores into consideration, the course is useful for teaching the conditions for aging well. A strong relationship was found between level of knowledge and "Teacher's clarity", "Interest of the exercises," "Usefulness of the exercises," and "Satisfaction with the lesson." It should be stressed that the knowledge achievement correlated positively and significantly with the opinions expressed about several features of the teaching styles and materials used. Participants were asked about their perceived changes; they reported that those more important were: "Enjoying life in general," "Thinking positively," "Improving memory," "Feeling self-efficacy," and "Pleasant events and well-being." Finally, "Vivir con Vitalidad" and "Vital Ageing-M" participants found the course very interesting; the course satisfied "fairly well" or "totally" the expectations of 98.8% of the participants and 96.7% considered that the knowledge acquired had been useful or will be useful in the future and that they would recommend the program to their family members and friends.

In summary, based on the theoretical and empirical approaches developed from the paradigm of optimal, successful, or active aging, "Vivir con Vitalidad®" (Fernández-Ballesteros, 2002) and "Vital Ageing-M®" have had positive evaluation results but much more research is required in order to disseminate this project (see Fernández-Ballesteros, 2005).

Population-Based Projects

Community-Based Projects

California Active Aging Project

- *Basic Principles.* Social Ecological model to mobilize communities to action (including stakeholders in planning and implementation) and dissemination and translation of evidence-based/evidence-informed best practices.

- *Objectives.* To educate, enable, and encourage Californians over 50 years of age to have healthier lives by promoting physical activity and creating social and physical environments that support active aging (e.g., Hooker, 2002).
- *Structure.* Active Aging Community Task Forces (AACTF) are the local agencies providing the program for persons over 50 years. Central program staff provides technical assistance to AACTF.
- *Evaluation.* Hooker et al. (2005) reported whether local agencies could implement a community-based program. Over the 5-year period, 25 AACTS conducted 36 workshops to train exercise class instructors. Thirteen local agencies participated in this evaluation study. These agencies implemented a choice-based telephone-assisted physical-activity promotion program for older adults. At baseline, participants developed their own physical-activity programs through an individualized planning session based on preference, health status, readiness to change, and available community resources. Afterwards, participants were followed-up for one year through telephone calls. As a result of the these efforts, 153 new exercise classes for older adults were created and an additional 81 formerly established classes for older adults incorporated new components (strength and mobility exercises). These classes served approximately 7,200 persons with an age range of 70 – 84 years across communities.

In sum, the authors reported that the program was useful for developed community coalitions and the AACTFs established fulfilled their objectives.

Active For Life® (AFL)

- *Theoretical Base.* Guidelines for physical activity updated by the American College of Sports Medicine and the American Heart Association.
- *Objective.* To learn how to deliver research-based physical activity programs to large numbers of mid-life and older adults, and to sustain such programs through existing community institutions.
- *Target Population.* Adults ages 65 and older, and those aged 50–64 with chronic conditions.
- *Actions*:
    1. At least 30 minutes of aerobic activity on at least 5 days each week, or at least 20 minutes of vigorous-intensity aerobic activity on at least 3 days each week is the minimum goal. This aerobic activity, whether of moderate or vigorous intensity, is in addition to routine, light-intensity activities of daily living.
    2. Muscle-strengthening includes resistance (weight) training in the regular fitness routine. This type of activity should include 10 to 15 repetitions of exercises that use major muscle groups on 2 or more nonconsecutive days each week.

3. Flexibility training 2 days a week, and balance exercises to reduce the risk of falls, should also be incorporated into the fitness programs of people aged 65 and older.
- *Sponsor*. Active for Life National Program Office, which operates out of The Texas A&M Health Science Center School of Rural Public Health.

The Active Ageing South Australia

- It is a strategic, operational, and marketing plan for 2004–2007 in line with the "Physical Activity Strategy for South Australia."
- The *vision* for Active Ageing SA is to be a key provider for the physical activity needs of the aging population.
- Three *objectives* are stated in the Plan:
   1. Increasing opportunities for *participation* in physical activity for the aging population, including for disadvantaged people and groups.
   2. *Representation* of the physical activity needs of the aging population, including for disadvantaged people and groups.
   3. Support of *research* and the application of *research knowledge*.
- *Strategic actions* are given, which provide guidance for the Board and staff:
   1. The development of initiatives, programs, and projects state-wide and beyond.
   2. Strengthening the organization's key communication roles and functions.
   3. Strengthening the effectiveness of programs and services for active-aging and continuing to promote key health-promotion messages.
   4. Strengthening collaborative partnerships with local and state governments and organizations in the fields of recreation, health, fitness, research, and aged care, including groups from multilingual backgrounds.
   5. Development of a membership base and membership services.
   6. Strengthening collaborative partnerships and representation with relevant tertiary bodies, research and professional organizations.
   7. Promotion/development of new initiatives and programs incorporating applied research.

International Organizations: The European Union

"Active Ageing" European Union Policy

- It is a *general policy* developed as a response to the challenge posed by population aging in Europe.

- It has as final *goal* that mandatory retirement (MR) should be abolished in EU as has been done in other Western countries (USA, Canada, Australia).
- At the intermediate EU level, active aging has two main *objectives* to be met by 2010:
  1. To increase the employment rate of older workers by 50% (Stockholm target) and
  2. To increase by 5 years the effective average exit age from the labor market (Barcelona target).
- *Principles*:
  1. Demographics: MR is outdated in a society where people live longer and do less physical labor than in the past.
  2. Workforce shortages: MR does not prevent skill and labor force shortages and "brain drain."
  3. Human rights: MR denies older people equal protection and treatment under law and permits direct discrimination based on age.
  4. Economic theories: there are no good economic reasons to retain MR in place for the economy at large.
  5. Social justice: MR harms those poor groups who need to continue working.
  6. Public opinion: there is a global rejection of MR ages.
- *Evaluation (Indicators):* Percentage of older workers, Mean age of retirement, nonmandatory retirement regulation. The impact of this Policy will be evaluated in the year 2010.

Other International Efforts

The International Council on Active Aging (ICAA)

- It was founded in the belief that unifying the efforts of the organizations focused on older adults benefits both the people they reach and the organizations themselves. Today, the vision is shared by over 7,500 organizations connected to the ICAA network.
- Whether retirement community, seniors center, or fitness club, all ICAA members share a common interest in reaching older adults with active-aging messages, facilities, programs, and guidance. The ICAA supports these professionals and organizations with education, information, resources, and tools so they can achieve optimal success with this market.

After our review and examples showed we must conclude that most of the active-aging projects consist of the promotion of physical exercise and only one (the European Union Policy on Active Aging) refers to labor implications. Promoting physical exercise is related to bio-psycho-social functioning but no information is provided about the multidimensional impact of active-aging projects. However, if we consider the definitions of active aging reviewed in Chapter 3, active aging cannot be reduced to any of its components. Only self-help books and the Vital Aging Project refer to multiple domains for promoting active aging.

Concluding Remarks

A first conclusion is that promoting positive aging implies a long process throughout the life cycle, which requires the optimization of all individual bio-psycho-social functions with the final goal to minimize decline throughout adulthood and in old age, as well as the compensation of common declines and impairment. Behavioral habits or lifestyles (not smoking, low alcohol consumption, diet, high physical activity), schooling, professional training, lifelong learning, cultural availability of activities, social promotion policies, and many other components provided by the environment (from physical, cultural, and political points of view) promote aging well. In sum, it can be concluded that, at the population level, educational, health, social, and protection systems can be considered part of active-aging programs. Only through population indicators such as disability free life expectancy and healthy life expectancy can lifelong population active-aging programs be evaluated.

At the micro level, is the individual who actively makes decisions about different courses of action during his/her life and, therefore, it is extremely difficult, or even impossible, to make conclusions about the extent to which he/she has been involved in active promotion programs or to what extent these programs have been successful through the process of successful aging. The only conclusion is that the acceleration or deceleration of decline is influenced by human agency – that is, both by the individual and his/her behaviors – who ages in interaction with the environment and its politically supportive or devastating actions.

Nevertheless, since health is one of the most important ingredients of positive aging, health promotion and illness prevention programs are basic for positive aging. From this respect, several problematic issues can be emphasized:
1. It can be concluded that there is no general data about effectiveness, efficacy, or efficiency of healthy-aging promotion programs for different reasons:
    a. They imply a lifelong learning processes and long-term outcomes and
    b. They require complex evaluation designs.
2. Although there is a broad consensus about the multidisciplinarity of successful aging, most of the healthy- and active-aging programs are devoted only to the promotion of lifestyles and, concretely, to promoting physical activity (taking into consideration, moreover, that physical activity increases social activity).

3. There are very few promotion programs devoted to promoting behavioral and psychological conditions, for example, cognitive activity, positive emotions, etc., for the four behavioral and psychological domains discussed in this book. Although there are examples of positive effects of intervention and training programs for concrete aspects of successful aging in each one of the four domains of aging well – fitness and nutrition, cognition, emotion and motivation, and social functioning – there are very few multidomain-bases intervention programs. Also, although there are some positive results in multidomain or multidimensional programs at an individual level there are no follow-up studies for assessing long-term effects.

Three main conclusions should be emphasized:
1. Because the positive-aging process is lifelong – from physical exercise to cognitive activity – it is never too late for introducing individual changes and public policies that increase human development and decrease the risk of decline and impairment. These individual changes and public policies must take into consideration the multidimensionality implied in active aging.
2. It is necessary to distinguish multiple levels, that is, population, community, and individual active-aging promotion programs. At the level of community, public policies must promote positive aging in the population taking into consideration that it is never too late for enhancing human health and human development. At the individual level, positive aging must be integrated throughout the educational system in order to make the individual conscious of his/her power and control over his/her life.
3. Finally, the process of aging well, at the individual, community, and population level, depends on complex psychological self-regulation functioning because the individual is always an active agent who requires the exercise of control.

Conclusions

1. During the last decades of the twentieth century, from an evidence-based point of view, a "new paradigm" or "revolution" in the field of the study of aging and, in a broad sense, in the science of gerontology started: a positive view. This positive view of aging adopted several verbal labels: "healthy," "successful," "optimal," "vital," "positive," "productive," "active," or, simply "Aging well" or "Good life." This positive view of aging is based on well-established *plasticity* of human being and on *individual differences* throughout the aging process in the balance of growth, maintenance, and decline of human bio-psycho-social functioning. *These individual differences are not at random; the person is an actor in his/her process of aging.*
2. This view of aging is more an active and proactive view than a simplistic or positive reductionism, as has been considered by some authors. Scientific literature of this new paradigm does not show ignorance about age concomitants with biological systems deterioration, increment of illness prevalence, cognitive decline, or impairment, and the occurrence of negative events such as loss of position, family, and friends being very frequent in old age is not neglected. Positive aging is not the attempt to look "younger," eliminating time traces on the body. This renewed view has four main assumptions:
   a. Human organisms age at different rates as a function of the interaction between the individual and his/her life circumstances;
   b. Individuals have different forms of aging and coping with decline, impairment, and losses;
   c. Some of the negative consequences of aging are determined by illness (not only by age) and, as is well known, illness (and other negative age-covariants such as disability), can be prevented and their consequences or eliminated or postponed, and
   d. Plasticity and modifiability is a human life condition throughout the life cycle, including old age.
3. Demographic projections predict a worldwide increase in life expectancy at birth and an increase of older people. Since age is associated to illness and disability, a consequence of population aging would be an increase in disability prevalence with a correspondent increase in health and social costs. At the same time, disability also constitutes an increased family burden. There is an important debate regarding the degree to which an increase in life expectancy (years of life) will increase years with disability, in other words, whether adding years of life is going to determine more years of disability at the end of life. This issue is extremely important in order to determine whether positive aging in the population will be

increased, reduced, or remain stable. A review of the field supports the idea that disability is being reduced in recent decades supporting the compression of morbidity and disability, at least in most of the settings assessed, but it is urgent to introduce new policies for increasing disability-free life expectancy and healthy life expectancy; not just life expectancy. That is, much more should be done not only for extending life but to extending good life.

4. Implicit, working, and empirical definitions concur that active aging is a *multidimensional bio-psycho-social concept* embracing not only biomedical but also psychological and social components. Implicit theories *support the dissemination of this concept*. Therefore, active aging cannot be reduced either to subjective appraisal or to biomedical output such as survival or disability, or to any of its other components. Also, active aging must not be confounded with other subjective concepts such as well-being or life satisfaction, nor with other complex and multidimensional concepts such as quality of life. Active aging could be defined as *the process of optimization of physical (including health), psychological (cognition and emotion and motivation), and social functioning of the individual throughout the aging process*. The output of this process is *high physical and mental functioning, enhanced emotional-motivational regulation, and high social interaction and participation*. This process emerges from the transitive relationship between the individual agent and the socioenvironmental systems. Since the process of aging affects both the individual, the community, and the population, active aging has also several perspectives and, therefore, can claim the interest of people, community, and entire society.

5. Since active (successful, optimal, active, or productive) aging is a new concept, it is important to emphasize that *posited determinants are provisional*. The most important criticism emerging from the already mentioned confusion between positive aging indicators and determinants is that most of the reviewed definitions are make it easy to confound *explanans* (or independent variables) and *explanandum* (or dependent variables) of active aging. Many more longitudinal and cohort research and experimental and evaluation studies are required in order to avoid misleading conceptualizations.

6. In order to clarify an empirical definition of positive aging and its potential determinants, both at the population, community, and individual levels, as well as to introduce the life cycle as temporal dimension, a framework is proposed distinguishing multidimensional, individual distal and proximal factors as well as micro, meso, and macro-contextual levels. From this model, four behavioral and psychological domains relevant for the study of active aging emerged: *behavioral health and physical fitness; optimal cognitive functioning; emotional-motivational (affect, control, and coping) functioning, and social relationships and participation*. Empirical evidence about the importance of behavioral and psychological factors for active aging organizes and articulates these four domains. Most important, these four domains can be trained, improved, and enhanced through empirically based behavioral interventions.

7. Some conclusions can be derived from these four domains:
   a. In the field of *behavioral health and fitness*: Not smoking, drinking moderately, and regular exercising (cardiovascular work outs, flexibility, and endurance) improve physical and mental health and well-being. Elders with positive behavioral habits show four times less disability than those who smoke, drink too much, do not exercise, and are obese. Physical exercise training programs have positive effects even in very old age. Aerobic exercise preserve and compensate gray and white substance in those areas of the brain that shrink with age. Finally, psychological conditions such as self-efficacy enlarge the impact and adherence to physical exercise training regimens.
   b. In the field of *cognitive functioning*: There is empirical evidence that physical and cognitive activities, training, and interventions improve cognitive functioning, reduce cognitive decline, and are protective factors against dementia (including Alzheimer's disease). More frequent *cognitive activity* throughout life is associated with decrease in the annual rate of cognitive decline and is also linked with risk of dementia. Effects of *training in cognitive functioning* are of a magnitude equivalent to the decline expected in the elderly without dementia. *Memory training* gives significant size effects both in objective memory tests as well as in subjective memory functioning. The promotion of cognitive activity and the development and evaluation of standardized and well-planning cognitive trainings and interventions is a pending matter for cognitive neuropsychology.
   c. In the field of *emotional-motivational functioning (affect, control, and coping)*: It is well established that *positive affect* reduces the probability of mortality in older individuals and increases survival; highly activated positive emotions were associated with increases in positive cardiovascular response as well as improve endocrine and immune functioning. Positive attitudes toward life is a protective factor from becoming frail. Positive self-stereotypes or self-images about aging have positive effects in health and survival. Self-efficacy for aging and sense of control predict recovery and healthy aging. Active coping styles are highly associated with physical and mental health and recovering from stressful situations. Finally, evidence-based interventions have been developed for promoting these emotional-motivational conditions, though much more evaluation research should be done here.
   d. In the field of *social functioning and participation*: Social ties not only are essential for psychological well-being and life satisfaction in old age, but also have a role in longevity and health. The association between social relationships and disability prevalence, incidence, and recovery has been well established. Results yielded a strong, negative, and robust cross-sectional association between social engagement and disability; more socially active persons reported lower levels of disability than their counterparts. Social disengagement is a risk factor for cognitive impairment and social engage-

ment decreased the risk of cognitive impairment and dementia. Finally, the promotion of social participation has been largely empirically tested.
8. Promotion of active aging is the natural consequence of the supporting empirical evidence. Our review showed that all psychological and behavioral conditions for positive aging could be trained and be enhanced. Since positive aging is a lifelong learning process, a first problematic issue is the difficulty in evaluating active-aging promotion programs. Second, active-aging promotion programs cannot be reduced to health or to physical exercise trainings; their final goal should be the bio-psycho-social development of the individual throughout his/her life aging process. Nevertheless, on the basis of the evidence presented here, it can be concluded that never is late to start introducing behavioral changes for improving physical fitness, cognition, a sense of control, well-being and coping, or social participation. The involvement of the individual as an "actor" in his/her aging process is decisive for improving the existing promotion program. Finally, although there are examples of effective programs in some of the components of active aging, there is not yet enough data about the effectiveness, efficacy, and efficiency of active-aging promotion. In fact, positive-aging promotion is the most intelligent answer to the "salient revolution" of an aging world and it is the best help for preventing disability in old age. International agencies, governments (at local, community, and state levels), nongovernmental organizations, and individuals, are all committed to promote active aging throughout the life cycle and in old age.

References

Abeles, P.R., Gift, H.C., & Ory, M.G. (Eds.). (1994). *Aging and quality of life.* New York: Springer.

Abraham, J.D., & Hansson, R.O. (1995). Successful aging at work: An applied study of selection, organization, optimization, and compensation through impression management. *Journal of Gerontology: Psychological Sciences, 50B,* P94–P103.

Adlard. P.A., Perreau, V.M., Pop, V., & Cotman, C.W. (2005). Voluntary exercise decrease amyloid load in a transgenic model of Alzheimer's disease. *Journal of Neuroscience, 25,* 4217–4221.

Adler, N.E., & Snibbe, A.C. (2003). The role of psychosocial processes in explaining the gradient between SES and health. *Current Directions in Psychological Science, 12,* 119–123.

Akiyama, H., Antonucci, T., Takahashi, K., & Langfahl, E.S. (2003). Negative interactions in close relationships across the lifespan. *Journal of Gerontology: Psychological Sciences, 58B,* P70–P79.

Albert, M.S., Savage, C.R., Blazer, D., Jones, K., Berckman, L., Seeman, T., & Rowe, J.W. (1995). Predictors of cognitive change in older persons: McArthur studies of successful aging. *Psychology and Aging, 10,* 578–589.

Aldag, L.D. (1997). Is use of selective optimization with compensation associated with successful aging? *Dissertation Abstract International: Science and Engineering, 58,* 2150.

Aldwin, C.M., Sutton, K.J., & Lachman, M. (1996). The development of coping resources in adulthood. *Journal of Personality, 64,* 837–873.

Aldwin, C.M., & Park, C.L. (2004). Coping and physical health. An overview. *Psychology and Health (Special Issue), 19,* 277–282.

Aldwin, C.M., Levenson M.R., & Gilmer, D.F. (2004). The interface between physical and mental health. In C.M. Aldwin & D.F. Gilmer (Eds.), *Health, illness, and optimal aging: Biological and psychosocial perspectives.* Thousand Oaks, CA: SAGE.

Aldwin, C.M., & Gilmer, D.F. (Eds.). (2006). *Health, illness, and optimal aging: Biological and psychosocial perspectives.* Thousand Oaks, CA: Sage.

Almeida, O.P., Norman, P., Hankey, G., Jamrozik, K., & Flikcker, L. (2006). Successful mental health aging: Results from a longitudinal study of older Australian men. *American Journal of Geriatric Psychiatry, 14,* 27–35.

Andersen, B.T., & Haley, W.E. (1997). Clinical geropsychology: Implication for practice in medical settings. *Journal of Clinical Psychology in Medical Settings, 4,* 193–205.

Andrews G.J., Clark, M., & Luszcz, M. (2002). Successful aging in the Australian longitudinal study of aging: Applying the MacArthur model cross-nationally. *Journal of Social Issues, 58,* 749–765.

Anderson, N.B., & Anderson, P.E. (2003). *Emotional longevity: What really determines how long you live.* New York: Viking.

Anstey, K., & Christensen, H. (2000). Education, activity, health, blood pleasure and apolipoprotein as a predictor of cognitive change in old age: A review. *Journal of Gerontology, Biological Sciences, 46,* A163–177.

Antonucci, T., Sherman, A., & Akiyama, H. (1996). Social network, support and integration. In J. Birren (Ed.), *Encyclopedia of gerontology* (pp. 505–516). New York: Pergamon.

Antonucci, T.C., Okorodudu, C., & Akiyama, H. (2002). Well-being among older adults on different continents. *Social Issues, 58,* 617–627.

Arkin, S.M. (2001). Alzheimer rehabilitation by students: Intervention and outcomes. *Neuropsychological Rehabilitation, 11,* 273–317.

Aspinwall, L.G., & Shelley, T.E. (1997). A stitch in time: Self-regulation and proactive coping. *Psychological Bulletin, 121,* 417–436.

Aspinwall, L.G., Richter, L., & Hoffman, R.R. (2001). Understanding how optimism "works": An examination of optimists' adaptive moderation of belief and behavior. In E.C. Chang (Ed.), *Optimism and pessimism: Theory, research and practice* (pp. 217–238). Washington DC: American Psychological Association.

Atchley R.C. (1989). A continuity theory of normal aging. *The Gerontologist, 29,* 183–190.

Atchley R.C. (1999). *A continuity and adaptation theory in aging. Creating positive experiences.* Baltimore, MD: John Hopkins University Press.

Atlantis, E., Chow, C.M., Kirby, A., & Fiatarone, M. (2004). An effective exercise-based intervention for improving mental health and quality of life measures: A randomized trial. *Preventive Medicine, 39,* 432–434.

Ausman, L.M., & Russell R.M. (1994). *Nutrition in the elderly. Modern nutrition in health and disease.* Philadelphia, PA: Lea Febiger.

Avlund, K., Holstein, B.E., Mortensen E.L. (1999). Active life in old age. Combining measures of functional ability and social participation. *Dan Medicine Bulletin, 46,* 345–349.

Ball, K. Berch, D.B., Helmers, K.F. Jobe, J.B., Leveck, M.D., Marsiske, M. et al. (2002). Effects of cognitive training interventions with older adults. *Journal of the American Medical Association, 288,* 2271–2281.

Ball. K., Edwards, J.D., & Ross, L.A. (2007). The impact of speed of processing training on cognitive and everyday functions. *Journal of Gerontology: Psychological Science, 62B,* 19–31.

Baltes, M.M., & Baltes, P.B. (Eds.). (1986). *The psychology of control and aging.* Hillsdale, NJ: Erlbaum.

Baltes, M.M., Kühl, K.P., & Sowarka, D. (1992). Testing for limits of cognitive reserve capacity: A promising strategy for early diagnostic of dementia? *Journal of Gerontology: Psychology Sciences, 17,* 165 167.

Baltes, M.M., Kühl, K., Gutzmann, H., & Sowarka, D. (1995). Potential of cognitive plasticity as a diagnostic instruments: A cross-validation and extension. *Psychology and Aging, 10,* 167–172.

Baltes, M.M., & Carstensen, L.L. (1996). The process of successful aging. *Aging and Society, 16,* 397–422.

Baltes, M.M., & Baltes, P.B. (1997). Normal versus pathological cognitive functioning in old-age: Plasticity and testing-the-limits of cognitive/brain reserve capacity. In P.B. Baltes (Ed.), *Demènce et longevité.* Berlin: DTB.

Baltes, P.B. (1987). Theoretical propositions of life-span developmental psychology: On the dynamic between growth and decline. *Developmental Psychology, 23,* 611–626.

Baltes, P.B., & Schaie, K.W. (1974). The myth of the twilight years. *Psychology Today, 40,* 35–38.

Baltes, P.B., & Schaie, K.W. (1976). On the plasticity of intelligence in adulthood and old age. *American Psychologist, 31,* 720–725.

Baltes, P.B.Reese, H.W., & Nesselroad, J.R. (1977). *Life span developmental psychology: Research methods in developmental psychology.* Monterey, CA: Brooks Cole.

Baltes, P.B., & Willis, S.L. (1982). Plasticity and enhancement of intellectual functioning in old age. Penn State's Adult Development and Enrichment Project (ADEPT). In I.M. Craik & S.E. Trehud (Eds.), *Aging and cognitive processes* (pp. 352–389). New York: Plenum.

Baltes P.B., & Baltes, M.M. (Eds.). (1990a). *Successful aging: Perspectives from the behavioral sciences.* Cambridge, UK: Cambridge University Press.

Baltes, P.B., & Baltes, M.M. (1990b). Psychological perspectives on successful aging: The model of selective optimization with compensation. In P.B. Baltes & M.M. Baltes (Eds.), *Successful aging: Perspectives from the behavioral sciences* (pp. 1–35). Cambridge, UK: Cambridge University Press.

Baltes, P.B., & Kliegl, R. (1992). Further testing of limits of cognitive plasticity. Negative age differences in a mnemonic skill are robust. *Developmental Psychology, 28,* 121–125.

Baltes, P.B., & Mayer, K.U. (Eds.). (1999). *The Berlin aging study. Aging from 70 to 100.* Cambridge, UK: Cambridge University Press.

Baltes P.B., & Smith, P. (2003). New frontiers in the future of aging: From successful aging of the young old to the dilemmas of the fourth age. *Journal of Gerontology: Psychological Sciences, 49,* 123–135.

Bandura, A. (1986). *Social foundation of thoughts and actions.* Englewood Cliffs, CA: Prentice Hall.

Bandura, A. (1997). *Self-efficacy. The exercise of control.* New York: Freeman and Co.

Bandura, A. (2005). The primary of self-regulation in health promotion. *Applied Psychology. An International Review, 54,* 245–254.

Bassuk, S.S., Glass, T.A., & Berkman, L.F. (1999). Social disengagement and incident cognitive decline in community-dwelling elderly persons. *Annals of Internal Medicine, 131,* 165–173.

Bath, P.A., & Deeg, D. (2005). Social engagement and health outcomes among older people: Introduction to a special section. *European Journal of Ageing, 2,* 24–31.

Bath, P.A., & Gardiner, A. (2005). Social engagement and health and social care use and medication among older people. *European Journal of Ageing, 2,* 56–64.

Batty, G.D., & Deary, I.J. (2004). Early life intelligence and adult health. *British Medical Journal, 329,* 585–586.

Bearon, L.B. (1996). Successful aging: What does the "goodlife" look like? *The Forum, 3,* 1–7.

Bernis C. (2007). Senescence, aging populations and old age. In B. Pavel, S. Charles, & E. Rebato (Eds.), *Essentials of biological anthropology* (pp. 270–281). Prague: Charles University, The Karolinum Press.

Bennett, K.M. (2005). Social engagement as a longitudinal predictor of objective and subjective health. *European Journal of Ageing, 2,* 48–56.

Benyamini, Y., & Lomranz, J. (2004). The relationship of activity restriction and replace-

ment with depressive symptoms among older adults. *Psychology and Aging, 19,* 363–366.
Berk, D.R., Hubert, H.B., & Fries, J.F. (2006). Associations of changes in exercise level with subsequent disability among seniors: A 16-year longitudinal study. *The Journals of Gerontology: Biological and Medical Sciences, 61,* 97–102.
Berkman, L.F., & Syme, S.L. (1979). Social networks, host resistance and mortality: A nine year follow-up study of Alameda County residents. *American Journal of Epidemiology, 109,* 186–204.
Berkman, L.F., Seeman, T.E., Albert, M. (1993)l: High, usual and impaired functioning in community-dwelling older men and women: Findings from the MacArthur Foundation Research Network on Successful Aging. *Journal of Clinical Epidemiology, 46,* 1129–1140.
Berkman, L.F. (1985). The relationship between social networks and social support to morbidity and mortality. In S. Cohen & S.L. Syme (Eds.), *Social support and health* (pp. 242–263). New York: Academic Press.
Berlin, J.A., & Colditz GA. (1990). A meta-analysis of physical activity in the prevention of coronary heart disease. *American Journal of Epidemiology, 13,* 17–46.
Bertera, E.M. (2003). Physical activity and social network contacts in community dwelling older adults. *Activities, Adaptation and Aging, 27,* 113–127.
Bijnen, F.C.H., Feskens, E.J.M., Caspersen, C.J., Nagelkerke, N., Mosterd, W.L., & Kromhout, D. (1999). Baseline and previous physical activity in relation to mortality in elderly men. *American Journal of Epidemiology, 150,* 1289–1296.
Birren, J. (Ed.). (1996). *Encyclopedia of gerontology. Aging, age, and the aged.* New York: Pergamon.
Blair, S.N. (1992). How much physical activity is good for health? *Annual Review of Public Health, 13,* 99.
Blair, S.N. (1995). Changes in physical fitness and all-cause mortality: A prospective study of healthy and unhealthy men. *Journal of American Medical Association, 272,* 1093.
Blanchard-Fields, F. Camp, C., & Casper-Jahnke, H. (1995). Age differences in problem-solving styles. *Psychology and Aging, 10,* 173–180.
Blazer, D.G. (2006). Successful aging. *American Journal of Geriatric Psychiatry, 14,* 2–5.
Bogers, R.P., Tijuis, M.a.R., Van Gelder, B.M., & Kromhout, D. (Eds.). (2006). *Final report of the HALE (Healthy Aging: A Longitudinal Study in Europe Project).* Bilthoven, NL: Centre for Prevention and Health Services Research.
Bonanno, G.A. (2004). Loss, trauma, and human resilience. *American Psychologist, 59,* 20–28.
Bond, L., Culter, S., & Grams, A. (Eds.). (1995). *Promoting successful and productive aging.* Newbury Park, CA: Sage.
Bosma, H., van Boxtel, M.,Ponds, R., Houx, P. Burdof, A., & Jolles, J. (2003). Mental work demands protect against cognitive impairment: MAAS prospective cohort study. *Experimental Aging Research, 29,* 33–45.
Börsch-Supan, Jürges, J. (Ed.). (2005). *Health, aging and retirement in europe methodology.* Mannheim, Germany: Research Institute of the Economy of Aging.
Bortz, W.M. (1982). Disuse and aging. *Journal of American Medical Association, 248,* 1203–08.

Bouchard, C., Shepard, R.J., & Stephens, T. (1994). *Physical activity, fitness and health: international proceedings and consensus statement.* Champaign, IL: Human Kinetics.

Bowling, A. (2006). Lay perceptions of successful aging: Findings from a national survey of middle aged and older adults in Britain. *European Journal of Ageing, 4,* 57–58.

Bowling, A. (2007). Aspiration for older age in the 21st century: What is successful aging? *International Journal of Aging and Human Development, 64,* 263–297.

Brandstädter, J., & Renner, G. (1990). Tenacious goal pursuit and flexible goal adjustments: Explication and age-related analysis of assimilative and accommodative strategies of coping. *Psychology and Aging, 5,* 58–67.

Brenes, B. (2003). Cognitive training may improve targeted cognitive functions in older adults. *Evidence Based Mental Health, 6,* 54.

Brim, O.G., Ryff, C.D., & Kessler, R.C. (2004). *How healthy are we? A national study of well-being at midlife.* Chicago: University Chicago Press.

Bronfenbrenner, V. (1977). Toward an experimental ecology of human development. *American Psychologist, 32,* 513–531.

Brosse, A.L., Sheets, E.S., Lett, H.S., & Blumenthal, J.A. (2002). Exercise and the treatment of clinical depression in adults: Recent findings and future directions. *Sports Medicine, 32,* 741–60.

Bruunsgard, H., & Pedersen, B.K. (2000). Special features for the Olympics: Effects of exercise on the immune system in the elderly population. *Immunology and Cell Biology, 78,* 523–531.

Bukov, A., Maas, I., & Lampert, T. (2002). Social participation in very old. *Journal of Gerontology: Psychological Sciences, 57B,* P510–517.

Bull, V.L. (2005). Successful aging and the Chinese-American elder. *Dissertation Abstract International, 65,* 4434.

Burke, G.L., Arnold, A.M., & Bild D.E.(2001). Factors associated with healthy aging: The cardiovascular health study. *Journal of American Geriatric Society, 49,* 254–262.

Burns, M.O., & Seligman, M.E.P. (1989). Explanatory style across lifespan: Evidence for stability over fifty-two years. *Journal of Personality and Social Psychology, 56,* 471–477.

Butler, R. (1969). Ageism: Another form of bigotry. *The Gerontologist, 9,* 212–252.

Butler, R., & Gleason, H.P. (1985). *Enhancing vitality in later life.* New York: Springer.

Butt, D.S., & Beiser, M. (1987). Successful aging: A theme for international psychology. *Psychology and Aging, 2,* 87–94.

Cahn-Weiner, D.A., Malay, P.F., & Rebok, G.W. (2003). Results of a randomized placebo-controlled study of memory training for mildly impaired Alzheimer's Disease patients. *Applied Neuropsychology, 10,* 215–223.

Callaghan, P. (2004). Exercise: A neglected intervention in mental health care? *Journal of Psychiatric and Mental Health Nursing, 11,* 476–83.

Callahan, C.M., & McHorney, C.A. (2003). Successful aging and the humility of perspective. *Annals of Internal Medicine, 139,* 389–390.

Cambois, E., Robine, J.M., & Hayward, M.D. (2001), Social inequalities in disability-free life expectancy in the French male population, 1980–1991. *Demography, 38,* 513–524.

Canadian Fitness and Life Style Institute. (2001). *Physical activity monitor.* Ottawa: Canadian Fitness and Life Style Institute.

Caprara, G.V., & Cervone, D. (2000). *Personality. determinants, dynamics, and potentials.* New York: Cambridge University Press.

Caprara, G.V., Caprara, M.G., & Steca, P. (2003). Personality's correlates of adult development and aging. *European Psychologist, 8,* 129–130.

Carnero-Pardo, C. (2000). Educación, demencia y reserva cerebral [Education, dementia, and brain reserve]. *Revista de Neurología, 31,* 584–592.

Carroll, D.K. (1995). The importance of self-efficacy expectations in the elderly patients recovering from coronary artery bypass surgery. *Heart and Lung, 24,* 50–59.

Carstensen, L.L. (1991). Selective theory: Social activity in life-span context. In *Annual Review of Gerontology and Geriatrics (Vol. II).* New York: Springer.

Carstensen, L.L. (1993). Motivation for social contact and lifespan: A theory of socioemotional selectivity. In J. Jacobs (Ed.), *Nebraska symposium on motivation developmental perspectives on motivation.* Lincoln: University Nebraska Press.

Carstensen, L.L., & Turk-Charles, S. (1994). The salience of emotion across the adult lifespan. *Psychology and Aging, 9,* 259–264.

Carstensen, L.L., Isaacowitz, D.M., & Charles, S.T. (1999). taking time seriously: A theory of socioemotional selectivity. *American Psychologist, 54,* 165–181.

Carstensen, L.L., Mayr, U., Pasupathi, M., & Nesselroade, J.R. (2000). Emotional experience in everyday life across the adult lifespan. *Journal of Personality and Social Psychology, 79,* 644–655.

Cassel, M. (2002). Use it or lose it: Activity may be the best treatment for aging. *Journal of American Medical Association, 288,* 2333–2335.

Cattell R.B. (1971). *Abilities: Their structure, growth and action.* Boston: Houghton Mifflin.

Center for Disease Control and Prevention. (2003). Public health and aging. United States and worldwide. *Journal of American Medical Association, 289,* 1371–1373.

Center for Disease Control and Prevention. (2004). Strength training among adults. *American Family Physician,* April 1.

Center for Disease Control and Prevention. (2005). *Health, United States, 2004.* Washington, DC: National Center for Health and Statistics.

Chiperfield, J.G., Perry, R.P., & Weiner, B. (2003). Discrete emotions in later life. *Journal of Gerontology: Psychological Sciences, 58,* P23–P34.

Chodosh, J. Reuben, D.B., Albert, M.S., & Seeman, T.E. (2002). Predicting cognitive impairment in high-functioning community-dwelling older persons: MacArthur studies of successful aging. *Journal of American Geriatric Society, 50,* 1051–1060.

Chovan, M., & Chovan, W. (1985). Stressful events and coping responses among older adults in two sociocultural groups. *Journal of Psychology, 110,* 253–260.

Christensen, H., Hedzi-Pavlovic, D., & Jacomb, P. (1997). The psychometric differentiation of dementia from normal aging: A meta-Analysis. *Psychological Assessment, 2,* 147–155.

Clare, L., Wilson, B.A., & Carter, G. (2003). Cognitive rehabilitation as a component of early intervention in Alzheimer's Disease: A single case study. *Aging Mental Health, 7,* 5–6.

Cohen, C.I., Teresi, J., & Holmes, D. (1985). Social network, stress and physical health. A longitudinal study on an inner-city elderly population. *Journal of Gerontology, 40,* 478–486.

Cohen, C.I., Teresi, J., & Holmes, D. (1986). Assessment of stress-buffering effects of social networks on psychological symptoms in an inner-city elderly population. *American Journal of Community Psychology, 14,* 75–91.

Clark, P.G., Nigg, C.R., Greene, G., Riebe, D., & Saunders, S.D. (Members of the SENIOR

Project Team). (2002). The study of exercise and nutrition in older Rhode Islanders (SENIOR): Translating theory into research. *Health Education Research, 17,* 552–561.

Cohen S., & Syme, S.L. (Eds.). (1985a). *Social support and health.* New York: Academic Press.

Cohen, S., & Syme, S.L. (1985b). Issues in the study of social support. In S. Cohen & S.L. Syme (Eds.), *Social support and health.* New York: Academic Press.

Cohen, S. (1988). Psychosocial models of the role of social support in the etiology of physical disease. *Health Psychology, 7,* 269–297.

Colcombe, S., & Kramer, A.F. (2003). Fitness effects on the cognitive function of older adults: A meta-analytic study. *Psychological Science, 14,* 125–130.

Colcombe, S.J., Erickson, K.I., Raz, N., Webb, A.G. Cohen, N.J., Edward McAuley, E., & Kramer, A.F. (2003). Aerobic fitness reduces brain tissues loss in aging human. *Journal of Gerontology: Biological and Medical Sciences, 58A,* M176–189.

Colcombe, S.J. Erickson, K.I., Scalf, P.E., Kim, J.S., Prakash, R., McAuley, E. et al. (2006). Aerobic exercise training increases brain volume in aging humans. *Journal of Gerontology: Biological and Medical Sciences, 61A,* M1166–1170.

Collins, A.L., & Smyer, M.A. (2006). Evolving trends in long-term care: the ecology of selective optimization with compensation. In L. Hyer & R.C. Intrieri (Eds.), *Geropsychological interventions in long term care.* (pp. 37–62). New York: Springer.

Conn, V.S., Minor, M.A., Burks, K., Rantz, M.J., & Pomeroy, S.H. (2003). Integrative review of physical activity intervention research with aging adults. *Journal of American Geriatrics Society, 51,* 1159–68.

Cook, T.D. (1985). Postpositivist critical multiplism. In S. Shotland & M.V. Mark (Eds.), *Social science and social policy.* Palo Alto, CA: Sage.

COP/EFPA. (2002). *Psychology, psychologists and agi*ng. Madrid: Colegio Oficial de Psicólogos and the European Federation of Psychologists Associations.

Costa, D. (2002). Changing chronic disease rates and functional decline among older men. *Demography, 39,* 119–137.

Costa, P.T., & McCrae, R.R. (1997). Longitudinal stability of adult personality. In R. Hogan, Johnson, J., & Briggs, S. (Eds.), *Handbook of personality psychology* (pp. 269–290). San Diego, CA, Academic Press.

Cotman, C.W., & Berchtold, N.C. (2002). Exercise: A behavioral intervention to enhance brain health and plasticity. *Trends Neuroscience, 25,* 295–301.

Crimmins, E.M. (2001). Mortality and health in human lifespans. *Experimental Gerontology, 36,* 885–897.

Crimmins, E.M., Saito, Y., & Reynolds, S. (1997). Further evidence on recent trends in the prevalence and incidence of disability among older Americans from two sources: The LSOA and the NHIS. *Journal of Gerontology: Biological Sciences, 52,* 59–71.

Crowe, M., Andel, R. Pedersen, N.L., Johansson, B., & Gatz, M. (2003). Does participation in leisure activities lead to reduced risk of Alzheimer's disease? A prospective study of Swedish twins. *Journal of Gerontology: Psychological Sciences, 58B,* P249–255.

Cummings, E., & Henry, W.E. (1961). *Growing old: The process of disengagement.* New York: Basic book.

Cheung, S.L.K. (2005). Three dimension of survival curve. *Demography, 42,* 243–258.

Danner, D.D., Snow, D.A., & Friesen, W.V. (2001). Positive emotions in early life and longevity: Finding from the Nun study. *Journal of Personality and Social Psychology, 80,* 804–13.

Davidson, R. (2000). Affective neuroscience and psychophysiology: Toward a synthesis. *Psychophysiology, 40,* 655–665.

Davis-Berman, J. (1989). Physical self-efficacy, perceived physical status, and depressive symptomatology in older adults. *The Journal of Psychology, 124,* 207–215.

Daviglus, N.L, Lin, K., Pirzada, A., Yan, L.L., D.B., & Garside, D.B. (2003). Body Mass Index in middle age and health-related quality of life in older age. *Archive of Internal Medicine, 163,* 2460–2468.

Day, A.T.& Day, L.H.(1993). Living arrangements and "successful" aging among ever-married American white women 77–87 years of age. *Aging and Society, 13,* 365–387.

Deary, I.K., & Der, G. (2005). Reaction time explain IQ's association with death. *Psychological Science,16,* 64–69.

D'Epinay, C.J.L., & Bickel, J.J. (2003). Do "young-old" exercisers feel better than sedentary persons. A cohort study in Switzerland. *Canadian Journal of Aging, 22,* 155–165.

De Vellis, B.M., & De Vellis, R.F. (2001). Self-efficacy and health. In A. Baum, T.A. Revenson, & J.E. Singer (Eds.), *Handbook of health psychology.* Mahwah, NJ: Erlbaum.

Denney, N.W. (1982). Aging and cognitive changes. In B.B. Wolman (Ed.), *Handbook of developmental psychology.* New Jersey: Prentice Hall.

Depp, C.A., & Jeste, D.V. (2006). Definitions and predictors of successful aging: A comprehensive review of larger quantitative studies. *American Journal of Geriatric Psychiatry, 14,* 6–20.

Diehl, M. (1998). Everyday competence in later life: Current status and future directions. *The Gerontologist, 38,* 422–433.

Diener, E., & Diener, C. (1996). Most people are happy. *Psychological Science, 7,* 181–185.

Diener, E.(1999). Introduction to the special section on the structure of emotions. *Journal of Personality and Social Psychology, 76,* 803–804.

Díez-Nicolás, J. (1996). *Los mayores en la Comunidad de Madrid* [The elderly in the Madrid region]. Madrid: Obra Social Caja de Madrid.

Draganski, B., Gasert, C., Busch, V. Schuierert, G., Bogdhan, U., & May, A. (2004). Changes in gray matter induced by training. *Nature, 427,* 311–312.

Draganski, B., Gaser, C., Kempermann, G., Kuhn, H.G., Winkler, J., Büchel, C., May, D., & May, A. (2006). Temporal and spatial dynamics of brain structure changes during extensive learning. *Journal of Neurosciences, 26,* 6314–6317.

Dunlosky, J. Cavallini, E., Roth, H., McGuire, C.L., Vecchi, T., & Hertzog, C. (2007). Do self-monitoring interventions improve older adult learning? *Journal of Gerontology: Psychological Sciences, 62B,* 70–76.

Eizenman, D.R., Nesselroade, J.R., Featherman D.L., & Rowe, J.W. (1997). Intraindividual variability in perceived control in a older sample: The Mac arthur Successful Aging Studies. *Psychology and aging, 12,* 489–502.

Ekman, P., & Davidson, R.J. (1994). *The nature of emotions: Fundamental questions.* New York: Oxford University Press.

Elias, J.W., & Wagster, M.V. (2007). Developing context and background underlying cognitive intervention/training studies in older populations. *Journal of Gerontology: Psychological Sciences, 62B,* 5–10.

Erikson, E.H., & Erikson, J.M., & Kivnick, H. (1986). *Vital involvement in old age: The experience of old age in our time*. London: Norton.

EURODIET. (2000). *www.eurodiet.med*.

European Communities Council. (2007). *Joint report on social inclusion and social protection. Countries profiles*. Brussels: European Communities.

Fernández-Ballesteros, R. (1986). Hacia una vejez competente [Toward a competent aging]. In M. Carretero, A. Marchesi, & J. Palacios (Eds.), *Psicología evolutiva* [Developmental psychology], Vol. III. Madrid: Alianza.

Fernández-Ballesteros, R. (Ed.). (1992). *Mitos y realidades sobre la vejez y la salud* [Myths and realities about age and health]. Barcelona: SG Editores.

Fernández-Ballesteros, R. (1996). *Psicología y envejecimiento* [Psychology and aging]. Madrid: Servicio de Publicaciones de la Universidad Autónoma de Madrid.

Fernández-Ballesteros, R. (2000). Gerontología social: Introducción [Social gerontology: Introduction]. In R. Fernández-Ballesteros (Ed.), *Gerontología social* [Social gerontology]. Madrid: Editorial Pirámide.

Fernández-Ballesteros, R. (Ed.). (2002a). *Vivir con vitalidad* [Living with vitality]. 5 Vols. Madrid: Pirámide.

Fernández-Ballesteros, R. (2002b). Envejecimiento satisfactorio [Satisfactory aging]. In P. Zarco & J.M. Martínez Lage (Eds.), *Corazón, cerebro y envejecimiento* [Heart, brain, and aging]. Madrid: Triacastela.

Fernández-Ballesteros, R. (2003). Light and dark in the psychology of human strengths. The example of psychogerontology. In L.G. Aspinwall & U.M. Staudinger (Eds.), *A psychology of human strengths* (pp. 131–149). Washington, DC: American Psychological Association.

Fernández-Ballesteros, R. (2004). Self-reports questionnaires. In S. Haynes & Heiby, E. (Eds.), *Behavioral assessment* (pp. 194–221). In M. Hersen (Ed.), *A comprehensive handbook of psychological assessment*, Vol. 3. New York: Wiley & Son.

Fernández-Ballesteros, R. (2005). Evaluation of "VITAL AGEING-M": A psychosocial program for promoting optimal aging. *European Psychologists, 10*, 146–156.

Fernández-Ballesteros, R. (2006). Geropsychology: An applied field for the 21st century. *European Psychologist, 11*, 312–324.

Fernández-Ballesteros, R. (Ed.). (2007). *GeroPsychology. An European perspective for an aging world*. Göttingen, Germany: Hogrefe & Huber.

Fernández-Ballesteros, R. (2007). Methodological and theoretical cultivation in cross-European research on ageing. *European Journal of Ageing, 4*, 97–100.

Fernández-Ballesteros, R., Díaz, P., Izal, M., & Hernández, J.M. (1988). "Conflict situations in elderly people." *Psychological Reports, 63*, 171–176.

Fernández-Ballesteros, R., & Calero, M.D. (1995). Training effects in intelligence of older persons. *Archives of Gerontology and Geriatrics, 20*, 135–148.

Fernández-Ballesteros, R., Van de Vijver, J., & Hambleton, R.K. (1999). Protocol adaptation procedures. In H.J.J. Schroots, R. Fernández-Ballesteros, & G. Rudinger (Eds.), *Aging in Europe* (pp. 169–184). Amsterdam: IOS Press.

Fernández-Ballesteros, R., & Calero, M.D. (2000). "The assessment of learning potential. The EPA instrument." In C.S. Lidz & J. Elliot (Eds.), *Dynamic assessment: Prevailing models and applications* (pp. 293–324). Greenwich: JAI.

Fernández-Ballesteros, R., Díez-Nicolás, J., Caprara, G.V., Barbaranelli, C., & Bandura, A.

(2002). Self-efficacy and collective efficacy: Structural relationships. *Applied Psychology: An International Review, 51,* 107–121.

Fernández-Ballesteros, R. Zamarrón, M.D., Tárraga, L., Moya, R., & Iñiguez, J. (2003). Learning potential in healthy, mild cognitive impairment subjects and in Alzheimer patients. *European Psychologist, 8,* 148–160.

Fernández-Ballesteros, R., & Marquez, M.O. (2003). Self-report (general). In R. Fernández-Ballesteros (Ed.), *Encyclopedia of psychological assessment* (Vol. II, pp. 871–877). London: Sage.

Fernández-Ballesteros, R., Zamarrón, M.D., Rudinger, G., Schroots, J., Drusini, A., Heikinnen, E. et al. (2004). Assessing competence. The European survey on aging protocol. *Gerontology, 50,* 330–347.

Fernández-Ballesteros, R., Caprara, M.G., & García, L.F. (2004). Vivir con Vitalidad-M: Un programa europeo multimedia [Vital Ageing-M: A multimedia European program]. *Intervención Social, 13,* 63–84.

Fernández-Ballesteros, R., Caprara, M.G., García, L.F., & Iñiguez, J. (2005). Promoción del envejecimiento activo: Efectos del programa "Vivir con Vitalidad" [Promoting active aging: Effects of "Vital Ageing" program]. *Revista de Geriatría y Gerontología, 50,* 330–347.

Fernández-Ballesteros, R., Zamarrón, M.D., & Tarraga, L. (2005). Learning potential: A new method for assessing cognitive impairment. *International Psychogeriatrics, 17,* 119–128.

Fernández-Ballesteros, R., Zamarrón, M.D., Calero, M.D., & Tárraga, L. (2007). Cognitive plasticity and cognitive impairment. In R. Fernández-Ballesteros (Ed.), *GeroPsychology. An European perspective for an aging world* (pp. 146–163). Göttingen, Germany: Hogrefe & Huber.

Fernández-Ballesteros, R., Kruse, A., Zamarrón M.D., & Caprara, M.G. (2007). Quality of life, life satisfaction, and positive aging. In R. Fernández-Ballesteros (Ed.), *GeroPsychology. An European perspective for an aging world* (pp. 196–223). Göttingen, Germany: Hogrefe & Huber.

Fernández-Ballesteros, R., & Botella, J. (2007). Self reports measures. In A.M. Nezu & C.M. Nezu (Eds.), *Evidence-based outcome research: A practical guide to conducting randomized controlled trials* (pp. 95–123). Oxford, UK: University Press.

Fernández-Ballesteros, R., García, L., Blanc, D., Efklides, A., Kornfeld, R., Lerma, A.J. et al. (2008). Lay concept of aging well: Cross-cultural comparisons. *Journal of the American Geriatric Society, 56,* 950–951.

Ferrucci, L., Izmirlian, G., Leveille, S.G., Phillips, C.L., Corti, M.C., Brock, D.B. et al. (1999). Smoking, physical activity and active life expectancy. *American Journal of Epidemiology, 149,* 645–653.

Fiatarone, M., O'Neill, E.F., Ryan, N.D., Clemens, K.M., Solares, G.R., & Nelson, M.E. (1994). Exercise training and nutritional supplementation for physical frailty in very elderly people. *New England Journal of Medicine, 330,* 1769–1775).

Finch, C.E. (1996). Variations in senescence and longevity include the possibility of negligible senescence. *Journal of Gerontology: Biological Sciences, 53A,* 235–239.

Fisher, B.J. (2002). Successful aging and life satisfaction: A pilot study for conceptual clarification. *International Journal of Aging and Human Development, 41,* 239–250.

Fisher, N.M., Pendergast, D.R., Gresham, G.E., & Calkins, E. (1991). Muscle rehabilitation:

Its effect on muscular and functional performance of patients with knee osteoarthritis. *Archives of Physical Medicine and Rehabilitation, 72,* 367–364.

Floyd, M., & Scogin, F. (1997). Effects of memory training on the subjective memory functioning and mental health of older adults: A meta-analysis. *Psychology and Aging, 12,* 150–161.

Fogel, R.W. (2005). Changes in the disparities in chronic diseases during the course of the XX century. *Perspective in Biology and Medicine, 48,* S150.

Folkman, S., & Moskowitz, J.T. (2000). Positive affect and the other side of coping. *American Psychologist, 55,* 647–654.

Folstein, M.F., Folstein, S.E., & Mchugh, P.R. (1975). Mini mental state. A practical method for grading the cognitive state of patients for the clinician. *Journal Psychiatric Research, 12,* 189–198.

Ford, A.B., Haug, M.R., & Stange, K.C. (2000). Sustained personal autonomy: A measure of successful aging. *Journal of Aging and Health, 12,* 470–489.

Fratiglioni, L., Paillard-Borg, S., & Winbland, B. (2004). An active and socially integrated lifestyles in late life might protect against dementia. *Lancet Neurology, 3,* 343–53.

Fredrickson, B.L. (2000). Cultivating positive emotions to optimize health and well-being. *Prevention & Treatment, 3,* 1–17.

Fredrickson, B.L. (2001). The role of positive emotions in positive psychology. *American Psychologist, 56,* 218–226.

Fredrickson, B.L., & Losada, M.F. (2005). Positive affect and the complex dynamics of human flourishing. *American Psychologist, 60,* 678–686.

Freedman, V.A., Crimmins, E.C.M., Schoeni, R.F., Spillman, B.C., Kramarow, E., Land, K. et al. (2004). Resolving inconsistencies in trends in old-age disability: Report from a technical working group. *Demography, 41,* 417–441.

Freund, A.M. (2006). Age-differential motivational consequences of optimization versus compensation focus in younger and older adults. *Psychology and Aging, 21,* 240–252.

Freund, A.M., & Baltes, P.B. (2000). The orchestration of selection, optimization, and compensation: An action-theoretical conceptualization of a theory of developmental regulation. In W.J. Perrig & A. Grob (Eds.), *Control of human behavior, mental processes and consciousness* (pp. 35–58). Mahwah, NJ: Erlbaum.

Freund, A.M., & Baltes, P.B. (2002). Life-management strategies of selection, optimization and compensation as strategies of selection, optimization and compensation: Measurement by self-report and construct validity. *Journal of Personality and Social Psychology, 82,* 642–662.

Freund, A.M., & Baltes, P.B. (2007). Toward a theory of successful aging: Section, optimization and compensation. In R. Fernández-Ballesteros (Ed.), *GeroPsychology. An European perspective for an aging world* (pp. 239–244). Göttingen, Germany: Hogrefe & Huber.

Freund, A.M., & Riediger, M. (2003). Successful aging. In R.M. Lerner, A. Easterbrooks, & J. Mistry (Eds.), *Comprehensive handbook of psychology. Volume 6: Developmental psychology* (pp. 601–628). New York: Wiley.

Fries, J.F. (1989). *Aging well.* Reading, MA: Addison-Wesley.

Fries, J.F. (2002). Reducing disability in older age. *Journal of American Medical Association, 288,* 3164–3166.

Fries, J.F., & Crapo, L.M. (1981). *Vitality and aging.* New York: Freeman.

Fries, J.F., Singh, G., Morfeld, D., Hubert, H.B., Lane, N.E., & Brown, B.W. (1994). Running and the development of disability with age. *Annals of Internal Medicine, 121*, 502–509.

Fries, J.F. (2003). Measuring and monitoring success in compressing morbidity. *Annals of Internal Medicine, 139*, 445–459.

Friis, R.H., Nomura, W.L., Ma, C.J., & Swan, J.H. (2003). Socioepidemiologic and health-related correlates of walking for exercise among the elderly: Results from the longitudinal study of aging. *Journal American Physical Activity, 11*, 1–11.

Fritsch, T., Smyth, K.A., Debanne, S.M., Petot, G.P., & Friedland, R.P. (2005). Participation in novelty-seeking leisure activities and Alzheimer's disease. *Journal of Geriatric Psychiatry and Neurology, 18*, 134–141.

Fritsch, T., McClendon, M.K.J., Smyth, K.A., Lerner, A.J., Friedland, R.P., & Larsen, J.D. (2007). Cognitive functioning in healthy aging: The role of reserve and lifestyles factors early in life. *The Gerontologist, 47*, 307–322.

Fukukawa, Y., Navashima, C., Tsuboi S., Kozakai, R., Doyo, W., Nino, N. et al. (2004). Age differences in the effect of physical activity on depressive symptoms. *Psychology and Aging, 19*, 346–351.

Gallacher, J., Bayer, A., & Ben Shlomo, Y. (2005). Commentary: Activity each day keeps dementia away – Does social interaction really preserve cognitive function. *International Journal of Epidemiology, 34*, 872–873.

Gatz, M. (2005). Educating the brain to avoid dementia: Can mental exercise prevent Alzheimer disease? *Public Library Of Science, Medicine, 2*, 7.

Garfein A.J., & Herzog A. (1995). Robust aging among the young-old, old-old, and oldest-old. *Journal of Gerontology: Psychological Sciences, 50B*, S77–S87.

Geronimus, M. (2001). Inequality in life expectancy, functional status and active Life expectancy. *Demography, 38*, 227–251.

Gelder van B.M., Tijhuis, M.A.R., Kalmijn, S., Giampaoli, S., Nissinen, A., & Kromhout, D. (2004). Physical activity in relation to cognitive decline in elderly men: The fine study. *Neurology, 63*, 2316–2321.

Gergen, M., & Gergen, K. (2001). Positive aging: New images for a new age. *Age International, 27*, 3–23.

Gething, L., Gridley, H., Browning, C., Helmes, E., Luszcz, M., Turner, J. et al. (2003). The role of psychologists in fostering the well-being of older Australians. *Australian Psychologists, 38*, 1–10.

Giampapa, V., Pero, R., & Zimmerman, M. (2004). *The antiaging solution: Five simple steps to looking and feeling young.* Milano: Lennart Sane Agency.

Gibson, J.J. (1979). *The ecological approach to visual perception.* Hilldale, NJ: Erlbaum.

Giltay, E.J., Geleiinjse, J.M., Zitman, F.G., Hoekstra, E.G., & Schonten, E. (2004). Dispositional optimism and all-cause and cardiovascular mortality in a prospective cohort of elderly Dutch men and women. *Archive of General Psychiatry, 61*, 1126–1135.

Glasgow, R.E., Vogt, T.M., & Boles, S.M. (1999). Evaluating the public health impact pf health promotion interventions: The RE-AIM Framework. *American Journal of Public Health, 89*, 1322–1327.

Glass, T.A. (2003). Assessing the success of successful aging. *Annals of Internal Medicine, 139*, 282–283.

Glei, D.S., Landau, D.A., Goldman, N., Yi-Li, C., Rodriguez, G., & Weinstein, M. (2005). Participating in social activities helps preserve cognitive function: An analysis of longitudinal, population-based study of the elderly. *International Journal of Epidemiology, 34,* 864–71.

Gottfredson, L.S., & Deary, I.J. (2004). Intelligence predicts health and longevity, but why? *Current Direction in Psychological Science, 13,* 1–4.

Gould, R.L. (1977). *Ontogeny and phylogeny.* Cambridge, MA: Harvard University Press.

Gould, R.L. (1981). *The mismeasure of man.* New York: Norton.

Gregg, D.W. (1992). Human wealth-span: The financial dimensions of successful aging. In N.E. Cutler, D.W. Gregg, & M.P. Lawton (Eds.), *Aging, money and life satisfaction: Aspects of financial gerontology* (pp. 169–182). New York: Springer.

Greve, W., & Staudinger, U.M. (2006). Resilience in later adulthood and old age. In D. Cicchetti & D.J. Cohen (Eds.), *Developmental psychopathology, Vol. 3. Risk, disorders and adaptation* (pp. 796–840). Hoboken, NJ: Wiley.

Gross, J.J., Carstensen, L.L., Pasupathi, M., Tsai, J., Gotestam, C., & Hsu, A. (1997). Emotion and aging: Experience, expression, and control. *Psychology and Aging, 12,* 290–99.

Grundy, E., & Bowling, A. (1999). Enhancing the quality of extended life years: Identification of the oldest old with a very good and very poor quality of life. *Aging Mental Health, 3,* 199–212.

Guralnik, J.M., & Kaplan, G.A. (1989). Predictors of healthy aging: Prospective evidence from the Alameda County study. *American Journal of Public Health, 79,* 703–708.

Hagberg, J.M., Montain, S.J., Martin, W.H., & Ehsani, A.A. (1989). Effect of exercise training in 60- to 69-year-old person with essential hypertension. *American Journal of Hypertension, 7,* 115.

Hardy, M.A. (2002). The transformation of retirement in the twentieth century in America: From discontent to satisfaction. *Generations, 26,* 9–16.

Harris, A.H., & Thoresen, C.E. (2005). Volunteering os associated with delayed mortality in older people: Analysis of the longitudinal study of aging. *Journal of Health Psychology, 10,* 739–752.

Harman, D., Hollidays, R., & Meydani, M. (1998). *Toward prolongation of the healthy lifespan.* New York: New York Academy of Sciences.

Hatziandreu, E.I., Koplan, J.P., Weinstein, M.C., Caspersen, C.J., & Warner, K.E. (1988). A cost effectiveness analysis of exercise as a health promotion activity. *American Journal of Public Health, 78,* 1417–1421.

Hausdorff, J.M., Levy, B.R., & Wei, J.Y. (1999). The power of ageism on physical function of older persons: Reversibility of age-related gait changes. *Journal of American Geriatrics Society, 17,* 1346–1349.

Havighurst, R.J. (1963). Activity theory of aging. In R.H. Williams, C. Tibbits, & W. Donahue, W. (Eds.), *Process of aging* (Vol. 1, pp. 299–320). New York: Atherton Press.

Haveman-Nies, A., De Groot, L.C., & Van Staveren, W.A. (2003). Dietary quality, life styles factors and healthy aging in Europe: The SENECA study. *Age and Aging, 32,* 427–34.

Hazzard, W.R.(2000). The department of internal medicine: Hub of the academic health center response to the aging imperative. *Annals of Internal Medicine, 133,* 293–296.

Heckhausen, J., & Schulz, R. (1995). A life-span theory of control. *Psychological Review, 102,* 284–304.

Hermanson, B., Omenn, G.S., Kronmal, R.A., & Gersh, B.J. (1988). Beneficial six-year outcome of smoking cessation in older men and women with coronary artery disease. *New England Journal of Medicine, 319,* 1365.

Herzog, A.R., Khan, R.L., Morgan, J.N. Jackson, J.S., & Antonucci, T.C. (1989). Age differences in productive activities. *Journal of Gerontology: Social Sciences, 44,* S129–148.

Higgins, E.T., Grant, H., & Shah, J. (1999). Self-regulation and quality of life: Emotional and non-emotional life experiences. In D. Kahneman, D. Diener, & N. Schwartz (Eds.), *Well-being: The foundations of hedonic psychology* (pp. 244–267). New York: Sage Foundation.

Higgins, M.W., Enright, P.L., Kronmal, R.A., Schenker, M.B., Anton-Culver, H., & Lyles, M. (1993). Smoking and lung function in elderly men and women. *Journal of American Medical Association, 269,* 2741–2748.

Hogan D.B., Fung T.S., & Ebly E.M. (1999). Health, function, and survival of a cohort of very old Canadians: Results from the second weave of the Canadian Study of Health and Aging. *Revue Canadienne de la Santé Publique, 90,* 338–342.

Hohaus, L. (2007). Remembering to age successfully: Evaluation of a successful aging approach to memory enhancement. *International Psychogeriatric, 19,* 137–150.

Holahan, C.K., & Holahan, C.J. (1987). Self-efficacy, social support, and depression in aging: A longitudinal analysis. *Journal of Gerontology: Psychological Sciences, 42,* 65–68.

Holmes, T.H., & Rahe, R.H. (1967). The social readjustment Rating Scale. *Journal of Psychosomatic Research, 11,* 213–218.

Hooker, S.P. (2002). California Active Aging Project. *Journal of Aging and Physical Activity, 10,* 354–359.

Hooker, S.P., Seavey, W. Weismed, C.E., Harvey, D.J., Stewart, A.L. Gillis, D.E. et al. (2005). California active aging community grant program: Translating science into practice to promote physical activity in older adults. *Annals of Behavioral Medicine, 29,* 155–165.

Hooker, S.P., & Cirill, L.A. (2006). Evaluation of community coalitions ability to create safe, effective exercise classes for older adults. *Evaluation and Program Planning, 29,* 242–250.

Horn, J.L. (1989). Models of intelligence. In R.L. Linn (Ed.), *Intelligence: Measurement, theory and public policy* (pp. 29–73). Urbana, IL: University of Illinois Press.

Hoyer, W.J., & Verhaeghen, P. (2006). Memory aging. In J.E. Birren & K.W.Schaie (Eds.), *Handbook of the psychology of aging* (6th ed., pp. 209–224). New York: Academic Press.

Hubert, H.B., Bloch, D.A. Oehlert, J., & Fries, J.F. (2002). Life styles habits and compression of morbidity. *Journal of Gerontology: Medical Sciences, 57,* M347–351.

Hsu, H.C. (2006). Exploring elderly people's perspectives on successful aging in Taiwan. *Aging and Society, 27,* 87–102.

Hyer, L., & Intrieri, R.C. (Eds.). (2006). *Geropsychological interventions in long-term care.* New York: Springer.

Institute of Medicine Committee on Assuring the Health of the Public in the 21st Century. (2002). *The future of the public's health in the 21st century.* Washington, DC: National Academy.

Inui, T.S. (2003). The need for an integrated biopsychosocial approach to research on successful aging. *Annals Internal Medicine, 139,* 391–94.

Isaacowitz, D.M. (2005). An attentional perspective on successful socio-emotional aging: Theory and preliminary evidence. *Research in Human Development, 2,* 115–132.

Jackson, N., & Waters, E. (2005). Criteria for the systematic review of health promotion and public health interventions. *Health Promotion International, 20,* 367–374.

Jagger, C., Matthews, R., Matthews, F., Robinson, T., Robine, J.-M. (2007). The burden of disease on disability-free life expectancy in later life. *Journal of Gerontology: Biological Sciences, 62A,* 408–414.

Jernigan, D.H., Monteiro, M., Room, R., & Saxena, S. (2000). Toward a global alcohol policy: Alcohol, public health, and the role of WHO. *Bulletin of the World Health Organization, 74,* 491.

Jeste, D.V. (2005). Feeling fine at a hundred and three. Secret of successful aging. *American Journal of Prevention Medicine, 28,* 323–24.

Jeune, B., & Vaupel, J.W. (1995). *Exceptional longevity: From prehistory to the present.* Odense, DK: Odense University Press.

Jopp, D., & Smith, J. (2006). Resources and life-management strategies as determinants of successful aging: On the protective effect of selection, optimization, and compensation. *Psychology and Aging, 21,* 253–265.

Jorm, A.F., Christiansen, H., & Henderson, S. (1998). Factors associated with successful aging. *Australian Journal of Ageing, 17,* 33–37.

Joseph, J.A., Schukitt-Hale, B., Denisova, N.A., Prior R.L., Cao, G., & Martin et al. (1998). Long-term dietary strawberry, spinach, or vitamin E supplementation retards the onset of age-related neuronal signal-transduction and cognitive behavioral deficits. *Journal of Neuroscience, 18,* 8047–8055.

Judd, J., Frankish, C.J., & Moulton, G. (2001). Setting standards in the evaluation of community-based health promotion programs. A unifying approach. *Health Promotion International, 16,* 367–380.

Juengst, E.T. (2005). Can aging be interpreted as a healthy, positive process? In M.L. Wykle, P.J. Whitehouse, & D.L. Norris, *Successful aging through the lifespan. Intergenerational issues in health* (pp. 3–19). New York: Springer.

Kahana, E., & Kahana, B. (2001). Conceptual and empirical advances in understanding aging well through proactive adaptation. In V. Bergtson (Ed.), *Adulthood and aging: Research on continuities and discontinuities* (pp. 18–41). New York: Springer.

Kahana, E., & Kahana, B. (2003). Contextualizing successful aging: New direction in ag-old search. In R. Settersten Jr. (Ed.), *Invitation to the life course. A new look at old age* (pp. 225–255). Amityville, NY: Baywood Pub.

Kahana, E. King, C. Kahana, B., Menne, H., Webster, N.J., Dan, A., Kercher, K., Bohne, A., & Lechner, C. (2005). Successful aging in the face of chronic disease. In M.L. Wykle, P.J. Whitehouse, & D.L. Norris *Successful aging through the lifespan. Intergenerational issues in health* (pp. 101–126). New York: Springer.

Kalache, A., & Kickbusch, I (1997). A global strategy for healthy aging. *World Health, 4,* 4–5.

Kamen-Siegel, L., Rodin, J., Seligman, M.E.P., & Dwyer, J. (1991). Explanatory style and cell-mediated immunity. *Health Psychology, 10,* 229–235.

Kamimoto, L.A., Easton, A.N., Maurice, E., Husten, C.G., & Macera, C.A. (1999). Surveillance for five health risks among older adults – United States, 1993–1997. *CDC-MMWR, 48,* 89–130.

Kane, R. (2003). The Contribution of geriatric health services research to successful aging. *Annals of Internal Medicine, 139,* 460–462.

Kang, J.H. (2004, July). From green and leafy to a sharper brain. *The New York Times.*

Kang, J.H., Ascherio, A., & Grodstein, F. (2005). Fruit and vegetable consumption and cognitive decline in aging women. *Annals of Neurology, 57,* 713–720.

Kannisto, V. (1996). *Advancing the frontier of survival*. Odense, DK: Odense University Press.

Kaplan, G.A., Salonen, J.T., Cohen, R.D., Brand, R.J., Syme, S.L., & Puska, P. (1988). Social connections and mortality from all causes and from cardiovascular disease: Prospective evidence from eastern Finland. *American Journal of Epidemiology, 128,* 370–380.

Kaplan, G.A., Seeman, T.E., Cohen, R.D., Knudsen, L.P., & Guralnik, J.M. (1987). Mortality among the elderly in the Alameda County Study: Behavioral and demographic risk factors. *American Journal of Public Health, 77,* 307.

Kaplan, R.M. (2000). Two pathways to prevention. *American Psychologist, 55,* 382–396.

Keys, A. (1980). *A multivariate analysis of death and coronary disease*. Cambridge, MA: Harvard University Press.

Keys, A. (1995). Mediterranean diet and public health: Personal reflexion. *American Journal of Clinical Nutrition, 61*(Suppl. 6), 1322lS–1323S.

King, L., Baker, A., Burton, C., & Velazquez, L. (2004). *Change, happiness, and maturity: Narrative accounts of the good things in life*. Paper presented at the American Psychological Association, Honolulu, August.

Klein, W.C., & Bloom, M. (1997). *Successful aging. Strategies for healthy living*. New York: Plenum.

Kliegl, R., Smith, J., & Baltes, P.B. (1989). Testing-the-limits in the study of adult age differences in cognitive plasticity of a mnemonic skill. *Developmental Psychology, 25,* 247–256.

Knight, T., & Ricciardelli, L.A. (2003). Successful aging: Perceptions of adults aged between 70 and 1001 years. *International Journal of Aging and Human Development, 56,* 223–246.

Knoefel, J.E., & Jankowiak, J. (2006). Can our leisure activities help to prevent cognitive decline? Patient page. *Neurology, 66,* E21–E22.

Knoops, K.T., Kim T.B., Knoops, M.S., Lisette C.P. de Groot, G.M., Kromhout, D. et al. (2004). Mediterranean diet, life style factors, and 10-year mortality in elderly European men and women: The HALE project. *Journal of American Medical Association, 292,* 1433–9.

Kramer, A.F., Hahn, S., & Cohen, N. (1999). Aging, fitness, and neurocognitive function. *Nature, 140,* 418–419.

Kramer, A.F., Bherer, L., Colcombe, S.J., Dong, W., & Greenough, W.T. (2004). Environmental influences on Cognitive and Brain Plasticity During Aging. *Journal of Gerontology, 59,* A940–57.

Krause, N. (1987). Life stress, social support, and self-esteem in an elderly population. *Psychology and Aging, 2,* 349–356.

Kubik, S.J. (2006). What is normal aging? *Gerontechnolgy, 5,* 56–59.

Kubzansky, L.D., Berkman, L.F. Glass, T.A., & Seeman, T.E. (1998). Is educational attainment associated with shared determinants of health in the elderly? Findings from Mac Arthur studies of successful aging. *Psychosomatic Medicine, 60,* 578–585.

Kubzansky, L.D., Sparrow, D., Voconas, P., & Kawachi I. (2001). Is the glass half empty or half full? A prospective study of optimism and coronary heart disease in the Normative Aging Study. *Psychosomatic Medicine, 63,* 910–916.

Labouvie-Vief, G., & DeVoe, M., & Bulka, D. (1989). Speaking about feelings: Conceptions of emotions across the lifespan. In K.W. Shaie (Ed.), *Annual review of gerontology and geriatrics* (pp. 172–194). New York: Springer.

Labouvie-Vief, G., Hakim-Larson, J., DeVoe, M., & Shoeberlein, S. (1989). Emotions and self-regulation. *Human Development, 32,* 279–299.

Labouvie-Vief G., & DeVoe, M. (1991). Emotional regulation in adulthood and later life: A developmental review. *Psychology and Aging, 4,* 425–437.

Labouvie-Vief G., & Marquez, M. (2004). Dynamic integration: Affect optimization and differentiation in development. In D.Y. Dai & R.G. Sternberg (Eds.), *Motivation, emotion and cognition: Integrative perspectives on intellectual functioning and development* (pp. 237–272). Mahwah, NJ: Erlbaum.

Lachman, M.E., & Leff, R. (1989). Perceive control and intellectual functioning in the elderly: A 5 year longitudinal study. *Developmental Psychology, 25,* 722–728.

Lachman, M.E. (1986). Personal control in later life: Stability, change, and cognitive correlates. In M.M. Baltes & P.B. Baltes (Eds.), *The psychology of control and aging* (pp. 207–236). Hillsdale, NJ: Erlbaum.

Lachman, M.E., Weaver, S.L., Bandura, M.M., Elliot, E., & Lewkowicz, C.J. (1992). Improving memory and control beliefs through cognitive restructuring and self-generating strategies. *Journal of Gerontology: Psychological Sciences, 47,* P293–P299.

Lamb V., & Myers G. (1999). A comparative study of successful aging in three Asian countries. *Population Research and Policy Review, 18,* 433–449.

Land, K. (2001). Models and indicators. *Social Forces, 80,* 381–410.

Landefeld, C.S.(2003). Improving health care for older persons. *Annals of Internal Medicine, 139,* 421–424.

Larson, E.B., Wang, L., Bowen, J.D., McCormick, W.C., Teri, L., Crane, P. et al. (2006). *Annals of Internal Medicine, 144,* 73–81.

Laurin, D., Verreault, R., Lindsay, J., MacPherson, K., & Rockwood, K. (2001). Physical activity and risk of cognitive impairment and dementia in elderly persons. *Archives of Neurology, 58,* 498–504.

Lawton, M.P. (1975). The Philadelphia Geriatric Center Moral Scale (PGCMS). *Journal of Gerontology, 30,* 85–89.

Lawton, M.P. (1983). Environment and other determinants of well-being in older people. *The Gerontologist, 13,* 349–357.

Lazarus, R.S. (1991). *Emotion and adaptation.* New York: Oxford University Press.

Lazarus, R.S. (2003). The Lazarus Manifiesto for positive psychology and psychology general. *Psychological Inquiry, 14,* 172–189.

Lazarus, R.S., & Folkman, S. (1984). *Stress, appraisal and coping.* New York: Springer.

Lehr, U. (1980). *Psicologìa de la senectud* [Psychology of the elderly]. Barcelona: Herder.

Lehr, U. (1982). Socio-psychological correlates of longevity. *Annual Review of Gerontology and Geriatric, 3,* 102–147.

Lehr, U. (2003). A model of well-being in old age and its consequences for further longitudinal studies. In J.J.F. Schroots (Ed.), *Aging, health, and competence* (pp. 293–300). Amsterdam: Elsevier.

Lehr, U., Seiler, E., & Thomae, H. (2000). Aging in a cross-cultural perspective. In A.L. Comunian, U.P. Gielen (Eds.), *International perspectives on human development* (pp. 571–589). Lengerich: Pabst.

Lennartsson, C. (1999). Social ties and health among the very old in Sweden. *Research on Aging, 21,* 657–681.

Leon, A.S., Connett, J., & the MRFIT Research Group (1991). Physical activity and 10.5 year mortality in the Multiple Risk Factor Intervention Trial (MRFIT). *International Journal of Epidemiology, 20,* 690.

Lerner, R.M. (1984). *On the nature of human plasticity.* New York: Cambridge University Press.

Leveille S., Guralnik, J.M., & Ferrucci, L. (1999). Aging successfully until death in old age: Opportunities for increasing active life expectancy. *American Journal of Epidemiology, 149,* 654–664.

Leventhal, H., & Patrick-Miller, L. (2000). Emotions and physical illness: Causes and indicators of vulnerability. In M. Lewis & J.M. Havilands-Jones (Eds.), *Handbook of emotions* (2nd ed., pp. 523–537). New York: Guilford.

Levy, B.R. (2003). Mind matters. Cognitive and physical effects of aging stereotypes. *Journal of Gerontology, Psychological and Social Sciences, 58,* P203–211.

Levy, B.R., & Langer, E. (1994). Aging free from negative stereotypes: Successful memory among the American deaf and in China. *Journal of Personality and Social Psychology, 66,* 935–943.

Levy, B.R., Slade, M.D., & Kasl, S.V. (2002). Longitudinal benefit of positive self-perceptions of aging on functioning health. *Journal of Gerontology: Psychological and Social Sciences, 57,* 1–9.

Levy, B.R., Slade, M.D., Kunkel, S.R., & Kasl, S.V. (2002). Longevity increased by positive self-perceptions of aging. *Journal of Personality and Social Psychology, 83,* 261–270.

Li, C., Zhang, M., He, Y., & Zhang, K. (2001). Impact if healthy behavior on successful aging: A 5-year follow-up study among community elderly. *Chinese Mental Health Journal, 51,* 325–326.

Liang, J., Shaw, B.A., & Krause, N.M. (2003). Changes in functional status among older adults in Japan: Successful and usual aging. *Psychology and Aging, 18,* 684–695.

LIFE Study Investigators. (2006). Effects of physical activity intervention on measures of physical performance: Results of Life styles Interventions and Independence for Elders Pilot (LIFE-P) study. *Journal of Gerontology: Biological and Medical Sciences, 61A,* 1157–1165.

Lindenberger, U., & Reischies, F.M. (1999). Limits and potentials of intellectual functioning in old age. In P.B. Baltes & K.U. Mayer (Eds.), *The Berlin aging study. Aging from 70 to 100* (pp. 329–360). Cambridge, UK: Cambridge University Press.

Litwin, H. (2005). Correlates of successful aging: Are they universal? *International Journal of Aging and Human Development, 61,* 313–333.

Litwin, H. (2007). What really matters in the social network-mortality association? A multivariate examination among older Jewish-Israelis. *European Journal of Aging, 4,* 71–82.

Lopez, M.D. (in press). Asesoramiento gerontológico [Gerontological counseling]. In R. Fernández-Ballesteros (Ed.), *Psicogerontología aplicada* [Applied geropsychology]. Madrid: Pirámide.

Lubitz, J. (2004). *Getting older, staying healthier: The demographics of health care. Testimony.* Washington, DC: US Senate.

Lubitz, J., Cai, L., Kramarow, E., & Lentzner, H. (2003). Health, life expectancy, and health care spending among the elderly. *New England Journal of Medicine, 349,* 1048–55.

Lum, T.Y., & Lightfoot, E. (2005). The effects of volunteering on physical and mental health of older people. *Research on Aging, 27,* 31–35.

Lupien, S.J., & Wan, N. (2004). Successful aging: From cell to self. *Philosophical Transaction of the Royal Society of London: Biological Sciences, 359,* 1413–1426.

Lyketsos, C.G., Chen, L.S., & Antony, J.C. (1999). Cognitive decline in adulthood: An 11.5-year follow-up of the Baltimore Epidemiological Catchments Area Study. *American Journal of Psychiatry, 156,* 58–65.

Lyubomirsky, S., King, L., & Diener, E. (2005). The benefits of frequent positive affect: Does happiness lead to success? *Psychological Bulletin, 131,* 803–855.

MacCorquodale, K., & Meehl, P.E. (1948). On a distinction between hypothetical constructs and intervening variables. *Psychological Review, 55,* 97–107.

Maes, S., & Karoly, P. (2005). Self-regulation assessment and intervention in physical health and illness: A review. *Applied Psychology, 54,* 267–299.

Magai, C., Consedine, N.S., Krivoshekova, Y.S., Kudadjie-Gyamfi, E., & McPherson, R. (2006). Emotional experience and expression across the adult lifespan: Insights from a multimodal assessment study. *Psychology and Aging, 21,* 303–317.

Maier, H., & Klumb, P.L. (2005). Social participation and survival at older ages: Is the effect driven by activity content or context? *European Journal of Ageing, 2,* 31–40.

Maier, H., & Smith, J. (1999). Psychological predictors of mortality in old age. *Journal of Gerontology, 54,* P-44–54.

Maier, S.F., Waltkins, L.R., & Fieshner, M. (1994). Psychoneuroimmunology. The interface between behavior, brain and immunity. *American Psychologist, 49,* 1004–17.

Manton, K.G. (1982). Changing concepts of morbidity and mortality in the elderly population. *Milbank Memorial Fund Quarterly. Health and Society, 60,* 183–244.

Manton, K.G. (1997). Changes in the age dependence of mortality and disability: Cohort and other determinants. *Demography, 34,* 135–157.

Manton, K.G., & Gu X. (2001). *Changes in the prevalence of chronic disability in the United States black and non-black population above age 65 from 1982 to 1999.* Proceedings of the National Academy of Sciences of United States of America, 10.1073, 111152298.

Manton, K.G., Gu, X., & Ukraintseva, S.V. (2005). Declining prevalence of dementia in the US elderly population. *Advances in Gerontology, 16,* 30–37.

Manton, K.G., Lamb, V.L., & XiLiang, G. (2007). Medicare cost effects of recent U.S. disability trends in the elderly: Future implications. *Journal of Aging and Health, 19,* 359–381.

Marcus, B.H., Dubbert, P.M., Forssyth, L.H., Stone, E.J., McKenzie, T.L., Dunn, A.L., & Blair, S.N. (2000). Physical activity behavior change. Issues in adoption and maintenance. *Health Psychology, 19*(Suppl.), 32–41.

Marin, B., & Zaidi, A. (Eds.). (2007). *Mainstreaming aging.* Vienna: European Centre, Ashgate.

Martínez-Lage, J.M. (2002). La polémica etiqueta diagnóstica de leve deterioro cognitivo en las personas mayores [The debate about the mild cognitive impairment label in the elderly]. In J. Manuel Ribera Casado & P. Gil Gregorio (Eds.), *Función mental y envejecimiento* [Mental function and aging]. Madrid: Editores Médicos, S.A.

Martínez-Lage, J.M., & Khachaturian, Z.S. (Eds.). (2001). *Alzheimer XXI: Ciencia y sociedad* [Alheimer XXI: Science and society]. Barcelona: Masson.

Mathers, C.D. (2003). Cause-deleted health expectancies. In J.M. Robine, C. Jaegger, C.D.

Mathers, E.M. Crimmins, & R.M. Suzman (Eds.), *Determining health expectancies* (pp. 149–175). West Sussex: Wiley.

Mathers, C.D., Vos, T., & Stevenson, C. (1999). *The burden of disease and injury in Australia.* Canberra: AIHW.

Matsubayashi, K., Ishine, M., Wada, T., & Okumiya, K. (2006). Older adults' view of "successful aging": Comparison of older Japanese and Americans. *Journal of American Geriatrics Society, 54,* 184–185.

Mayne, T.J. (2001). Emotions and health. In T.J. Mayne & G.A. Bonnanno (Eds.), *Emotions. Current issues and future directions* (pp. 361–397). New York: Guilford.

McAuley, L., Elavsky, S., Jerome, G.J., Konopack, J.F., & Marquez, D.X. (2005). Physical activity-related well-being in older adults: Social cognitive influences. *Psychology and Aging, 2005,* 205–302.

McConatha, J.T., & Huba, H.M. (1999). Primary and Secondary, and emotional control across adulthood. *Current Psychology: Developmental, Learning, Personality, and Social, 18,* 164–170.

McCrae, R.R. (2002). The maturation of personality psychology: Adult personality development development and psychological well-being. *Journal of Research in Personality, 36,* 81–90.

McLeod, J.D. (1996). Life events. In J. Birren (Ed.), *Encyclopedia of gerontology* (pp. 41–52). San Diego: Academic Press.

Mendes de Leon, C.F., Glass, T.A., & Berkman, L.F. (2003). Social engagement and disability in a community population of older adults. *American Journal of Epidemiology, 157,* 633–642.

Mendes de Leon, C.F. (2005). Social engagement and successful aging. *European Journal of Aging, 2,* 64–66.

Menec, V.H. (2003). The relation between everyday activities and successful aging: A 6-year longitudinal study. *Journal of Gerontology: Psychological Sciences, B58,* S74–82.

Meslé, F., & Vallin, J. (2003). Increase in life expectancy and concentration of ages at death. In J.M. Robine, C. Jaegger, C.D. Mathers, E.M. Crimmins, & R.M. Suzman (Eds.), *Determining health expectancies* (pp. 13–34). West Sussex: Wiley.

Miller, T. (2001). Increasing longevity and medicare expenditures. *Demography, 38,* 215–226.

Minkler, M. (1985). Social support and health of the elderly. In S. Cohen & S.L. Syme (Eds.), *Social support and health* (pp. 199–212). New York: Academic Press.

Moe, E.L., Elliot, D.L., Goldberg, L., Kuehl, K.S., Stevens, V.J., Breger, R.K.R. et al. (2002). Promoting health lifestyles: Alternative models' effects (PHLAME). *Health Education Research, 17,* 586–596.

Molden, D.C., & Dweck, C.S. (2006). Finding "meaning" in psychology. Lay theories approach to self-regulation, social perception, and social development. *American Psychologist, 61,* 192–203.

Montross, L.P., Depp, C., Daly, J., Reichstadt, J., Golshan, S., Moore, D. et al. (2006). Correlates of self-rated successful aging among community-dwelling older adults. *American Journal of Geriatric Psychiatry, 14,* 43–51.

Motta, M., Bennati, E., Ferlito, L., Malaguarnera, M., & Motta, L. (2005). Successful aging in centenarian: Myths and reality. *Archives of Gerontology and Geriatrics, 40,* 241–151.

Moore, A.J., & Stratton, D.C. (2002). *Resilient widowers: Older men speak for themselves.* New York: Springer.

Moos, R.H. (Ed.). (1986). *Coping with life crises. An integrated approach.* New York: Plenum.

Moos, R.H. (1981). Environmental choice and control in community care settings for older people. *Journal of Applied Social Psychology, 11,* 23–43.

Moos, R.H., & Schaffer, J.A. (1986). Life transitions and crises: A conceptual overview. In R.H. Moos (Ed.), *Coping with life crises. An integrated approach.* New York: Plenum.

Morrow-Howell, N., Hinterlog, J., Rozario, P.A., & Tang, F. (2003). Effects of volunteering on the well-being of older adults. *Journal of Gerontology: Social Sciences, 58B,* S137–145.

Motivala, S.J., Sollers, J., Thayer, J., & Irwin, M.R. (2006). Tai Chi acutely decrease sympathetic nervous system activity in older adults. *Journal of Gerontology: Medical Sciences, 61A:* 1177–1180.

Mroczek, D.K., & Kolarz, C.M. (1998). The effect of age on positive and negative affect: A developmental Perspective on Happiness. *Journal of Personality and Social Psychology, 75,* 1333–49.

Multiple Risk Factor Intervention Trial Research Group. (1982). Multiple factor intervention trial. Risk factor changes and mortality results. *Journal of American Medical Association, 248,* 1465.

Murberg, T.A., Furze, G., & Brus. E. (2003). Avoidance coping styles predict mortality among patients with congestive heart failure: A 6-year follow-up study. *Personality and Individual Differences, 36,* 575–766.

Murphy, J.M., Monson, R.R., Olivier, D.C., Sobol, A.M., & Leighton, A.H. (1987). Affective disorders and mortality. *Archives General Psychiatry, 44,* 473–480.

Murrell, S.A., Norris, F.H., & Grote, C. (1988). Life events in older adults. In L.H. Cohen (Ed.), *Life events and psychological functioning* (pp. 233–247). Newbury Park, CA: Sage.

Nelson, M.E. et al. (1994). Positive effects of weight-bearing exercise and estrogen on bone mineral density in older women. *Journal of American Medical Association, 272,* 1909.

Netz, Y., Wu, M-J. Becker, B.J., & Tenenbaum, G. (2005). Physical activity and psychological well-being in advance age: A meta-analysis of intervention studies. *Psychology and Aging, 20,* 272–284.

Neugarten, B.L. (1970). Dynamics of transition of middle age to old age: Adaptation and the life cycle. *Journal of Geriatric Psychiatry, 4,* 71–87.

Neugarten, B.L. (1977). Personality and aging. In J.L. Birren & K.W. Schaie (Eds.), *Handbook of the psychology of aging* (pp. 71–87). New York: Van Nostrand Reinhold.

Newman, A.B., Arnold, A.M., & Naydeck, B.L. (2003). "Successful aging": Effect of subclinical cardiovascular disease. *Archive Internal Medicine, 163,* 2315–2322.

Newth, S., & DeLongis, A. (2004). Individual differences, mood and coping with chronic pain in rheumatoid arthritis: A daily process analysis. *Psychology & Health, 19,* 283–305.

Noack, H. (1987). Concept of health and health promotion. In T. Abelin, Z.J. Brzezinski, & V.D.L. Carstairs (Eds.), *Measurement in health promotion and protection* (pp. 5–28). Copenhagen: World Health Organization.

Noice, H., Noice, T., & Staines, G. (2004). A sort-term intervention to enhance cognitive and affective functioning in older adults. *Journal of Aging and Health, 16,* 562–585.

Nusselder, W.J. (2003). Compression of morbidity. In J.M. Robine, C. Jaegger, C.D. Mathers, E.M. Crimmins, & R.M. Suzman (Eds.), *Determining health expectancies* (pp. 35–58). West Sussex: Wiley.

Nusselder, W.J., Looman, C.W.N., Marang-van de Mheen, P.J., van de Mheen, H., & Mackenbach, J.P. (2000). Smoking elimination produces compression of morbidity. *Journal of Epidemiology and Community Health, 54*, 566–574.

Nusselder, W.J., & Peeters, A. (2006). A. successful aging: Measuring the years lived with functional loss. *Journal of Epidemiology and Community Health, 60*, 448–455.

Nyberg, L. (2005). Cognitive training in healthy aging. In R. Cabeza, L. Nyberg, & D.C. Park.(Eds.), *Cognitive neuroscience of aging* (pp. 309–324). New York: Oxford University Press.

Olazarán, J., Muñiz, R., & Reisberg, B. (2004). Benefits of cognitive-motor intervention in MCI and mild to moderate Alzheimer Disease. *Neurology, 63*, 2348–2353.

Olshansky, S.J., Carnes, B.A., & Desesquelles, A. (2001). Prospects of human longevity. *Science, 291*(5508), 1491–1492.

Oman, D., Thorensen, C.E., & McMahon, K. (1999). Volunteerism and mortality among the community-dwelling elderly. *Journal of Health Psychology, 4*, 301–316.

Orrell, M.W., & Davis, A.D.M. (1994). Live events in the elderly. *International Review of Psychiatry, 6*, 59.

Ory, M.G., Jordanb, P.J., & Bazzarre, T.(2002). The Behavior Change Consortium: Setting the stage for a new century of health behavior-change research. *Health Education Research, 17*, 500–511.

Osler, M., Anderson A.M., Due, P., Lund, R., Damsgaards, M.T., & Holstein, B.E. (2003). Socioeconomic position in early life, birth weight, childhood cognitive function and adult mortality. A longitudinal study of Danish men born in 1953. *Journal of Epidemiology and Health, 57*, 681–686.

Ostir, G.V., Markides, K.S., Black, S.A., & Goodwin, J.S. (2002). Emotional well-being predict subsequent functional independence and survival. *Journal of American Geriatrics Society, 48*, 473–478.

Ostir, G.V., Ottenbacher, K.J., & Markides, K.S. (2004). Onset of frailty in older adults and the protective role of positive affect. *Psychology and Aging, 19*, 402–408.

Pahor, M. Blair, S., Espeland, M., Fielding, R., Gill, T., Guralnik, J. et al. (2006). Effects of a physical activity intervention on measures of physical performance: Results of the Lifestyle Interventions and Independence for Elders Pilot (LIFE-P) Study. *Journal of Gerontology: Biological and Medical Sciences, 61A*, M1157–M1165.

Palmore E (1979). Predictors of successful aging. *The Gerontologist, 19*, 427–431.

Park, D.C., Polk, T., Mikels, J.A., Taylor, S.F., & Marzhuetz, C. (2001). Cerebral aging: Integration of brain and behavioral models of cognitive function. *Dialog of Clinical Neurosciences, 3*, 151–164.

Park, D.C., Gutchess, A.H., Meade, M.L., & Stine-Morrow, E.A.L. (2007). Improving cognitive function in older adults: Nontraditional approaches. *Journal of Gerontology: Psychological Sciences, 62B*, 45–52.

Peel, N.M., McClure, R.J., & Bartlett, H.P.(2005). Behavioral determinants of health aging. *American Journal of Prevention Medicine, 28*, 298–304.

Penley, J.A., Tomaka, J., & Wiebe, J.S. (2002). The association of coping to physical and psychological health outcomes: A meta-analytic review. *Journal of Behavioral Medicine, 25*, 551–603.

Pennix, B.W., Guralink, J.M., Ferucci, L., Simonsick, E.M., Deeg, D.J.H., & Wallance R.B. (1998). Depressive symptoms and physical decline in community-dwelling older persons. *Journal of American Medical Association, 279,* 1720–26.

Peres, K., Jagger, C., Lievre, A., & Barberger-Gateau, P. (2005). Disability-free life expectancy of older French people: Gender and education differentials from the PAQUID cohort. *European Journal of Ageing, 2,* 225–233.

Perry, D. (1995). Researching the aging well process. *American Behavioral Scientist, 39,* 152–171.

Petersen, R.C. (2001). Marcadores neuropsicológicos del deterioro cognitivo ligero en la fase inicial de la enfermedad de Alzheimer. In J.M. Martínez Lage & Z.S. Khachaturian (Eds.), *Alzheimer XXI: Ciencia y Sociedad.* Barcelona: Masson.

Peterson, C., & Stunkard, A.J. (1989). Personal control and health promotion. *Social Science and Medicine, 28,* 819–28.

Peterson, C. (1999). Personal control and well-being. In D. Kahnneman, E. Diener, & N. Schwarz (Eds.), *Well-being: The foundation of hedonic psychology* (pp. 288–301). New York: Sage Foundation.

Peterson, C., Seligman, M.E.P., Yurko, K.H., Martin, L.R., & Friedman, H.S. (1998). Causal explanation as a risk factor for depression: Theory and evidence. *Psychological Review, 91,* 347–74.

Peterson. C., Seligman, M.E., & Vaillant, G.E. (1988). Pessimistic explanatory style is a risk factor for physical illness. A thirty five year longitudinal study. *Journal of Personality and Social Psychology, 55,* 23–27.

Pfeiffer, E., & Pfeiffer, L.A. (1975). A short portable, mental status questionnaire for the measurement of organic brain deficit in elderly patients. *Journal of American Geriatric Society, 23,* 433–441.

Phelan, E.A., Anderson, L.A., Lacroix, A.-Z., & Larson, E.B. (2004). Older adults's views of "successful aging". How do they compare with researcher's definitions? *Journal of American Geriatric Society, 52,* 211–16.

Plomin, R., & Thompson, L. (1986). Life-span developmental behavior genetics. In P.B. Baltes, D.L. Featherman, & R.M. Lerner (Eds.), *Life-span development and behavior* (Vol. 8, pp. 1–31). Hillsdale, NJ: Erlbaum.

Podewils, L.J., Guallar, E., Kuller, L.M., Fried, L.P., Lopez, O.L., & Carlson, M. (2005). Physical activity, APOE genotype, and dementia risk: Finding from the Cardiovascular Health Cognition Study. *American Journal of Epidemiology, 161,* 639–51.

Podewils, L.J., & Guallar, E. (2006). Mens sana in corpore sano. *Annals in Medicine, 144,* 135–136.

Ponzo, Z. (1992). Promoting successful aging: Problems, opportunities, and counseling guidelines. *Journal of Counseling and Development, 71,* 210–213.

Pressman, S.D., & Cohen, S. (2005). Does positive affect influence health? *Psychological Bulletin, 131,* 925–971.

Puggaard, L., Larsen, J.B., Stovring, H., & Jeune, B. (2000). Maximal oxygen uptake, muscle strength and walking speed in 85-year-old women: Effects of increased physical activity. *Aging, 12,* 180–189.

Pushkar, D., Arbuckle, T., Rousseau, F.L., & Bourque, P. (2003). Réussir sa viellesse: La vision des aînés [Successful aging: The eye of the beholder]. *Revuew Québécoise de Psychologie, 24,* 155–174.

Quayhagen, M.P., Quayhagen, M., & Czaja, S.J. (2000). Coping with dementia: Evaluation of four nonpharmacological interventions. *International Psychogeriatric, 12*, 249–265.

Ramamurti, P.V., Jamuna, D., & Reddy, L.K. (1992). Improving human resources among the elderly: Effects of an intervention. *Journal of Personality and Clinical Studies, 8*, 77–79.

RAND. (2002). *Evidence report and evidence-based recommendations: Health risk appraisal and medicare.* Washington, DC: Department of Health and Human Services.

Raz, N., & Rodriguez, K.M. (2006). Differential aging of the brain: Patterns, cognitive correlates and modifiers. *Neuroscience and Biobehavioral Reviews, 30*, 730–748.

Rardak, Z., Kaneko, T., Tahara, S., Nakamoto, H., Pucsok, J., Sasvari, M. et al. (2001). Regular exercise improves cognitive function and decreases oxidative damage in rat brain. *Neurochemistry International, 38*, 17–23.

Rebok, G.W., & Balcerak, L.J. (1989). Memory self-efficacy and performance differences in young and old adults. *Developmental Psychology, 25*, 714–721.

Rebok, G.W., Carlson, M.C., & Langbaum, J.B.S. (2007). Training and maintaining memory abilities in healthy older adults: Traditional and novel approaches. *Journal of Gerontology, 62B*, 53–61.

Reed, D.M., Foley, D.J., White, L.R., Heimovitz, H., Burchfield, C.M., & Masaki, K. (1998). Predictors of healthy aging in men with high life expectancies. *American Journal of Public Health, 88*, 1463–1467.

Reis, A., & Castro-Caldas, A. (1997). Illiteracy: A cause for biased cognitive development. *Journal of International Neuropsychological Society, 3*, 444–450.

Renaud S., Lorgeril, M., Delaye, J., Guidollet, J., Jacquard, F., Mamelle, N. et al. (1995). Cretan Mediterranean diet for prevention of coronary heart disease. *American Journal of Clinical Nutrition, 61*(Supplement), 1360S–7S.

Richards, M., & Sacker, A. (2003). Lifetime antecedents of cognitive reserve. *Journal of Clinical and Experimental Neuropsychology, 25*, 614–624.

Riediger, M., Li, S.C., & Lindenberger, U. (2006). Selective optimization with compensation as developmental mechanisms of adaptive resources allocation: Review and preview. In J.E. Birren & K.W. Schaie (Eds.), *Handbook of the psychology of aging. 6th edition* (pp. 289–315). New York: Academic Press.

Roberts, B.W., & Del Vecchio, W.F. (2000). The rank-order consistency of personality traits from childhood to old age: A quantitative review of longitudinal studies. *Psychological Bulletin, 126*, 3–25.

Roberts, B.W., Walton, K.E., & Bogg, T. (2005). Conscientiousness and health across the life course. *Review of General Psychology, 9*, 156–168.

Roberts, S.B., & Hays, N.P. (1998). Older people. Nutritional requirements. In M.J. Sadler, J.J. Strain, & B. Caballero (Eds.), *Encyclopedia of human nutrition* (Vol. III, pp. 1–4). London: Academic Press.

Robine, J.M. (2001). Redefining the stages of the epidemiological transition by a study of the dispersion of lifespans: The case of France. *Population, An English Selection, 23*, 173–194.

Robine, J.M. (2003). Life course, environmental change, and lifespan. *Population Development Review, 29*(Supplement), 229–238.

Robine, J.M., Mormiche, P., & Sermet, C. (1998). Examination of the causes and mechanisms of the increase in disability-free life expectancy. *Journal of Aging and Health, 10,* 171–191.

Robine, J.M., Jaegger, C. Mathers, C.D., Crimmins, E.M., & Suzman, R.M. (Eds.). (2003). *Determining health expectancies.* West Sussex: Wiley.

Robine, J.M., & Michel, J.P. (2004). Looking forward to a general theory on population aging. *Journal of Gerontology: Biological Sciences, 59A,* 590–597.

Rodin, J. (1986). Aging and health: Effects of the sense of control. *Science, 233,* 1272–1276.

Rodin, J., Timko, C., & Harris, S. (1977). The construct of control: Biological and psychological correlates. In M.P. Lawton & G.L. Maddoz (Eds.), *Annual review of gerontology and geriatrics* (Vol. 5, (pp. 80–96). New York: Springer.

Roff., L.L., & Atherton, C.R. (1990). *Promoting successful aging.* Chicago: Nelson Hall.

Rosen, W.G., Mohs, R.C., & Davis, K.L. (1984). A new rating scale for Alzheimer's disease. *American Journal of Psychiatry, 11,* 1356–1364.

Rosenzweig, M.R., & Bennett, E.L. (1996). Psychobiology and plasticity: Effects of training and experience on brain and behavior. *Behavioral Brain Research, 78,* 57–65.

Ross, N.P., & Havens, B. (1991). Predictors of successful aging: A 12-year study of Manitoba elderly. *American Journal of Public Health, 81,* 63–68.

Rothermund, K., & Brandstadter, J. (2003). Coping with deficits and losses in later life: From compensatory action to accommodation. *Psychology of Aging, 18,* 896–905.

Rowe, J.W., & Khan, R.L. (1987). Human aging: Usual and successful. *Science, 237,* 143–149.

Rowe, J.W., & Khan, R.L. (1997). Successful aging. *The Gerontologist, 37,* 433–440.

Rowe, J.W., & Khan, R.L. (1998). *Successful aging.* New York: Random House.

Rozanski, A., Blumental, J.A., & Kaplan, J. (1999). Impact of psychological factor on the pathogenesis of cardiovascular disease and implications for therapy. *Circulation, 99,* 2192–2217.

Ryff, C.D. (1989a). Beyond Ponce de Leon and life satisfaction: New directions in quest of successful aging. *International Journal of Behavioral Development, 12,* 35–55.

Ryff, C.D. (1989b). In the eye of the beholder: Views of psychological well-being among middle-aged and older adults. *Psychology and Aging, 4,* 195–210.

Ryff, C., & Singer, B. (2003). The role of emotion on pathways to positive health. In R. Davidson, K. Scherer, & H. Goldsmith (Eds.), *Handbook of affective sciences* (pp. 1083–1104). New York: Oxford University Press.

Rudinger, G., & Thomae, H. (1990). The Bonn longitudinal study of aging: Coping, life adjustment and life satisfaction. In P.B. Baltes & M.M.Baltes (Eds.), *Successful aging* (pp. 265–295). Cambridge UK: Cambridge University Press.

Ruiz, B.A., Dibble, S.L., & Gillis, C.L., & Gortner, S.R. (1992). Predictors of general activity 8 weeks after cardiac surgery. *Applied Nursing Research, 5,* 59–65.

Rutter, M. (1987). Psychosocial resilience and protective mechanisms. *American Journal of Orthopsychiatry, 57,* 316–331.

Saczynski, J.S., Willis, S.L., & Schaie, K.W. (2002). Strategy use in reasoning training with older adults. *Aging, Neuropsychology and Cognition, 9,* 48–60.

Saczynski, J.S., Pfeifer, L.A., Masaki, K., Korf, E.S., Laurun, D., White, L. et al. (2006). The effect of social engagement on incident dementia. *American Journal of Epidemiology, 163,* 433–440.

Salmon, P. (2001). Effects of physical exercise on anxiety, depression, and sensitivity to stress: A unified theory. *Clinical Psychology Review, 21,* 33–61.

Salovey, P., Rothman, A.J., Detweiler, J.B., & Steward, W.T. (2000). Emotional states and physical health. *American Psychologist, 55,* 110–121.

Salthouse, T.A. (1996). Speed mediation of adult age differences in cognition. *Developmental Psychology, 29,* 722–738.

Salthouse, T.A. (2006). Mental exercise and mental aging. *Perspectives on Psychological Science, 1,* 68–79.

Salthouse, T.A., Babcock, R.L., & Miles, M. (2002). The role of cognitive stimulation on the relations between age and cognitive functioning. *Psychology and Aging, 17,* 548–557.

Savaskan, E. Olivieri, G., Meier, F., Seifritz, E. Wirz-Justice, A., & Muller-Spahn, F. (2003). Red wine ingredient resveratrol protects from beta-amyloid neurotoxicity. *Gerontology, 49,* B280–B283.

Scalf, P.E., Colcombe, S.J., McCarley, J.S., Erickson, K.I., Alvarado, M., Kim, J.S., Wadhwa, R.P., & Kramer, A.F. (2007). The neural correlates of and expanded functional field of view. *Journal of Gerontology: Psychological Sciences, 62B,* 32–44.

Scarmeas, N., Levy, G., Tang, M.-X, Manly, J., & Stern, Y. (2001). Influence of leisure activity on the incidence of Alzheimer's disease. *Neurology, 57,* 2236–2242.

Schaie, K.W. (1990a). Late-life potential and cohort differences. In M. Perlmutter (Ed.), *Late life potential* (pp. 43–62). Washington, DC: Gerontological Society of America.

Schaie, K.W. (1990b). Optimization of cognitive functioning: Predictions based on cohort-sequential and longitudinal data. In P.B. Baltes & M.M. Baltes (Eds.), *Successful aging: Perspectives from the behavioral sciences* (pp. 94–117). Cambridge, UK: Cambridge University Press.

Schaie KW. (1996). *Intellectual development in adulthood: The Seattle longitudinal study.* New York: Cambridge University Press.

Schaie, K.W. (2005a). *Developmental influences on adult intelligence: The Seattle longitudinal study.* New York: Oxford University Press.

Schaie, K.W. (2005b). What can we learn from longitudinal studies of adult development? *Research on Human Development, 2,* 133–158.

Schaie, K.W., & Willis, S.L. (1986). Can decline in adult intellectual functioning be reversed? *Developmental Psychology, 22,* 223–232.

Scheidt, R.J., Humphreys, D.R., & Yorgason, J.B. (1999). Successful aging: What's not like? *Journal Applied Gerontology, 18,* 277–282.

Scheider, M.F., Weintraub, J.K., & Carver, C.S. (1986). Coping with stress: Divergent strategies of optimists and pessimists. *Journal of Personality and Social Psychology, 51,* 1257–1264.

Schoenback, V.J., Kaplan, B.H., Fredman, L., & Kleinbaum, D.G. (1986). Social ties and mortality in Evans County, Georgia. *American Journal Epidemiology, 123,* 577–501.

Schoenfeld, D.E., Malmrose, L.C., Blazer, D.G., Gold, D.T. (1994). Self-rated health and mortality in the high-functioning elderly: A closer look at healthy individuals: MacArthur Field Study of Successful Aging. *Journal of Gerontology: Medical Sciences, 49M,* 109–115.

Schooler, C., & Mulatu, M.S. (2001). The reciprocal effects of leisure time activities and intellectual functioning in older people: A longitudinal analysis. *Psychology and Aging, 16,* 466–482.

Schroots, J.J.F. (1995). Psychological models of aging. *Canadian Journal of Aging, 14,* 40–44.

Schulz, R., & Heckhausen, J. (1996). A life model of successful aging. *American Psychologist, 51,* 702–714.

Seals, D.R., Hagberg, J.M., Hurley, B.F., Ehsani, A.A., & Holloszy, J.O. (1984). Effects of endurance training on glucose tolerance and plasma lipid levels in older men and women. *Journal of American Medical Association, 252,* 654.

Seeman, T.E., Kaplan, G.A., Knudsen, L., Cohen, R., & Guralnik, J.M. (1987). Social network ties and mortality among tile elderly in the ALAMEDA County Study. *American Journal of Epidemiology, 126,* 714–723.

Seeman, T.E., Charpentier, P.A., Bekman, L.F., & Tinetti, M.E. (1994). Predicting changes in physical performance in high-functioning elderly cohort: MacArthur studies of successful aging. *Journal of Gerontology: Biological and Medical Sciences, 49,* M97–M108.

Seeman, T.E., Berkman, L.F., Charpentier, P.A., Blazer, D.G., Albert, M.S., & Tinetti, M.E. (1995). Behavioral and psychosocial predictors of physical performance: Mac Arthur studies of successful aging. *Journal of Gerontology: Biological and Medical, 50,* M177–M183.

Seeman, T., McAvay, G. Merrill, S., Albert, M., & Rodin, J. (1996a). Self-efficacy beliefs and change in cognitive performance: Mac Arthur studies of successful aging. *Psychology and Aging, 11,* 538–551.

Seeman, T.E., Bruce, M.L., & McAvay, G. (1996b). Social network characteristics and onset of ADL disability: MacArthur Studies of Successful Aging. *Journal of Gerontology: Psychological Sciences, 51,* S191–200.

Seeman, T.E., McEwen, B.S., Singer, B.H., Albert, M.S., & Rowe, J.W. (1997a). Increase in urinary cortisol excretion and memory declines: MacArthur studies of successful aging. *Journal Clinical Endocrinology Metabolic, 82,* 2458–2465.

Seeman, T.E. Singer, B.H., Rowe, J.W., Horwitz, R.I., & McEwen, B.S. (1997b). Price of adaptation: Allostatic load and its health consequences. *Archives of Internal Medicine, 157,* 2259–2268.

Seeman, T.E., McEwen, B.S., Rowe, J.W., & Singer, B.H. (2001). Allostatic load as a marker of cumulative biological risk: MacArthur studies of successful aging. *Proceeding National Academy Science USA, 98,* 4770–4775.

Seeman, T.E., Lusignolo, T.M., Albert, M., & Merkman, L. (2001). Social relationships, social support, and patterns of cognitive aging in healthy, high-functioning older adults: MacArthur Studies of Successful Aging. *Health Psychology, 20,* 243–255.

Segerstrom, S.C. (2001). Optimism, goal conflict, and stressor-related immune change. *Journal of Behavioral Medicine, 24,* 441–467.

Segerstrom, S.C., & Miller, G.E. (2004). Psychological stress and the human immune system: A meta-analytic study of 30 years of inquiry. *Psychological Bulletin, 130,* 601–630.

Seligman, M.E.P., Steen, T.A., Park, N., & Peterson, C. (2005). Positive psychology progress: Empirical validation of interventions. *American Psychologist, 60,* 410–21.

Serra-Majem, L., Bertmomeu, I., & Bach, A. (2007). La dieta mediterranea: Una sinópsis [Mediterranean diet: A synthesis]. *Alimentación, Nutrición y Salud, 14,* 76–80.

Shaw, L.J., Krause, N.M., Vlaum, B., Kobayashi, E., Fukaya, T., Sugihara, Y. et al. (2003). Changes in functional status among older adults in Japan: Successful and usual aging. *Psychology and Aging, 18,* 684–95.

Sherman, F.T.(1997). Exercise at midlife. How and why to prescribe it for sedentary patients. *Geriatrics, 52,* 71–80.

Siegrist, J. Knesebeck, O., & Pollack, C.E. (2004). Social productivity and well-being of older people. A sociological exploration. *Social Theory and Health, 2,* 243–263.

Singer, T., Lindenberger, U., & Baltes P.B. (2003). Plasticity of memory for new learning in very old age: A story of major loss? *Psychology and Aging, 18,* 306–317.

Skinner, E.A. (1995). *Perceived control, motivation, and coping.* Thousand Oaks, CA: Sage.

Smith, J., & Baltes P.B. (1999). Trends and profiles of psychological functioning in very old age. In P.B. Baltes & K.U. Mayer (Eds.), *The Berlin aging study: Aging from 70 to 100* (pp. 197–226). New York: Cambridge University Press.

Snow, L., & Pan, C.X. (2004). How physicians think about successful aging? *Annals Internal Medicine, 140,* 137.

Snowdon, D.A. (2003). Healthy aging and dementia: Findings from the Nun Study. *Annals Internal Medicine, 139,* 450–54.

Solinge, H. van, & Henkens, K. (2007). Involuntary retirement: The role of restrictive circumstances, timing, and social embeddedness. *Journal of Gerontology, 62B,* S295–304.

Spector, A., Orrell, M., Davies, S., & Woods, B. (2001). Can reality orientation be rehabilitated? Development and piloting of an evidence-based program of cognition-based therapies for people with dementia. *Neuropsychological Rehabilitation, 11,* 377–397.

Spector, A., Thorgrimsen, I., Woods, B., Royan, L., Davies, S., Butterwoeth, M. et al. (2003). Efficacy of an evidence-based cognitive stimulation therapy program for people with dementia. *British Journal of Psychiatry, 183,* 248–254.

Staats, A.W. (1971). *Child learning, intelligence, and personality.* New York: Harper & Row.

Staats, A.W. (1975). *Social behaviorism.* New York: Dorsey.

Staats, A.W. (1996). *Personality and behavior.* New York: Springer.

Stanton, A.L., Danoff-Burg, S., Cameron, C.L., Bisho, M., Collins, C.S., Kirk, S.B., Sworowski, L.A., & Twilman, R. (2000). Emotionally expressive coping predicts psychological and physical adjustment to breast cancer. *Journal of Consulting and Clinical Psychology, 12,* 16–23.

Staudinger, U., Freund, A.M., Linden, M., & Maas, I. (1999). Personality and life regulation: Facets of psychological resilience in old age. In P.B. Baltes & K.L. Mayer (Eds.), *The Berlin aging study. Aging from 70 to 100* (pp. 302–328). Cambridge, UK. Cambridge University Press.

Stearns, S.C., Bernard, S.L., Fasick, S.B., Schwartz, R., Ory, M.G., & DeFriese, G.H. (2000). The economic implications of self-care: The effect of lifestyle, functional adaptations, and medical self-care among a national sample of Medicare beneficiaries. *American Journal of Public Health, 90,* 1608–1612.

Steel, K. (1997). Editorial research on aging. An agenda for all nations individually and collectively. *Journal of American Medical Association, 278,* 1374–1375.

Steen, B. (2000). Preventive nutrition in old age: A review. *Journal of Nutrition Health and Aging, 4,* 114–119.

Stek, M.L., Vinkers, D.J., Gussekloo, J., Beekman, A.T.F., van der Mast, R.C., & Westendorp, R.G.J. (2005). Is depression in old age fatal only when people feel lonely? *American Journal of Psychiatry, 162,* 178–80.

Stern, Y. (2003). The concept of cognitive reserve: A catalyst for research. *Journal of Clinical and Experimental Neuropsychology, 25,* 589–93.

Sternberg, R.J. (1990). *Metaphors of mind.* New York: Cambridge University Press.

Stine-Morrow, E.A.L., Parisi, J.M., Morrow, D.G., Greene, J., & Park, D.C. (2007). An engagement model of cognitive optimization through adulthood. *Journal of Gerontology: Psychological Sciences, 62B,* 62–69.

Stowell, J.R., Kiecolt-Glaser, J.K., & Glaser, R. (2001). Perceived Stress and cellular immunity: When doping count. *Journal of Behavioral Medicine, 24,* 323–339.

Strawbridge, W.J., Cohen, R.D., & Shema, S.J. (1996). Successful aging: Predictors and associated activities. *American Journal of Epidemiology, 144,* 135–141.

Strawbridge, W.L. (2002). Successful aging and well-being: Self-reports compare with Rowe & Khan. *The Gerontologist, 42,* 727–733.

Sturman, M.T., Morris, M.C., Mendes de Leon, C.F., Bienias, R.S. Wilson, R.S., & Evans, D.A. (2005). Physical activity, cognitive activity, and cognitive decline in a biracial community population. *Archives in Neurology, 62,* 1750–1754.

Sulander T., Helakorpi S., Rahkonen O., Nissinen A., & Uutela A. (2003). Changes and associations in healthy diet among the Finnish elderly, 1985–2001. *Age and Ageing, 32,* 394–404.

Sunquist, K., Qvist, J. Sunquist, J., & Johansson, S.E. (2004). Frequent and occasional physical activity in the elderly: A 12-year follow-up, study of mortality. *American Journal of Preventive Medicine, 27,* 22–27.

Svensson, T., Dhlin, O. Hagberg, B., & Samuelsson, G. (1993). The Lund 80+ study: Some general findings. In J.J.F. Schroots (Ed.), *Aging, health and competence* (pp. 345–356). Amsterdam: Elsevier.

Syme, S.L. (2003). Psychosocial interventions to improve successful aging. *Annals Internal Medicine, 139,* 400–402.

Tárraga, L. (1994). Cognitive psychostimulation: A non-pharmacological therapeutic strategy in Alzheimer's Disease. In M. Selmes, J. Selmes, A. Portera, & A. Toledano (Eds.), *3rd annual meeting Alzheimer Europe updating of Alzheimer's disease.* Madrid: TG Forma.

Tárraga, L., Boada, M., Modinos, G., Espinosa, A., Diego, S., Morera, A. et al. (2006). A randomized pilot study to assess the efficacy o fan interactive, multimedia tool of cognitive stimulation in Alzheimer's disease. *Journal of Neurology and Neurosurgery Psychiatry, 77,* 1116–1121.

Tate, R.B., Lah, L., & Cuddy, E. (2003). Definition of successful aging by elderly canadian males: The Manitoba follow-up study. *The Gerontologist, 43,* 735–744.

Taylor, S.E., Kemeny, M.E., Reed, G.M., Bowers, J.E., & Gruenewald, T.L. (2000). Psychological resources, positive illusions and health. *American psychologist, 55,* 99–109.

Tedeschi, R.G., & Calhoun, L.G. (2004). Posttraumatic growth: Conceptual foundations and empirical evidence. *Psychological Inquiry, 15,* 1–18.

Thomae, H. (Ed.). (1975). *Patterns of aging: Findings from the Bonn Longitudinal Study of Aging.* Basel: Karger.

Timko, C., & Moos, R.H. (1989). Choice, control and adaptation among elderly residents of sheltered care settings. *Journal of Applied Social Psychology, 19,* 636–655.

Tinetti, M.E., Baker, D.I., McAvay, G., Claus, E.B., Garrett, P., Gottschalk, M. et al. (1994). A multifactorial intervention to reduce the risk of falling among the elderly people living in the community. *New England Journal of Medicine, 331,* 821–827.

Toobert, D.J. Strycker, L.A., Glasgow, R.E., Barrera, M., & Bagdale, J.D. (2002). Enhancing support for health behavior change among women at risk for heart disease. The Mediterranean lifestyle trial. *Health Education Research, 17,* 574–585.

Trichopoulou, A., Kouris-Blazos, A., Vassilakou, T., Gnardellis, C., Polychronopoulos, E., Venizelos, M. et al. (1995). Diet and survival of elderly Greeks: A link to the past. *American Journal of Clinical Nutrition, 61*(Supplement), 1346S–50S.

Trichopoulou, A., Costacou, T., Barnia, C., & Trichopoulos, D. (2003). Adherence to a Mediterranean diet and survival in a Greek population. *The New England Journal of Medicine, 348,* 2599–2608.

Turk, C., & Turk, S. (2005). Viewing injustice. Greater emotion heterogeneity with age. *Psychology and Aging, 20,* 159–164.

Turk, S., & Piazza, J.R. (2007). Memories of social interactions: Age differences in emotional intensity. *Psychology and Aging, 22,* 300–309.

UNECE. (2003). *Aging populations. Opportunities and challenges for Europe and North America.* Geneva: Author.

UN. (2002). *Madrid international plan of action on aging.* New York: Author.

United States of America. (2006). *Bureau of the Census, International data base.* Washington, DC: USA Pub.

Uotinen, V., Suutama, T., & Ruoppila, I. (2003). Age identification in the framework of successful aging. A study of older Finnish people. *International Journal of Aging and Human Development, 56,* 173–195.

Vaillant, G.E. (2002). *Aging well: Surprising guideposts to a happier life from the Landmark Harvard Study of Adult Development.* Boston: Little Brown.

Vaillant, G.E., & Vaillant, C.O. (1990). Natural history of male psychological health: XII. A 45-year study of predictors of successful aging at age of 65. *American Journal of Psychiatry, 147,* 31–37.

Vaillant, G.E., & Mukamal, K. (2001). Successful aging. *American Journal of Psychiatry, 158,* 839–847.

Valentijn, S.A.M., Hill, R.D., Van Hooren, S.A.H., Bosma, H., Van Boxel, M.P.J., Jolles, J. et al. (2006). Memory self-efficacy predicts memory performance: Results from a 6-year follow-up study. *Psychology and Aging, 21,* 165–172.

Van Elderen, T., Maes, S., & Dusseldorp, E. (1999). Coping with coronary heart disease: A longitudinal study. *Journal of Psychosomatic Research, 47,* 175–183.

Van Gelder, Tijhuis, M.A.R., Kalmijn, S., Giampaoli, S., Nissinen, A., & Kromhout, D. (2004). Physical activity in relation to cognitive decline in elderly men. *Neurology, 63,* 2316–21.

Van Kraayenoord, C. (2006). Editorial: Adulthood, aging and those with disabilities: Starting early with education. *International Journal of Disability, Development, and Education, 53,* 283–285.

Vaupel, J.W., & Jeune, B. (1995). The emergence and proliferation of centenarians. In B. Jeune & J.W. Vaupel (Eds.), *Exceptional longevity: From prehistory to the present* (pp. 11–24). Odense: Odense University Press.

Vaupel, J.W., Carey, J.P., Christensen, K., Johnson, T.E., Yashin, A.I., Holm, N.V. et al. (1998). Biodemographic trajectories of longevity. *Science, 280,* 855–840.

Vázquez, C. Hernangómez, L., & Hervás, G. (2003). Longevidad y emociones positivas [Longevity and positive emotions]. In L. Salvador-Carulla, A. Cano, & J.R. Cabo-Soler (Eds.), *Longevidad* [Longevity] (pp. 753–761). Madrid: Panamericana.

Verghese, J., Lipton, R.B., Katz, M.J., Hall, C.B., Derby, C.A., Kuslansky, G., Ambrose, A.F., Sliwinski, M., & Buschke, H. (2003). Leisure activities and the risk of dementia in the elderly. *New England Journal of Medicine, 348,* 2508–2516.

Verhaeghen, P., & Marcoen, A., & Grossens, L. (1993). Improving memory performance in the aged through mnemonic training. A meta-analytic study. *Psychology and Ageing, 7,* 242–251.

Verhaeghen, P. (2000). The interplay of growth and decline. Theoretical and empirical aspects of plasticity of intellectual and memory performance in normal old age. In R.D. Hill, L. Backman, & A.S. Neely (Eds.), *Cognitive rehabilitation in old age* (pp. 3–23). Oxford: Oxford University Press.

Verhaeghen, P. (2003). Aging and vocabulary scores. A meta-analysis. *Psychology and Aging, 18,* 332–336.

Vitaliano, P.P., Russo, J., & Niaura, R. (1995a). Plasma lipid and their relationships with psychosocial factors in older adults. *Journal of Gerontology: Psychological Sciences, 50,* P18–P24.

Vitaliano, P.P., Russo, J., Paulsen, V.M., & Bailey S.L. (1995b). Cardiovascular recovery from laboratory stress: Biopsychosocial concomitants in older adults. *Journal of Psychosomatic Research, 42,* 361–377.

Von Faber, M., Van der Wield, A.B., Van Excel, E., Gussekloo, J., Lagaay, A.M., Van Dongen, E.V. et al. (2001). Successful aging in the oldest old. *Archives of Internal Medicine, 161,* 2694–2700.

Wagner, M., Schütze, Y., & Land, F.R. (1999). Social relationships in old age. In P.B. Baltes & K.U. Mayer (Eds.), *The Berlin aging study: Aging from 70 to 100.* Cambridge, UK: Cambridge University Press.

Walker, A. (2005). A European perspective on quality of life in old age. *European Journal of Ageing, 2,* 2–12.

Wang, B.W., Ramey, D.R., Schettler, J.D., Hubert, H.B., & Fries, J.F. (2002). Postponed development of disability in elderly runners: A 13-year longitudinal study. *Archive of Internal Medicine, 162,* 2285–94.

Wang, H.X., Karp, A., Winbland, B., & Fratiglioni, L. (2002). Late-life engagement in social and leisure activities is associated with decrease risk of dementia: A longitudinal study from Kungsholmen project. *American Journal Epidemiology, 155,* 1081–1087.

Wang, H.X., Zhou, D.H.D., Li, J., Zhang, M., Demg, J., Tang, M. et al. (2006). Leisure activity and risk of cognitive impairment: The Chongqing aging study. *Neurology, 66,* 911–913.

Weiss, A., & Costa, P.T. (2005). Domain and facet personality predictors of all-cause mortality among medicare patients aged 65 to 100. *Psychosomatic Medicine, 67,* 724–733.

Weiss, A., Costa, P.T., Karuza, J., Duberstein, P.R., Friedam, B., & McCrae, R.R. (2005). Cross-sectional age differences in personality among medicare patients aged 65 to 100. *Psychology and Aging, 20,* 182–185.

Weissberg, R.P., Kumpfer, K.L., & Seligman, M.E.P. (2003). Prevention that works for children and youth. *American Psychologist, 58,* 425–432.

Welsh, K.A., Butters, N., Hughes, J.P., Mohs, R.C., & Heyman, A. (1992). Detection and staging of dementia Alzheimer's Disease. *Archive of Neurology, 49,* 448–452.

WHO. (1990a). *Diet, nutrition and the prevention of chronic diseases* Geneva: Author.

WHO. (1990b). *Healthy aging.* Geneva: Author.

WHO. (1997). The World Health Organization issues guidelines for promoting physical activity among older persons. *Journal of Aging and Physical Activity, 5,* 1–8.

WHO. (1999). *Making a difference.* Geneva: Author.

WHO. (2001). *Health and aging. A discussion paper.* Geneva: Author.

WHO. (2002). *Active aging. A policy framework.* Geneva: Author.

WHO. (2003). *The world health report 2002.* Geneva: Author.

WHO. (2004). *Changing history,* Geneva: Author.

Whooley, M.A., & Browners, W.S. (1998). Association between depressive symptoms and mortality in older women. Study of Osteoporotic Fractures Research Group. *Archive Internal Medicine, 138,* 129–35.

Whitebourne, S.K. (1985). *The aging body.* New York: Springer.

Whitebourne, S.K. (2005). Successful aging: Introductory perspectives. *Research and Human Development, 2,* 99–102.

Williams, R.H., & Witths, G.G. (1965). *Lives through the years: Styles of life and successful aging.* New York: Atherton.

Willigen, M.V. (2000). Differential benefits of volunteering across the life course. *Journal of Gerontology: Psychological and Social Sciences, 55,* S308–318.

Willis, L., Goodwin, J., Lee, K.O., Mosqueda, L., Garry, P., Liu, P. et al. (1997). Impact of psychosocial factors on health outcomes in the elderly. *Journal of Aging, 9,* 396–414.

Willis, S.L., & Nesselroade, C.S. (1990). Long-term effects of fluid ability training in old-old age. *Developmental Psychology, 26,* 905–910.

Wilson, R., Mendes de Leon, C.F., Barnes, L.L., Schneider, J.A., Bienias, J.L., Evans, D.A. et al. (2002). Participation in cognitively stimulating activities and risk of incident AD. *Journal of American Medical Association, 287,* 742–748.

Wilson, R.S., Bennett, D.A., Bienias, J.L., Mendes de leon, C.F., Morris, M.C., & Evans, D.A. (2003). Cognitive activity and cognitive decline in a biracial community population. *Neurology, 61,* 812–816.

Wilson, R.S., Krueger, K.R., Gu, L., Bienias, J.L., Mendes de Leon, C.F., & Evans, D.A. (2005). Neuroticism, extraversion, and mortality in a defined population of older persons. *Psychosomatic Medicine, 67,* 841–845.

Wilson, R.S., Mendes de Leon, C.F., Barnes, L.L., Schneider, J.A., Bienias, J.L., Evans, D.A., & Bennett, D.A. (2002). Participation in cognitively stimulating activities and risk of incident Alzheimer's disease. *Journal of American Medical Association, 287,* 742–748.

Wolf, S.L., O'Grady, M., Easley, K.A., Guo, Y., Kressig, R.W., & Kutner, M. (2006). The influence of Intense Tai Chi Training on physical performance and homodynamic outcomes in transitional frail, older adults. *Journal of Gerontology, 61A,* 184–189.

Woods, B. (1996). Cognitive approaches to the management of dementia. In R.G. Morris (Ed.), *The cognitive neuropsychology of Alzheimer-type of dementia.* New York: Oxford University Press.

Wurm, S., Tesch-Römer, C., & Tomasik, M.J. (2007). Longitudinal findings on aging-related cognitions, control beliefs, and health in later life. *Journal of Gerontology: Psychological Sciences, 62,* P156–P164.

Wykle, M.L., Whitehouse, P.J., & Morris, D.L. (Eds.). (2005). *Successful aging through the lifespan.* New York: Springer.

Yaakov, S. (2003). The concept of cognitive reserve: A catalyst for research. *Journal of Clinical and Experimental Neuropsychology, 25,* 259–593.

Yoon, G. (1996). Psychosocial factors for successful aging. *Australian Journal of Ageing, 15,* 69–72.

Zamarrón, M.D., Tárraga, L., & Fernández-Ballesteros, R. (2008). Plasticidad cognitiva en personas con la enfermedad de Alzheimer que reciben programas de estimulación cognitiva[Cognitive plasticity in Alzheimer's disease patients treated with cognitive stimulation programs]. *Psicothema, 20,* 432–437.

Zanetti, O. Binetti, G., & Magnini, E. (1997). Procedural memory stimulation in Alzheimer's Disease: Impact of training program. *Acta of Neurological Scandinavia, 95,* 152–157.

Zautra, A.J., Reich, J.W., & Newsom, J.T. (1995). Autonomy and sense of control among older adults: An examination of their effects on mental health. In L. Bond, S. Culter, & A. Grams (Eds.), *Promoting successful and productive aging* (pp. 153–170). Newbury Park, CA: Sage.

Zeng, Y. (2004). A new method for correcting underestimation of disability life expectancy. *Demography, 41,* 335–361.

Zunzunegui, M.V., Rodriguez-Laso, A., Otero, A., Pluijm, S.M.F., Nikula, S., Blumstein, Jyylhä, M., Minucuci, N., & Deeg, D. (2005). Disability and social ties: Comparative findings of the CLESA study. *European Journal of Ageing, 2,* 40–48.

Selected Websites on Active Aging

www.appliedgerontology.org/cag_Id.cfm
www.centerforhealthyaging.com
www.geron.org
www.geropsych.org
www.healthandage.com
www.icaa.cc
www.ilcusa.org/pub/news.htm
www.positiveaging.com
www.icpsr.umich.edu/NACDA
www.geron.psu.edu/sls
www.radcliffe.edu/murray
www.uam.es/geronto/html
www.uninettuno.it/Vitalagell/frameset.htm
www.cdc.gov/aging/publications.htm
www.caphysicalactivity.org/our_newsletter.html
www.fiftyplus.liverpool.gov.uk/information/active_aging/index.asp
www.icaa.cc/Awards/winners.htm
www.capegateway.gov.za/Text/2003/aging
www.activeagingsa.net.au/aboutus.html
www.tripdatabase.com/SearchResults.html?s=1&gk=Active+Aging+Promotion &itemId =249757
www.epa.gov/aging/resources/presentations/2007_0416-active-aging-and-healthy-communities
www.europeancenter.org
www.lnactiveaging.org/recognition_program/ten_strategies.html
www.healthypeople.gov/Publications/HealthyCommunities2001/healthy com01hk.pdf
www.abilitynotage.ca/index.php?option=com_content&task=category&section id=4&id =19&Itemid=26
http://eng.newwelfare.org/?p=237&page=6
www.monitoringris.org
http://50plus.com/display.cfm?authorsearch=yes&authorname=Gifford-Jones
www.imsersomayores.csic.es/
www.madrid.org/cs/Satellite?pagename=PMAY/Page/PMAY_home&language =es
www.50plus.org/
www.fifty-plus.net
www.capegateway.gov.za/Text/2003/aging.pdf
http://nurseweb.ucsf.edu/iha/Programs/Hlthy_Active.htm
www.tripdatabase.com/SearchResults.html?s=1&gk=Active+Aging+Promotion &itemId =249757
www.activeforlife.info/default.aspx

http://whqlibdoc.who.int
www.prevent.org
www.sparkpeople.com
www.who.int/ageing
www.agingblueprint.org
http://aspe.hhs.gov
http://vrchawaii.org/ActiveAging/
www.activeaging.org
www.inactiveaging.org
www.activeaging.com.au
http://health.msm.com/health-topics/aging
www.euro.who.int/ageing
www.aarpinternational.org
http://sbs.ucsf.edu/iha/chaa.htm

Rocío Fernández-Ballesteros (Editor)

GeroPsychology
European Perspectives for an Aging World

2007, 272 pages, hardcover, US $44.00 / € 34.95,
ISBN: 978-0-88937-340-2

A fascinating overview of the most important psychological research into aging, with special emphasis on training and professional issues as well as science.

Psychologists will have to play a leading role in dealing with the societal and personal implications of an aging population. This outstanding volume by leading experts shows how, by means of a comprehensive overview of the latest research into aging, its effects, and its implications for science, training, and profession. As this book shows, the aging of the population should be considered a positive phenomenon that reflects sociopolitical, educational, biomedical, and psychological development.

> "A ground-breaking textbook of fundamental importance and practical use for all those concerned with the impact of population aging, not only to European societies, but also throughout the world. The concepts and results outlined here have profound implications for practice, research, and policy."
> Alexandre Kalache, MD, PhD, Programme Head Ageing and Life Course (ALC) WHO

Table of Contents
Foreword by *R.K. Silbereisen* • 1. Geropsychology: Demographic, Socio-Political, and Historical Background by *R. Fernández-Ballesteros, M. Pinquart, P. Tordahl* • 2. Main Trends in Geropsychology in Europe: Research, Training, and Practice by *M. Pinquart* • 3. Age Identifications by *S.O. Daatland* • 4. Person-Environment Relations by *H.-W. Whal, S. Iwarsson* • 5. Semantic Memory in Healthy Aging by *H. Peraita* • 6. Affect and Emotions by *D. Moraitou, A. Efklides* • 7. Personality and Self-Beliefs by *M. Caprara, P. Steca, G.V. Caprara* • 8. Old-Old People: Major Recent Findings and the European Contribution to the State-of-the-Art by *C. Paul* • 9. Cognitive Plasticity and Cognitive Impairment by *R. Fernández-Ballesteros, M.D. Zamarrón, M.D. Calero, L. Tárraga* • 10. Cognitive Decline and Dementia by *S. Berg, A. Dahl, S. Nilsson* • 11. Demographic Change, the Need for Care and the Role of the Elderly by *U. Lehr, S. Re, J. Wilbers* • 12. Quality of Life, Life Satisfaction, and Positive Aging by *R. Fernández-Ballesteros, A. Kruse, M.D. Zamarrón, M. Caprara* • 13. Wisdom: Adult Development and Emotional-Motivational Dynamics by *U. Kunzmann* • 14. Toward a Theory of Successful Aging: Selection, Optimization, and Compensation by *A.M. Freund, P.B. Baltes*

30 Amberwood Parkway · Ashland, OH 44805 · USA
Tel: (800) 228-3749 · Fax: (419) 281-6883
Rohnsweg 25 · D-37085 Göttingen · Germany
Tel: +49 551 999 500 · Fax: +49 551 999 50 425
E-Mail: custserv@hogrefe.com

BF 724.8 .F47 2008
Fernández Ballesteros,
 Rocío.
Active aging

OCT 2 4 2008